Professionalism in the Interdisciplinary Early Years Team

Also available from Continuum

Professionalism in the Interdisciplinary Early Years Team

Supporting Young Children and Their Families

Edited by

Avril Brock
Carolynn Rankin

continuum

Continuum International Publishing Group

The Tower Building	80 Maiden Lane
11 York Road	Suite 704
London	New York
SE1 7NX	NY10038

www.continuumbooks.com

© Avril Brock, Carolynn Rankin and Contributors 2011

All rights reserved. No part of this publication may be reproduced or transmitted in any form or by any means, electronic or mechanical, including photocopying, recording, or any information storage or retrieval system, without prior permission in writing from the publishers.

Avril Brock, Carolynn Rankin and Contributors have asserted their right under the Copyright, Designs and Patents Act, 1988, to be identified as Author of this work.

British Library Cataloguing-in-Publication Data
A catalogue record for this book is available from the British Library.

ISBN: 978-1-4411-1408-2 (paperback)
         978-1-4411-3706-7 (hardcover)

Library of Congress Cataloging-in-Publication Data
A catalog record for this book is available from the Library of Congress.

Typeset by Newgen Imaging Systems Pvt Ltd, Chennai, India

Printed and bound in India

This book is dedicated to all those who work in interprofessional teams with young children and their families.

Contents

X Contents

List of Tables

List of Figures

List of Abbreviations and Acronyms

ASBO	Anti-Social Behaviour Order
BCS	British Cohort Study
BHPS	British Household Panel Survey
CAF	Common Assessment Framework
CAMHS	Child and Adolescent Mental Health Services
CC	Children's Centre
CGFS	Curriculum Guidance for the Foundation Stage
CILIP	Chartered Institute of Library and Information Professionals
CLLD	Communication, Language and Literacy Development
COS	Charity Organisation Society
CPAG	Child Poverty Action Group
CPD	Continuing Professional Development
CQC	Care Quality Commission
CSP	Chartered Society of Physiotherapy
CWDC	Children's Workforce Development Council
CWS	Children's Workforce Strategy
DCMS	Department for Culture, Media and Sport
DCSF	Department for Children, Schools and Families
DfE	Department for Education
DfEE	Department for Education and Employment
DfES	Department for Education and Science
DoH	Department of Health
DWP	Department of Work and Pensions
ECAT	Every Child a Talker
ECCE	Early Childhood Care and Education
ECEC	Early Childhood Education and Care
ECM	Every Child Matters
EE	Early Education
EEAG	Early Education Advisory Group
ELSA	English Longitudinal Study of Ageing

EPPE	Effective Provision of Preschool Education Project
EYE	Early Years Educators
EYP	Early Years Professional
EYPS	Early Years Professional Status
FACS	Families and Children Study
FE	Further Education
GCSE	General Certificate of Secondary Education
GP	General Practitioner
GSCC	General Social Care Council
GTC	General Teaching Council
HE	Higher Education
HPC	Health Professions Council
HV	Health Visitor
IFLA	International Federation of Library Associations
IFSW	International Federation of Social Work
IPL	Interprofessional Learning
Ippr	Institute for Public Policy Research
ITE	Initial Teacher Education
ITT	Initial Teacher Training
JAR	Joint Area Review
LSYPE	Longitudinal Study of Young Local Authority People in England
MCS	Millennium Cohort Study
MLA	Museums, Libraries and Archives
MP	Member of Parliament
NCDS	National Child Development Study
NCSL	National College of School Leadership
NFER	National Foundation for Educational Research
NHS	National Health Service
NPQICL	National Professional Qualification in Integrated Centre Leadership
NQT	Newly Qualified Teacher
NSPCC	National Society for the Prevention of Cruelty to Children
OECD	Organization for Economic Cooperation and Development
Ofsted	Office for Standards in Education
PCT	Primary Care Trust
PSED	Personal, Social and Emotional Development
QAA	Qualifications Assessment Authority
QCA	Qualifications and Curriculum Authority
QCDA	Qualifications and Curriculum Development Authority
QUANGO	Quasi-autonomous non-governmental organisation
RCSLT	Royal College of Speech and Language Therapists

REPEY   Researching Effective Pedagogy in the Early Years
SEN   Special Educational Needs
SENCO   Special Educational Needs Coordinator
SLCN   Speech, Language and Communication Needs
SLT   Speech and Language Therapists / Therapy
TAC   Team Around the Child
TDA   Teacher Development Agency
TIPS   Towards Interprofessional Practice
UK   United Kingdom
UNICEF   United Nations Children's Fund (formerly United Nations International Children's Emergency Fund)

List of Contributors

The editors

Avril Brock is a Principal Lecturer in the Carnegie Faculty at Leeds Metropolitan University in the UK. She works on Master's and undergraduate degree courses in Early Childhood Education and Childhood Studies and she has written books on bilingualism, early language development and play. Avril has worked in Initial Teacher Training since 1989. Formerly, she was a deputy head teacher, primary and early years teacher in West Yorkshire, often working with linguistically diverse children. Avril's PhD research on the professionalism of early years educators has become a longitudinal study resulting in a model of the seven dimensions of professionalism. This has now been explored across the professions of the early years inter-disciplinary team. Throughout her work in higher education, Avril has participated in several Socrates, Comenius and Erasmus European-funded international projects and is involved in international and interdisciplinary partnerships with colleagues in West Yorkshire and the United States of America.

Carolynn Rankin is a Senior Lecturer in the School of Applied Global Ethics, Faculty of Health and Social Sciences at Leeds Metropolitan University, UK. Carolynn lectures on Master's and undergraduate degree courses on the information society, global citizenship and research methods. She is a member of the Chartered Institute of Library and Information Professionals (CILIP) and is external examiner for the CILIP Chartership Board. Her current research interests include the social impact of information and library services and the role of the information professional. Carolynn has been invited to lecture to professional associations and conferences in Europe and Canada. She has directed national research projects including the National Year of Reading evaluation in Yorkshire and is currently undertaking research on the Sister Libraries programme of the International Federation of Library Associations. Carolynn was the lead author for *Delivering the Best Start: A Guide to Early Years Libraries*, published by Facet, and is editing a follow-up publication focusing on the challenges of delivering children's library services in the digital age.

The contributors

Pat Broadhead is Professor of Playful Learning at Leeds Metropolitan University, UK. After leaving school, she trained as a nursery nurse and then as an early years/primary teacher. Her doctorate focused on primary teachers' perceptions of good practice. She began her higher education career at the University of Leeds, where she led the Articled Teacher scheme (a two-year postgraduate route into teaching) and the one-year PGCE early years course. She worked at the Universities of York and Northumbria in the UK before coming to Leeds Metropolitan University. Her main research interests focus on children as playful learners in early years settings and supporting pedagogies. She has also researched effective schooling through school development planning and also wider aspects of the changing children's workforce.

Fiona Butler has worked with young children and their families as a librarian, childminder, early years teacher and Local Authority advisory teacher in the UK. As a result of her work within Children's Centres, she tutored and mentored Children's Centre leaders taking the National Professional Qualification in Children's Centre Leadership (NPQICL) and was involved in the development of the NPQICL training resources. She now leads a team of Improvement Partners dedicated to the development of high-quality Children's Centre services and the performance management process for the 58 Children's Centres in Leeds.

Nick Frost is Professor of Social Work (children, childhood and families) at the Faculty of Health, Leeds Metropolitan University, UK. He has researched in the fields of child welfare, family support and integrated working and has published widely, including, most recently, *Understanding Children's Social Care* (with Nigel Parton, Sage, 2009); *Beyond Reflective Practice* (as co-editor with Bradbury et al., 2010); and *Understanding Childhood and Families* (Continuum, 2011). Nick was a social worker with local authorities for 15 years before commencing his academic career.

Wendy Holland has over 30 years of teaching experience in mainstream nurseries, primary and special schools in the UK. From the 1970s onwards, her focus has been on inclusive provision and practice for children up to 8 years. Through the establishment of mother and toddler groups and playgroups for children with particular needs, integrated mainstream provision for hearing and hearing-impaired nursery- and primary-aged children, she has pursued her particular interests around the inclusion of parents/carers in the caring and educative process. The importance of the role of reflective practitioner as an agent for change is another of her interests and she is presently involved in the training and assessment of early years professionals at Bradford College in the UK. She also currently develops and produces modules for the BA(Hons) with Qualified Teacher Status degree and the BEd Studies degree in the Teaching, Health and Care sector at Bradford College, as well as supporting students engaged in a range of undergraduate and Master's level programmes.

Pam Jarvis is a qualified teacher, researcher and graduate psychologist. She is currently working on the Teaching, Health and Care team at Bradford College University Centre, and as a tutor at the Open University, UK, supporting education and child development students on a wide range of programmes at undergraduate and Master's degree levels. She additionally coordinates the Bradford College Early Years Professional Status academic programme. Pam was awarded a PhD in Education Studies by Leeds Metropolitan University, UK, in 2005, for a piece of research that explored children's play-based learning. Her most recent publications are: Jarvis, P., George, J., and Holland, W. (2010), *The Early Years Professional's Complete Companion* (Harlow: Pearson Longman); and Jarvis, P., and George, J. (2010), 'Thinking It Through: Rough and Tumble Play', pp. 164–78, in J. Moyles (ed.) *Thinking It Through: Reflecting on Playful Pedagogy in the Early Years* (Buckingham: Open University Press).

Kate Karban is a Senior Lecturer in Social Work at the University of Bradford, UK. She has extensive experience in social work practice, education and training with a particular emphasis on mental health and interprofessional working. Until 2009 she worked at Leeds Metropolitan University, where she was involved with Sue Smith in the development of the Interprofessional Learning programme in the Faculty of Health. Research experience includes the local evaluation of Sure Start programmes and she is currently involved in the evaluation of an independent living programme for people with mental health difficulties or learning disabilities, working with service user and carer researchers. She is also involved in a British Council-funded DelPHE link with Chainama College of Health Sciences in Zambia. Her publications include *Social Work and Mental Health* (Polity Press, 2011) and she is also joint convenor of the Social Work and Health Inequalities Network.

Tracey Marsh is a Senior Lecturer in Speech and Language Therapy at Leeds Metropolitan University, UK. Shortly after qualifying, she specialized in paediatric practice and was privileged to work in the early years sector during the key transformations surrounding Every Child Matters, Sure Start Local Programmes and subsequent transitions into Children's Centres. Tracey continues to work clinically, both in private practice and in clinical teaching contexts. She is passionate about her profession and endeavours to inspire and engage students with the same enthusiasm. Tracey has a long-standing interest in the development of the profession, continuing professional development, professional behaviour and professional standards. She is engaged in research in this area and sits on the Professional Development and Standards Board at the Royal College of Speech and Language Therapists, SLTs' professional body.

David Saltiel worked for many years as a social worker with children and families and as a manager in a range of settings in the statutory and voluntary sectors in the UK. Since 2005 he has been a Lecturer in Social Work in the School of Healthcare at the University of Leeds, UK, teaching undergraduate and postgraduate degree courses. His particular interests are in Social Work with children and families and interprofessional practice. He is currently pursuing doctoral research into decision making in child-protection social work.

Sue Smith provided academic leadership for the development of enterprise education for the HEFCE-funded Centre for Excellence in Teaching and Learning at the Institute of Enterprise in the UK until August 2010. She now works in the central Assessment Learning and Teaching Office at Leeds Metropolitan University, UK. After a clinical and management career in the

NHS, she moved into higher education and most recently worked as a principal lecturer and teacher fellow in the Faculty of Health. She has been the lead researcher in a diverse range of research projects, focusing on problem-based learning and interprofessional working for health and social-care students and tutors. She has published widely in the fields of education and health and has a specific interest in social enterprise, student-centred learning and creative interactive-learning approaches to encourage interprofessional working.

Foreword

This is a timely book written at a period of transition from a Labour policy of state intervention in services for families to Coalition policies of 'rolling back the state', drastically reducing the costs of public services and promoting localism. As the Coalition Government unravels New Labour policy and legislation in the field of children's services, the future of professionalism in interdisciplinary teams working for children looks uncertain.

During 13 years in power, Labour invested heavily in children's services, particularly in the early years sector. The imperatives of New Labour policy were: to ensure economic viability of families and communities, to tackle poverty and inequality, to confront intractable social and health problems and to rationalize and cut costs of public services. In order to achieve these aims, 'monolithic' public services had to be reformed. Reforms included reconfiguring the delivery of services in partnership with the private, voluntary and independent sector – the so-called 'third way'. Specialist services were also reconfigured into interdisciplinary teams, thus ensuring that communications and procedures around the delivery of education, welfare and health services for families with young children were to be 'joined up', more efficient and, in the long-term, more effective.

The flagship New Labour early years initiative to enact these policies and change ways in which professionals worked was a ten-year £500 million anti-poverty early intervention programme, Sure Start. Sure Start was to become a metaphor for changing public services and reconstructing the kinds of professionals delivering them. Sure Start Local Programmes were introduced from 1998. They were independent of local authorities, funded directly by the government and franchised to community programmes, charities or social enterprise businesses. Programmes were designed to target all the families with children under four in more than 500 of the most disadvantaged communities in England. Sure Start Local Programme professionals were charged with providing core services: outreach and home visiting; support for families and parents (including access to work and training opportunities); good quality play/early learning/childcare; and healthcare and support for children and parents with additional needs and/or disabilities. Professionals were required to work with communities to identify and respond to their needs and to be flexible in ways of delivering services. The ambitious aim was to improve the life chances of all families within a defined 'pram-pushing' locality.

But this bottom-up approach to service design and delivery was accompanied by a list of specific and challenging targets to be met by the programmes, for example, reduction in parents' smoking, higher percentage of parents in work, reduction in low birth weights and enhanced language development for all 3-year-olds. Thus a Labour Government introduced draconian systems of accountability for outcomes at a time when professionals were struggling with the new challenges of interdisciplinary and multi-agency teamwork. Complex systems of accountability (at local authority and government levels), inspection (by an 'independent' Ofsted) and regulation (to reduce risks and standardize procedures and protocols) sat uneasily alongside the rhetoric of passing power and decision making to Sure Start front-line workers and their local communities. In 2005 the government panicked at a lack of early evidence of significant gains in child outcomes. There were small but significant gains in parental outcomes such as higher levels of acceptance of children, less scolding and smacking and better-than-expected home-learning environments and by 2008 there was evidence of beneficial effects on both children and their families living in Sure Start neighbourhoods (see National Evaluation of Sure Start publications for 2005, 2007 and 2008 at www.ness. bbk.ac.uk). But governments want evidence of immediate impact, and from 2006, Sure Start Local Programmes were taken under local-authority control and re-branded as Sure Start Children's Centres.

Many other teams of professionals working for families, children and young people were charged with making interdisciplinary or multi-agency systems work. In this book there are accounts of health visitors, speech therapists, nursery officers, teachers, social and welfare workers and librarians coping with a maelstrom of changes in their roles and responsibilities in a wide range of settings. They had to espouse the new vocabulary of joined-up thinking, partnerships, social enterprise and market forces. They had to think long and hard about how to attract new users to their services, how to make their institutions user friendly, how to monitor usage, how to measure impact and how to cooperate with other agencies. The stories told by these professionals in this book bear witness to the emotional, intellectual and physical energy they expended during this period of radical change.

New forms of professionalism emerged from their struggles to adapt to new ways of working. Some were generated by teams working together – exchanging knowledge, sharing skills and learning to listen to alternative values and beliefs about how best to work with families and their children. Some were generated by the government as it became clear that the workforce had to be better trained and better qualified to cope with the complexity of making integrated services a reality. The Children's Workforce Development Council was set up to rationalize qualifications for the workforce delivering children's services. In this book a chapter covers the emergence of early years professionals, a graduate qualification designed to train lead officers in early years care and education settings. Another chapter includes a cogent discussion of the tensions between the respective roles and conditions of service of early years professionals and qualified teachers in early childhood settings. Other chapters explore the historical tensions between health visitors and midwives in maternity services and new tensions between generic family support workers and specialist health professionals in outreach work. Throughout this period of fluidity managers struggled with the vexed question of how best to deploy expensive specialist knowledge and expertise (such as health, education and social services staff). At the same time they were charged with upgrading the knowledge and expertise of less-well-paid generic practitioners (such as family support workers, outreach workers and nursery officers) to deliver front-line services. Despite all these challenges, the book attests that new forms of professionalism flourished and hopes were high that the quality of services for children, young people and their families was steadily improving.

However, such hopes depended on achieving long-term aims, and governments are driven by imperatives to produce short-term outcomes. Moreover, by 2009 the economic climate in the UK was dogged by debts, the credit crunch, banking crises and fear of a major recession. In 2010 a Conservative and Liberal Democrat Coalition Government took power. The imperatives of these unlikely partners were very different from those of Labour: to roll back the state, to free up families from 'nannying' and state surveillance, to dismantle national and local government agencies and to reduce public services and encourage the voluntary, independent and private sectors to fill the gaps left.

In quick succession the Coalition Government has symbolically changed the Department for Children, Schools and Families to the Department for Education, removed the ringfencing of funding for Sure Start Children's Centres and their requirement to provide childcare, downgraded the requirements for settings to employ qualified teachers or early years professionals, pledged to remove statutory requirements for local authorities to commission services through Children's Trusts and announced the closure of the Children's Workforce Development Council. The Coalition Government seems likely to promote specialist expertise to target those perceived as in need; teachers in schools are to concentrate on teaching and learning; health visitors or 'family nurses' will be the lead professionals with responsibilities for very young children; general practitioners are to commission local health services for their patients; social workers are to focus on child protection rather than safeguarding.

Professionals who have worked for 20 years to raise the status of those who work for children and their families, to enhance the quality of provision of services and, in the last decade, to learn how to work in integrated teams are reeling with the enormity of these changes. In such a period of instability, it is a good time for readers of this book to take stock of what it means to be a professional because what you were is forever who you are.

Angela Anning,
Emeritus Professor of Early Childhood Education,
University of Leeds, UK

Author Acknowledgements

This book would not have been written without our practitioner colleagues across the different professions.

Particular thanks go to all those who have given their voices to the case studies and examples mentioned in this book.

The contributing authors have willingly given their professional knowledge and experience and all have been so very prompt with their chapters and in answering any questions arising.

Many thanks to those who have provided or appear in photographs – Parklands Children's Centre; students on courses at Leeds Metropolitan University; the editors' extended family, in particular Kirsty, David, Melissa and Oscar; Jackie, Simon, James, Joe and Tom.

We do hope that JGJ and BR's patience will continue throughout our writing partnership.

Thanks to AJ for her contribution and to Neil Priestley for his help with the Bronfenbrenner diagram.

Publisher Acknowledgements

Belbin Team Role Summary Descriptions – permissions to use were granted by Elsevier on 16/12/10

The 'onion' diagram: children's services under New Labour (1997–2010) (DCSF)

Introduction

This book is about the professionalism of those who support young children and their families in the twenty-first century. The book explores this professionalism from the perspectives of those working in care, education, health, social work and libraries. These professionals work in interdisciplinary teams in settings such as children and family centres, schools, health centres and across a range of local-authority services.

The book commences by setting the scene for what it is to be a young child growing up in the twenty-first century in the UK. The social, cultural and political environment impacts on the child and the issues that concern the millennium family are explored through a decade of policy development.

The implementation of this government policy has required cooperation at strategic and operational levels and promoted multi-professional working across professional and organizational boundaries. There are complex issues associated with working in interdisciplinary teams when a range of professionals endeavour to work together to provide services for children and their families. The challenge is for organizations, agencies and managers to provide structures and systems that enable practitioners to effectively carry out their roles and responsibilities within a team ethos. Professionals are no longer restricted by particular spaces or areas of knowledge and interprofessionalism is the key to delivering services.

Having an understanding of the different professionals' expertise and values is important for maximizing effective interdisciplinary teamwork. The book examines the concept of *professionalism*, in particular seven dimensions of professionalism: knowledge, education and training, skills, autonomy, values, ethics and reward. An ethos of professionalism should foster understanding, facilitate a collaborative environment and generate closer working relationships for the benefit of young children and their families. It is imperative that professionals understand the nature of knowledge and practice of their counterparts from the different disciplines.

In practice there still may be a lack of cohesive interprofessional sharing of knowledge and of the values, beliefs and ethics of the professionals in different disciplines. Putting people together in the same office doesn't mean they will work and collaborate together. As one professional observed, 'We might be positioned together within one large open-plan office. However, this doesn't mean we collaborate effectively – we even have colour-coded coffee cups in the kitchen!' The way that the varied professionals are all trained and gain their work experience frames the way they think and operate; their background drives the way they deliver services to children and their families.

Thinking beyond boundaries and forming professional relationships can be supported through gaining an understanding of other professional backgrounds, thus dismantling any preconceived stereotypes. This book will provide information for readers about the professional identities of those working in an interdisciplinary team. An understanding of these wider influences has an impact on individual professionals' practice through challenging thinking and supporting advocacy for their own and children's rights to high-quality professional services.

The book contains chapters from professionals in each of the critical support services working with young children and their families. Professional perspectives are provided from the disciplines of care, education, health, social work, speech and language therapy and librarianship. Through gaining an understanding of the professionalism involved, the reader is able to connect to the key players who support young children.

This book celebrates the professionalism of the varied practitioners who work with young children. It is aimed at those who are still developing their knowledge and experience through undergraduate and postgraduate courses, as well as those undertaking continuing professional development courses. Interdisciplinary teaching is becoming more evident as courses share both knowledge and module delivery, enabling an understanding of the expertise of each professional. This book aims to be a valuable text for those working in and leading an interdisciplinary team in a range of settings. It is written by those who are well qualified in their respective disciplines and are involved in teaching and research. The contributing authors are based in the northern cities of Leeds and Bradford and all have close links with local children's services, drawing on the voices of those working in the front line of those services.

Part I
Introducing the Context for Professionalism

1

The Child in Context: Policy and Provision

Avril Brock

Chapter Outline

Introduction

This chapter sets the scene for what it is to be a young child in the twenty-first century in the UK through exploring social, cultural, environmental and political influences. The policy changes have been both numerous and rapid for the last quarter century and this chapter advocates scrutiny of the aims, values and assumptions behind the key policy developments that have impacted upon young children. The chapter explores what policy has been developed, what has informed it and what it means for the child, her family and the community in which she lives. It will reflect on the twenty-first-century 'millennium' family and examine issues relating to the complex relationships that children may experience within their immediate and extended home life. Each individual child will grow up in a particular social and cultural environment shaped by her home, family, friends and community. Race, ethnicity, culture, diversity and language will all play a part in forming her identity, aspirations and life prospects. Socio-economic status, geographical location, early childhood education and care settings all affect the context and environment in which a child grows up and evolves. These issues will be explored from the perspective of children's rights and listening to children's and their families' voices. The social, political and cultural environment influences how professionals work and how they develop their personal professional values and ethics in their work with young children and their families. The chapter therefore focuses on the child in context and starts the debate about professionalism.

Madeleine's case study

Why did my mum die when I was a baby? Why did my daddy marry my new mummy? Why can't grandma and grandad live with us? Why do they have to go home now? Why doesn't Josh and Tyler live with Uncle Steve and Aunty Jess? Did mummy and Aunty Jess live near their cousins when they were little? Why is Makayla's skin a different colour to her mummy? Why are families so complexicated?

Madeleine was aged 6 at the time of this dialogue and her challenging questions – for which she wanted answers – confounded her step-grandma who tried to answer them to the best of her ability. Philosophical discussions such as these commenced when Madeleine was 3 years old. She had attended day care at the local Sure Start Children's Centre from the age of 6 months. Her mother had been diagnosed with breast cancer during the pregnancy and the family was bereaved by the time Madeleine reached 16 months of age. Her grandparents had always been very involved with her upbringing and when she was four and a half she gained a total of six grandmothers across four generations when her father married again. It really makes you realize how important extended families are – the birthday, Easter, Christmas, Halloween and bonfire parties now involved different sets of step-cousins and in-laws gained through the various marriage connections. From a very early age Madeleine would talk about death, age, illness, relationships and friendship. She had a photo of her birth mother in her bedroom and albums with photographs throughout her early years, which were particularly perused when her baby brother was born so she could make comparisons. She had always wanted a baby brother and had been asking since she was three years old why she was an only child and why she didn't have siblings.

This brief visit to Madeleine's early years aims to indicate the 'complexicatedness' of young children and their families' lives. It raises issues of the impact of bereavement, the importance of extended family and relationships, the relevance of culture and in this case the celebration of festivals, the nature of early childhood education and care, and the importance of language and thinking in a young child's development. Within the first year of her life Madeleine had met various professionals specializing in health and early childhood education and care. A timeline of her significant events and involvement with professionals would resemble the example in Table 1.1.

There is no such concept as the 'average' or 'normal' child – the variables are too many and too complex as the pattern of each child's life experience can differ considerably. Smith (2009) raises questions as to what extent there is a constant core to childhood and if so, whether it is located in the child or in the social processes, which conceptualize and classify the distinctive features of childhood, and how, when identified, these can be balanced with those aspects which are variable and reflect wider social diversities. While bearing in mind this complexity, this chapter examines the key issues and policy drivers that affect the 'universal' child living in the UK in this century.

All children in the UK will have contact from birth with a range of health professionals – midwife, general practitioner, health visitor and dentist – and some children will encounter paediatricians, dieticians, physiotherapists or speech and language therapists. The majority of children will have early childhood education and care experiences with childminders, early years professionals (EYPs), nursery nurses or teachers. They will then enter the state education system, be educated in the independent sector or be home educated. Some children will have interventions from social services and may encounter a variety of social

Table 1.1 Madeleine's timeline

Age	Event	Professionals involved
Birth	Mother diagnosed with cancer.	Midwives GP Health visitor
6 months to 1 year	Entered day care in a Sure Start Children's Centre. Full time day care. Mother died when Madeleine was 16 months. Paternal grandparents very involved in care.	Nursery nurse/key worker Early years professional Early years teacher Children's Centre manager
3 years	Independent school kindergarten. After school club.	Class teacher Teaching assistants Head teacher
4 years	Joins and visits library with grandmother. Starts swimming lessons.	Librarians Swimming teachers
5 years	Father remarried and Madeleine is a bridesmaid. New extended family. Starts dancing lessons.	Vicar Dentist Dance teacher
6 years	Baby brother born.	Midwives Health visitor

My Famliy

Figure 1.1 Madeleine's drawing of her family

workers, outreach workers, police officers and even lawyers. Not all children will have had early literacy experiences with an early years librarian, yet the majority should have received an invitation to the library through the Bookstart Project (see Chapter 9).

Timelines of young children and their families will be presented in this chapter – they are based on 'real' children but anonymized – to provide a set of small case studies that reflect the involvement of different professionals and the range of interventions that some children experience in both minor and major ways. These case studies cannot reflect every eventuality, but they have been carefully selected to provide a breadth of 'events' to indicate how few young children and their families have straightforward lives. Children are very resilient and many have to cope with serious incidents that affect themselves and their families, but those who face three or more stressful life events, such as family bereavement, divorce or serious illness, are three times more likely than other children to develop emotional and behavioural disorders (CAMHS, 2008, p. 20). However, the aim of this book is not to focus on disadvantaged or hard to reach children or those in need, but to present and examine a whole range of issues that may have an impact on any child's early years.

Figure 1.2 A family celebration – a christening party

Bronfenbrenner's ecological theory

Bronfenbrenner (1979; 1989) was interested in the interconnectedness of the systems that affect children's lives and development and his model portrays a complex hierarchy of systems in which individual interactions between people are situated. His model of the universal child places her at the centre of concentric circles of influence: the family, the immediate context and the wider cultural context, and so indicates the influences that affect young children's life experiences.

- Macro-system: the historical/social/cultural/ecological environments at national policy level
- Exo-system: settings that do not involve the child as an active participant, but in which events by authority systems or inspection structures affect the micro-system
- Meso-system: interrelations between two or more settings in which the child actively participates – for example, home and nursery, childminder or Children's Centre
- Micro-system: the playgroup, nursery class, day-care or childminder setting where the child experiences a particular pattern of activities, roles and interpersonal relationships (adapted from Anning and Ball, 2008).

Bronfenbrenner's model demonstrates the significance of the macro-system on the micro-system and the relationships between individuals, actions, meanings, contexts, communities and cultural histories. He explains that children's development is best understood within the socio-cultural context of the family, educational setting, community and broader society. Children act simultaneously within these different groups, the contexts are interrelated and all have an impact on the developing child. Bronfenbrenner's main concern has been to examine how the groups or settings surrounding the child work and how the child is influenced by these systems. He sees children's own individual perceptions of their environments to be more important than what might be happening in reality.

This phenomenological approach demands the ability to listen to children, seeking to understand experiences through their eyes (Anning and Edwards, 1999). Grappling with different theories of how children perceive the world; how they think, learn and develop is important for professionals who work with young children, so that their professional knowledge is built on a critical understanding and incorporated into providing appropriate services for young children and their families. There are several adaptations of the Bronfenbrenner's social ecological model. Figure 1.3 builds on Bronfenbrenner's model to provide a new perspective on how professionals in both universal and targeted services connect to the nested layers of a child's world.

Constructs of childhood

In recent years early childhood has been high on the political agenda globally, shaping children's and their families' daily and future lives through policy development. This has evolved through the growing awareness of the significance of the first years of life for intellectual, social and emotional development and the growing interest and research in these early years from the disciplines of health, psychology, education, social policy, social care and neuropsychology. There has also been increased interest in recent years into the research and scholarship regarding constructs of childhood. James and Prout's (1997) paradigm for understanding childhood as a social construction is an example of an interpretive frame for contextualizing early childhood. They challenge the 'growing imposition of a particularly Western conceptualization of childhood' for all children and suggest that psychological explanations of child development have dominated childhood study until recently (James and Prout, 1997, p. 9). They argue that children's social relationships, cultures and learning cannot be divorced from contextual variables such as class, gender or ethnicity. Children must not be considered in isolation from their families and in Western society these are complicated organisms.

Generally, it is adults who debate the issues of rights for children, but their conceptions and interpretations may differ widely. In 1989 the United Nations endorsed the Convention on the Rights of the Child, which affords children the same range of civil, political, economic, social and cultural rights as adults. It requires that services for children develop policies that are responsive to the wide range of children's needs that encompasses all spheres of their lives

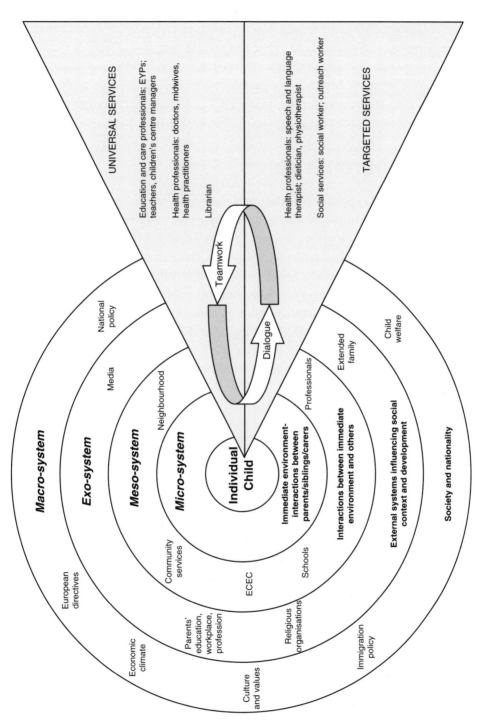

Figure 1.3 A child's world – a social ecological perspective of professional intervention

(Lewis and Lindsay, 2000). Children are seen as rightful recipients who should have the right to express views on all matters of concern to them. Inclusive practice means children should take part in any decision-making processes that concern them (Nutbrown and Clough, 2006) and they should be allowed to be active participants in the construction of their own lives (Jones et al., 2006). Have these aims yet been achieved? Do young children and their families really have much of a voice in the policy developments that affect their lives?

Giving children a voice

Giving children a voice began to become established as we entered the twenty-first century. The Childcare Act (2006) placed a duty on English local authorities to take into account children's views on the services they receive. A national charity – the Young Children's Voices Network – was established to promote listening to children and to support practitioners and in 2007 the Children's Society instigated the first independent inquiry into childhood in the UK, believing it to be important to understand children's life experiences. The Good Childhood Inquiry (a national inquiry commissioned by the Children's Society) gathered evidence from almost 3,000 sources, including 1,200 children. This determined six themes of friendship, family, health, learning, lifestyles and values. Friendship was found to be very important for children, both for their social and emotional development and sense of well-being, from the age of 2 years onwards. As stated in 'Summary 1 – Friends' of *The Good Childhood* report:

> Adults often underestimate the importance of friendship for children, and how friends help them to adjust to school, the arrival of new siblings and the experience of being bullied…. [B]eing separated from friends is often a deeply unhappy experience for children and can result in poorer mental health…. (Children's Society, 2009)

Young children gave evidence of how they thought playing with their friends was so important and demonstrated how they gained a sense of identity and belonging through sharing experiences as they played. Brock et al. (2009, p. 4) describe how 'play is crucially important for children's development, learning and well-being, reflecting the fact that the concept of play itself is infinitely flexible, offering choices and allowing for freedom of interpretation'. A range of perspectives of the role of play in children's lives is provided in *Perspectives of Play: Learning for Life* and when three of the authors working in the fields of psychology, education and playwork met to discuss a shared chapter, they realized they had 'different, but not incompatible standpoints and constructs for examining the complex concept of play' (Brock et al., 2009, p. 3). Children not only require time and space to play, their voices need to be heard and their needs and desires recognized by adults.

The Good Childhood survey demonstrates how it is important to provide a forum to allow children to contribute and state their interests and concerns. Fortunately, it is becoming more common to elicit children's voices although there is still a long way to go. Here are three inquiries that did so in 2008–2010:

- The Children and Mental Health Services (CAMHS, 2008) review found that children, young people and their families and carers wanted 'consistent relationships with people who can help and to be treated with dignity and respect'. A key objective of the review was to emphasize that the mental health and psychological well-being of all children are not the preserve of one profession or another, but should be through effective, well-integrated child- and family-centred services.
- The Lamb Inquiry for Special Educational Needs and Parental Confidence (2009) talked with parents of disabled children and children with special educational needs (SEN). They met some of the happiest parents in the country, who felt their children were well supported and making good progress, and some of the angriest, who found the education system to be a battleground when trying to get the needs of their child identified and met. The inquiry found that parents need to be listened to more; that the system needs to be more ambitious for their children; and that there should be a cultural shift in the way that schools, local authorities and other professionals work with parents and children.
- 'Support for all: The families and relationships green paper' (DCSF, 2010) sought the advice of parents, grandparents, young people, experts and voluntary agencies in developing the government's proposals. It raised several consultation questions asking families what more they could do to help create a culture where seeking help for family difficulties is considered socially acceptable. Which issues and services should be prioritized to strengthen and support families in a truly family-friendly manner?

In 2007 the UNICEF report on childhood in 21 of the world's wealthiest countries hit *The Independent* newspaper with the headline: 'Britain's children: unhappy, neglected and poorly educated' as the UK came twenty-fourth out of 24 countries. Two years later the Child Poverty Action Group (CPAG, 2009a) published a briefing drawn from the 2009 European league table of child well-being in European countries, when the UK came twenty-fourth out of the 29 countries. CPAG demanded that the government engaged in a frank analysis of why other countries are doing so much better for their children than the UK. Kate Green, CPAG chief executive, called for government cooperation:

All political parties must pledge to direct more of our national resources towards making children's lives better. We need to rethink the place of children in today's Britain and ensure the right to a good childhood is central to our national culture. … The report shows a clear link between high levels of child well-being and low levels of child poverty. If we fail to protect families during the downturn, progress on child well-being could go into reverse. (CPAG, 2009b)

How has contemporary UK policy impacted young children and their families and what is the way forward? The next sections in this chapter examine issues from the past, present and future to try to make sense of the complexities involved.

Reflecting on policy development

Table 1.5 illustrates the milestones of policy and initiatives that have impacted early childhood in the UK 1999–2010 and provides a timeline of critical events with particular focus on care and education, health and social work. The timeline does not demonstrate *all* the policy developments that have affected young children and their families in the UK within the last decade, but it does indicate that they are numerous and rapid.

> While there is much to be celebrated in the developing emphasis on improving and expanding services for young children (DfES, 2004), there is a real concern that the obfuscation of aims may inhibit the necessary and welcome emphasis on the needs of the child and on children's voices that has come to the fore since the Children Act 1989. (Warin, 2007)

Policies are developed in particular social, cultural, historical, ideological, political frameworks; therefore the following questions should be considered when implementing policy:

1. What is the aim behind its publication?
2. What are the values it is portraying and are there any underlying assumptions?
3. What effects will it have for individual professionals' role and for the children and families with whom they work?

Baldock et al. (2009) advise that you read a policy document carefully to determine any values that have informed it, as it may be rooted in a particular time frame and things may have changed. There may be inevitable tensions between government policy and the autonomy of local authorities and/or personal beliefs and values.

Challenge Point

Select a particular policy from Table 1.5 and download it from the relevant government website. Read and analyse the policy and see if you can answer the three questions above. Can you also examine the policy for its clarity regarding:

- underlying values
- broad objectives
- cost and resource implications
- feasibility of implementation
- compatibility with other policies
- relevance and appropriateness to the specific client group of young children and their families

Policy change needs to be implemented rationally and creatively and it should be suitably and sustainably funded. Early childhood has 'become increasingly recognized as an important part of the economic and socio-political fabric of the country' and prompted the wider debate about role, responsibility and value base of those who work with young children (Reed, 2008, p. 162). The challenge for professionals is in continuing to develop knowledge and build on experience to respond to new initiatives. It is important to understand, interpret, reflect on and implement these changes and to liaise with other professionals to be responsive to regional and local needs.

Challenge Point

The challenges arising from family policy developments are immense and questions to debate could include:

- Account taken of complex family circumstances?
- Families' and children's individual needs and rights?
- Professional tensions and identities of the key players?
- Differential knowledge, qualifications, status, pay and conditions of service in the children's workforce?
- Addressing poverty or subsidized child care?
- Parents and work – support or pressure?
- Parenting as a learnable set of skills?
- Work life balance – a woman's problem?

Do governments make assumptions that 'families can be serviced as an unproblematic unit of coherent needs' based on the 'underlying slippery nature of the concept of 'family' (Warin, 2007). Before we address specific policies, it is important first to reflect on the twenty-first-century family and the issues that concern them in contemporary society and everyday life?

Families and family structures

The Office for National Statistics (Social Trends web page at www.statistics.gov.uk/social-trends/) celebrated its four decades of social reporting in 2010. The website provides up-to-date statistics of social and economic data for important aspects of social existence from a range of government departments and other organizations to provide a comprehensive guide to UK society. The demographic forces that drives these trends include: households and families; labour market; housing; transport; lifestyles and social participation; income and wealth; expenditure; education and training; health; environment; and crime and justice. The social trends of the UK have obviously changed over the years and the health of the population, the number of older people in society, the number of children born and movement in and out of the country all contribute to political, economic, social and cultural demands and changes in lifestyle.

Challenge Point

Do the following statistics confirm what you already know or alter your perspectives, or are they meaningless because they are just numbers?

- In 2008 there were 61.4 million people resident in the UK, an increase of 23.2 million since the start of the twentieth century, and a number that is predicted to rise to 65 million in 2018.
- During 2008, England experienced a net loss to other countries in the UK of around 7,800 people, with an outflow of 100,600 people and an inflow of 92,800 people, whereas Scotland, Wales and Northern Ireland all experienced net gains. In 2007–2008, an estimated 554,000 people came to live in the UK for at least one year, a fall of around 41,000 people compared with 2006–2007. There were around 25,900 applications for asylum (excluding dependants) to the UK in 2008, an increase of 11 per cent on the previous year and the first annual increase since 2002.

Reflect on the following example in Table 1.2 that demonstrates the early experiences of Russian twin boys to gain a perspective of how complicated some young children's lives can be.

Table 1.2 Sean and Mark's timeline

Age	Event	Professionals involved
Pre-birth	English prospective parents instigate proceedings to prepare to adopt – start legalities; learn Russian; liaise with agencies.	Social services Social workers Lawyers Adoption agencies Modern foreign language teacher
Birth	Stephan and Mikhail (twins), born in Russia, enter state care system.	Midwives Social workers Carers
Birth to 1 year	Adoption takes place. Immigration to UK. Change of citizenship. Renamed Sean and Mark.	Doctors, including GP Social workers Solicitors Judge International agencies Health visitor
1–2 years	Developing social and emotional skills; communication and English language; physical development. Some delay in maturation due to 'immobility' in first year in care settings.	Social workers GP Speech and language therapist Podiatrist Physiotherapist
3–4 years	Enter nursery school.	Early years professional Nursery nurse Early years teacher
5 years	Enter English state education – primary school.	Early years teacher Head teacher Librarian

The concepts and structures of the family are constantly changing and professionals need to have knowledge and awareness of issues surrounding families. For example, a nuclear family consists of a father, mother and one or more children living together; a single parent family has either the mother or father caring for the children in the family; an extended family may comprise parents, grandparents, uncles, aunts and children; a reconstituted, blended or stepfamily has parents with children from a previous relationship. The word 'parent' can encompass a wide diversity and variety of parenting cultures and the social context within which families function can vary greatly. An understanding of families is crucial for those who work with young children – so how does life vary for different families? The *Focus on Families* report (Smallwood and Wilson, 2007) provides a comprehensive description of twenty-first-century families and brings together data from a variety of sources to describe the characteristics of UK families such as stepfamilies, extended families, multigenerational family households and same sex partnerships. The 'traditional' view of the family is of a married couple with children and this is still mainly the norm, but increasingly, families with children may consist of a cohabiting couple or a single parent. Recent trends include the delay of marriage and childbearing and an increase in divorce; cohabitation and births outside marriage have created 'reconstituted' families as family units break up and reform. Jay's timeline in Table 1.3 indicates the changes in both his family and his personal situation that have occurred in his life.

Table 1.3 Jay's timeline

Age	Event	Professionals involved
Birth	Illness as a baby. Mother and father unmarried and living apart.	Midwives Health visitor Paediatrician Nurses
1 year	Parents reunite and get married.	GP
3 years	Younger brother born. Parents divorce.	Midwives Solicitors
5 years	Begins full time schooling.	Class teacher Nursery nurse Head teacher School nurse
6 years	Bullied at school.	Teachers Head teachers
7 years	Changed school. Individual education plan created. Diagnosed with Asperger's syndrome Playing team football. Father remarried. Stepbrother born.	Child psychology team School psychologists Both parents and families working together

Bourdieu (1990) introduced the notion of social and cultural capital which are generated through a person's social relationships, networks and community strength. Each child will have levels of capital stock from her parents' financial circumstances and wealth; human and intellectual capital from education and knowledge; and social, identity and relationship capital gained through parents, extended family, neighbourhood and the infrastructure of services (Dex and Joshi, 2005). All these 'capitals' will contribute to a child's life chances and social esteem.

Britain's national longitudinal birth cohort surveys have been undertaken in 1946, 1958, 1970 and 2000. The Millennium Cohort Study (MCS) follows the lives of a sample of nearly 19,000 babies born in the UK through information collected from parents when the children were aged 9 months, 3 years and 4 years old. The study's broad objective was to create a new multipurpose longitudinal dataset, describing the diversity of backgrounds into which children were born in the new century. It contains sufficient samples of families in disadvantaged areas and in minority ethnic groups to allow analyses of country of origin, location in the UK, and ethnic minority. An initial survey recorded the circumstances of pregnancy, birth, the early months of life and the social and economic background of each family. 'These babies started out in life in a certain context – the initial conditions into which they were born and over which they had no control' (Dex and Joshi, 2005, p. 21). A second survey charted continuity and change in the child's family and parenting environment: 25 per cent of children gained a sibling; 6 per cent of families interviewed separated and 3 per cent of single parents gained a new partner who, in some cases, was the child's natural father. Two-thirds of non-resident natural fathers were in some form of contact and 56 per cent made some maintenance payments. Marriages had increased and the vast majority of the cohort families still comprised two natural parents, while 15 per cent of the families were headed by lone mothers.

The work of Economic and Social Data Service (ESDS) provides a web-based download service where a range of longitudinal data collections can be accessed:

- 1970 British Cohort Study (BCS70)
- British Household Panel Survey (BHPS)
- English Longitudinal Study of Ageing (ELSA)
- Families and Children Study (FACS)
- Longitudinal Study of Young People in England (LSYPE)
- Millennium Cohort Study (MCS)
- National Child Development Study (NCDS)

All this demonstrates the wealth of material that can be accessed to determine the demographic nature of UK contemporary society. While one may sometimes be sceptical of statistics, the MCS draws on information from families themselves. It is important to access peoples' voices to develop a depth of understanding of different family's needs and aspirations.

Table 1.4 Charlotte's timeline

Age	Event	Professionals involved
Birth	Family known to social services. Charlotte had her own social worker from birth. In and out of care between birth and age 3.	Midwives Health visitor Social workers
3 years	Family not providing appropriate care. Charlotte taken into care full time.	GP – for childhood illnesses but also annual physical check for bruises
4 years	Started pre-reception class based in a school – place offered due to situation. Behavioural problems – child psychologist involved. New foster/adoptive parents had CRB checks. School home visits (head teacher) to adopted family to see Charlotte in new situation and to interview adoptive mother.	Social workers Class teacher Nursery nurse Head teacher Child psychologist School nurse Police
5 years	Charlotte, birth parents, foster adoptive mother – each had own social worker. Officially adopted.	Head teacher Social workers Registered at new GP – physical checks Teachers

Parents want to remain in control of their family lives and be treated as active participants in meeting their children's needs (Broadhead et al., 2008). Furthermore, before implementing any policy a range of voices should be sought – not just those in national and local government, but also a range of professionals who work with families and the families and children themselves. Table 1.4 presents Charlotte's timeline where several family members and diverse professionals have been involved in ensuring Charlotte gets the best support and provision for a happy and safe life.

The Department for Children, Schools and Families (2008) produced an 'analytical' evidence paper, 'Families in Britain'. It acknowledged the power of this social institution for children, adults, communities and society and affirmed that it is the bedrock of society – nurturing, loving, encouraging and supporting children throughout their lives. While this paper realizes that families are 'private' institutions, it demonstrates how family decisions or circumstances will impact upon society and that government has a key role to play in addressing inequalities and providing appropriate and proportionate intervention. That 'strong families give children love, a personal identity and a secure base from which to explore life as they grow up' is affirmed in the Department for Children, Schools and Families 'Support for all: the families and relationships green paper'(DCSF 2010), which sets out a wide range of measures to support all families. This is timely as the 2010 interim findings of the 4Children organization's inquiry into family life shows that families feel key public services are not family friendly and they would like them to change. So what are some of the key issues for families?

Key issues for family well-being

Do researchers and policymakers have a limited understanding of family life and parenting among the broad variety of families that populate the UK? The Family and Parenting Institute has published a literature review that analyses quality issues surrounding the conceptual and practical challenges for 'family well-being'. A BBC poll in 2007 found that the family's future looked 'bright' despite dire political warnings about family breakdown. Interestingly this is 24 per cent higher than when the same question was asked in 1964! The survey questioned 1,001 adults, 95 per cent of whom said their families were important to them and they were very or fairly happy with their family life. However, 70 per cent of those surveyed believed that family life was more successful in their parents' generation.

Challenge point

The points below were some of the findings from the DCSF research conducted in 2008. Do you think a similar poll, conducted at the time of your reading this chapter, would elicit similar results?

- Women with preschool children reported greater satisfaction in more recent years.
- Take-up of formal childcare had increased, while use of informal childcare was relatively stable. Adults now spent a greater part of their leisure time with their children.
- Pressures to combine work and family life were greatest among couples with young children when both partners worked full time.
- Most fathers wanted to be more involved in childcare but still felt women were generally better carers.
- Fathers showed great interest in paternity leave and other policies to balance work and family life. Redundant.

The Organization for Economic Cooperation and Development (OECD) 2010 survey on family structures, women's employment and family policy in thirty-one countries placed the UK twelfth in public spending on early childhood care and education and third in public expenditure in family benefits and services. Throughout 2009/2010 the Family Commission asked 10,000 families in the UK to describe what mattered most to them, what life was like for them, what the future held for them and what support they felt they needed. Their report *Starting a Family Revolution: Putting Families in Charge* maps out a route to change the dynamic between family and state and aims to enable families to feel in control.

The complexity of family relationships

Parents surveyed for the BBC television documentary *The Family* (BBC, 2009) stated that their children were at the very centre of family life. As one parent on the programme said:

> Children often dominate the home in this generation – children are focus of conversation and parenting a focus of TV programmes. My mother is astonished at the amount of attention my children get. We consult them overmuch – they are allowed to have too much of an opinion.

Anthony Gibbons in the Reeth lectures observed that, historically, children were meant to be seen and not heard, but in a democratic society they should be allowed to speak out honestly and openly. 'Respect is still there in families but the relationship is more one of friendship'. The documentary raised the following issues: If parents' identity is so based on children, does this reduce objectivity and is it therefore difficult to use intuition? Has parenthood become a lifestyle choice and are children seen as an investment, as an extension of the parents themselves, to fulfil parents' aspirations and hopes?

Support from the extended family is crucial in times of need, but also for enhanced family well-being. Almost all of the MCS children in the second survey (2007) had at least one living grandparent and 25 per cent of grandparents provided some form of childcare. Over 80 per cent of the grandparents were born in the UK, the countries of Pakistan, India, Ireland and Bangladesh providing the main overseas origins (Hansen and Joshi, 2007). In one-fifth of South Asian families three generations lived together in one household. According to statistics from the Cabinet Office/Department for Children, Schools and Families (2008) nearly 40 per cent of grandparents lived within 15 minutes' travel and saw their grandchildren several times a week and 68 per cent of grandparents stated they felt very close to their grandchildren. Of the MCS families, 90 per cent had received financial support from grandparents and their help had an important influence on whether mothers of young children took employment, especially those with lower earnings potential and those who worked part time.

Some families believe they have been singled out by policymakers and media quite unfairly and that there has been too much intervention in their lives. Lone parents have been singled out as a target group for welfare reform, alongside measures to improve childcare availability and affordability (James, 2009). Yet the reasons for lone parenting are multiple and complex, including bereavement, child protection, divorce or separation, prison and illness.

There is a view that teenage parenthood ruins young people's lives and those of their children, yet research increasingly shows that parenthood is not necessarily a disaster and indeed can sometimes improve young people's lives. Alexander et al.'s (2010) research provides teenage parents with a voice and demonstrates that many teenage mothers are motivated to turn their lives around to provide for their children. Duncan et al. (2010) suggest there needs to be a refocus on the value of parenthood in itself, both for society and for individuals, which for teenage parents might 'focus on the positive experience of becoming a mother and father, and on young parents' own resilience and strengths'.

Every year more children are separated from a parent by prison than divorce. It is estimated that there are 160,000 children with a parent in prison each year and around 2,500 women prisoners are mothers (Hunter, 2008). One-third of mothers are lone parents which makes prison particularly traumatic and they may be more than 50 or 100 miles away from home. Half of incarcerated parents do not receive any visits from their children (Seymour and Hairston, 2001). Children with parents in prison are at a greater risk of depression and anxiety, have behaviour problems and experience a range of emotions such as fear, anger, sadness, loneliness, guilt and low self-esteem. This brief extract about Chloe indicates the impact of his father being in prison:

> 'I miss my Dad so much. When I feel lonely I listen to my CD and hearing his voice makes me feel better.' Chloe aged 7 (Storybook Dads, 2010).

It can be seen that families and family values are complex and the four timelines in this chapter illustrate a range of childhood traumas: the bereavement of a parent, illness, parents' divorce, diagnosis of Asperger's, parental abuse, foster adoption and migration. The next section examines the impact of income and the socio-economic issues that arise through a lack of limited finance coming into a household.

Socio-economic issues

The Institute for Public Policy Research (Ippr) (Ben-Galim and Lanning, 2010) reports that from 1998 to 2008 average household debt in the UK increased substantially and that rather than increasing families' opportunities it often created vulnerability. Ippr's (2010) research through in-depth interviews found that everyday occurrences of broken washing machines, leaking pipes, unexpectedly high bills or seasonal pressures such as Christmas and birthdays put considerable strains on finances. Families with low incomes are particularly vulnerable if they experience a sudden loss of income resulting from redundancies, relationship break-up or ill health. Mortgage holders are at risk of house repossession and Ippr argues for the government to address income inequality and job security, support social housing and promote affordable credit initiatives for low income families.

Families who are trapped in a cycle of poverty may be suffering from lack of employment, poor housing, overcrowding, lack of resources leading to poor health and diet, post-natal depression, mental health, learning difficulties (Raffo et al., 2007). Low socio-economic status does not mean low aspiration, but it is more likely there are barriers to achieving them (Hirsch, 2007). The gap in attainment is evidenced in Feinstein's (2003) research, which found that children from high socio-economic status at 22 months overtook the children from low socio-economic status as their age increased at 40 months, 5 years and 10 years of age. This was further substantiated by the Sutton Trust funded report (2010), which showed that children in the poorest fifth of families were already nearly a year behind children from middle income families in vocabulary tests. This research by Waldfogel and Washbrook (2010) indicates that children's educational achievements are strongly linked to parents' income and therefore a key barrier to social mobility.

Family policy in the time of the New Labour Government

The first five years of the New Labour Government saw unparalleled attention, resources and initiatives devoted to the early years as it 'rocketed onto the political, educational and research agenda' due to a commitment to reduce poverty and social exclusion (Taggert, 2004, p. 619). The Sure Start (Department for Education and Employment, 1999) community based local programmes were aimed at supporting children, families and communities in disadvantaged neighbourhoods. This cross-departmental government strategy was to improve and integrate the services of health care, education and community services. Sure Start's mandate was to promote the physical, intellectual and social development of preschool children to increase their chances of success when they began school. It aimed to access 'hard-to-reach parents' to increase opportunities for at-home parents to train for employment. The Working Families Tax Credit was created to provide financial support to families with low incomes and the Welfare-to-Work policy was to ensure childcare for lone parents. From 2002 the Sure Start community based local programmes were integrated into the Sure Start Children's Centres and the government promised there would be one centre located in every community.

The New Labour Government also focused on the role of parents and parenting interventions, which were highlighted through a range of policies including the Parenting Fund (2002), which allocated £25 million to support groups of parents, and the Education Act (2002), which gave powers to local authorities to prepare the way for Extended Schools to provide childcare, parenting support and other services (James, 2009).

The New Labour Government commenced the integration of children's services to create multi-agency teams of health, education, social services, law, youth work and child welfare professionals. This became more sharply focused in 2000 after the tragic death of Victoria Climbié, who was 'perceived to have "fallen through the cracks" of the implicated professional services' (Warin, 2007). The recommendations of the Laming Report (2003) were incorporated into Every Child Matters (ECM) (2004), which became one of the most important policies for children and children's services. All those who work with children and young people should have the knowledge and skills to do their utmost to help them develop and succeed across all the five ECM outcomes:

- being safe
- staying healthy

- enjoying and achieving
- making a positive contribution
- achieving economic well-being (Department for Education and Skills, 2004)

The focus on children and early intervention was demonstrated through the Children's Plan: Building Brighter Futures (2007), which set out objectives for achieving the Every Child Matters outcomes and the vision for reforming services for children. Joining up services was intended to work across professional boundaries in accessible locations for parents to provide both a safety net for the vulnerable and facilitate the potential of every child. The aim of the Children's Trust was to make high-quality arrangements for early intervention in the welfare of children and young people with additional needs through the implementation of integrated working practices across all children's services, including in schools and health. Critics of the New Labour Government policy disliked the emphasis on early intervention, declaring it to be highly instrumental and reflective of middle class values. Moss (2006) and Clarke (2006) argue that the policies have not addressed the complex underlying issues related to the poverty and self-esteem of families.

The evaluation of Sure Start's integrated services found they had 'a positive but limited effect', yet the initial evaluation suggested substantial benefits that met children, family and community needs 'without the stigma associated with specialist provision' (Sylva and Pugh, 2005, p. 20). Many feel it was unfortunate that time was not allowed for the 'bedding down, reflection and sense of ownership' of Sure Start (Jones et al., 2006, p. 212) and Belsky et al.'s (2007) longitudinal study found the community and neighbourhood environment at the heart of Sure Start to be a significant factor in enhancing children's well-being. However, Hirsch (2007, p. 8) found that some needy groups were not being reached due to availability and access, cultural barriers or parents' lack of literacy.

The Coalition Government, 2010

When the Coalition Government came to power in May 2010, the UK was emerging from a recession and was still feeling the effects of the banking and financial crisis. The reduction of the national debt was to be the main priority for the new government and they immediately indicated the changes to policy and the demands that society would have to meet to address the financial situation.

The Coalition Government rapidly began to introduce new reforms to education and health that would have long-reaching effects on families. Immediate policy shifts included the cutting of government QUANGOs; the deregulation of developments such as Contact Point; the Children's Trust Fund and the Children's Plan; changes to Serious Case Reviews and restrictions to local authority expenditure (Frost, 2011). The Department for Children,

Schools and Families was rapidly renamed the Department of Education emitting a strong ideological message reflecting an 'educated child' replacing New Labour's vision that promoted a 'holistic' child.

In a Comprehensive Spending Review (*The Foundation Years: Preventing Poor Children Becoming Poor Adults*) of October 2010, the chancellor announced the continuation of the Sure Start Children's Centres in disadvantaged areas, with services targeted to work more effectively to remove barriers for vulnerable families (Field, 2010). The poorest young members of society would be particularly supported and 130,000 disadvantaged two-year-olds would receive 15 hours a week of free nursery education, building on the pilot schemes introduced by New Labour. Health visitors were to be at the centre of the initiative, particularly supporting families who felt socially 'alienated' and those with SEN children. Families with low incomes would receive less financial support to pay for childcare, as the childcare element of the working tax credit would return to the 70-per-cent level.

Sir Paul Ennals, chief executive of the National Children's Bureau, gave his considered verdict on the Comprehensive Spending Review:

> times still look tough for children's services across a number of areas. ... The freezing of Sure Start budgets for four years means, in effect, at least 13 per cent real cuts by 2014. While this should be enough to retain the bulk of existing Children's Centres, and a universal offer, we will still see real reductions in many local services. Reductions to working families tax credit puts the financing of many childcare services at risk, especially in city areas where costs are high. ... Family support services, including play services, seem likely to have to rely on the new Early Intervention Grant. ... Children's social care – child protection and support for children in care – faces a rising tide of demand, which can only be met if the other services above are more deeply cut. (CYPN, 2010)

Ennals advised that everyone would need to adjust to the financial situation through creative thinking. Along with families, both public and private organizations would need to adjust to restricted budgets and the challenges would be to collect evidence and determine what worked effectively.

Towards the end of 2010, government minister Frank Field conducted The Independent Review on Poverty and Life Chances – a powerful review which acknowledged that the first five years of young children's lives are those which predicate their future life chances. The new strategy to meet the government's target of abolishing child poverty is detailed in the report *The Foundation Years: Preventing Poor Children Becoming Poor Adults*. The report has two overarching recommendations: to prevent poor children from becoming poor adults and to establish a set of life chances indicators that will measure how successful we are as a country in making life's outcomes more equitable for all children.

Megan Pacey, Chief Executive of Early Education (a leading national voluntary organization for early years practitioners and parents in the UK), welcomed this review:

> Early Education is delighted that opportunities for a child's cognitive, language and social and emotional development as well as support for parenting, good health services, Children's Centres and high quality early education and care have been identified as the issues that matter most. Shamefully, many of the decisions of the Coalition Government in the course of the Comprehensive Spending Review and subsequent announcements fly in the face of this overwhelming evidence. (Pacey, 2010)

Pacey believed that the removal of the ring-fencing of many early years grants would cause local authorities to reduce spending their entire Sure Start allocation on services for young children and their families and that the removal of the requirement for the Children's Centres to offer full day care would make it impossible to support many parents' return to study and work. Pacey was concerned about the sustainability of the existing high quality provision if qualified teachers and EYPs were removed. This concern drew on clear evidence from EPPE that trained teachers promote better intellectual and social and emotional outcomes for children, particularly among disadvantaged children.

The Allen (2011) report, compiled by cross political party cooperation, examined the effects of 'early intervention' in breaking the cycle of deprivation that can occur from generation to generation. The report recommended that early intervention should play a more central part in UK policy and practice to provide a social and emotional bedrock for current and future generations of babies, children and young people by helping them and their parents/caregivers before problems arise. It advised that the government should further develop existing policies in this field to make sure that all children have the social and emotional capability to be 'school ready' at five. The report's recommendations included: enabling vulnerable first-time mothers access to Family Nurse Partnerships; a national parenting campaign as part of the 'Big Society'; high-quality, benchmarked pre-school education for two, three and four-year-olds as part of a birth–five Foundation Stage; and a more coherent series of assessments for the birth–fives.

The Tickell Review (2011) of the Early Years Foundation Stage gathered evidence from a wide range of professionals working in the early years sector. Claire Tickell (2011) stated that its recommendations built on and improved the current statutory framework to create a revised EYFS that is more flexible and accessible to provide a strong foundation for all children and families. However there are concerns that play has less priority with a lack of depth of understanding of its complexity as a vehicle for learning in this review than in the original EYFS. Furthermore the reception year appears to be more of a preparation for year 1, which will also create less emphasis on learning through play.

The Final Report of the Munro Review of Child Protection (2011) finds that local areas should have more freedom to design their own child protection services. Munro states this is a radical shift from previous reforms that she believes had resulted in overmuch bureaucracy and a loss of focus on the needs of the child. Munro called this third and final report 'a child-centred system' to reflect that the effectiveness of help and the experiences of children, young people and families are central to her recommendations for reform. The report advocates the revision of statutory, multi-agency guidance to remove unnecessary prescription and to focus only on essential rules for effective multi-agency working. The recommendations include local authorities implementing sufficient prevention, identification and provision of early intervention; that the prescribed timescales for social work assessments should be removed; the OfSTED inspection framework should examine the effectiveness of all local services, including health, education, police, probation and the justice system, and that social workers should exercise more professional judgment, but also improve their expertise, knowledge and skills.

Munro aligns this report with those of Field (2010), Allen (2011) and Tickell (2011) on the effectiveness of early intervention with children and families through preventative services rather than reactive services. However there are worries from critics of the Coalition reforms that the focus on early intervention may lead to a pathologizing of disadvantaged families.

Frost (2011) believes that the two UK governments have two distinctly different and ideological models of childhood. New Labour promoted an ethos of regulation, assessment and measurement; social investment and professional involvement; holistic, planned and strategic approaches. The Coalition Government aims to provide less regulation; less social investment; an 'educated' child rather than the 'holistic' child; a more 'privatised' and less 'public' existence that has more localised variation.

Future challenges

Research and policy have documented the complex and powerful influences that home and community have on young children's educational and social achievement. There is therefore an increasing expectation that professionals will work in partnership with parents. However, it is important to consider the ethics involved through examining the breadth of possibilities and choices in what is offered to families and any 'taken-for-granted' constructions that might be promoted through policy development. Parents and families are not a homogeneous group; they are complex organisms with different individual needs, values and aspirations. There is still considerable debate surrounding the issue of supporting inclusion, and the concept of partnership with parents is often 'bandied about' without a full understanding of the promotion of true equity in services (Jones et al., 2006, p. 65). There are complex issues surrounding the expert–client relationship. Real partnerships are hard to achieve, requiring commitment and perspicacity from practitioners and there may be dilemmas, challenges and tensions for the professionals through the changing relationships, boundaries and power relationships.

There was a huge policy shift when the Labour Government, which came to power in 1997, recognized that children are connected to families and that it is no use intervening without taking into account family strengths and needs. Professionals have had to realize the implications of policy decisions and the rights of children and families. There are challenges and tensions for the government and for the professionals represented in this book. Will the Coalition Conservative and Liberal Government formed in May 2010 continue to support and defend families? Out of economic necessity will the government turn to a new model of community partnerships with more self-autonomy? Will it allow families to work together as was the ideal of the original Sure Start programmes? It might be more effective for individuals to be empowered to fight for their rights rather than relying on professional intervention.

It can be seen that there are definitely ethical dilemmas ahead regarding any decisions about future social policy. Table 1.5 exemplifies milestones of policy and initiatives that have impacted early childhood in the UK between 1999 and 2010. The following chapters will show how some of these key policies have impacted on professionals' knowledge and practice and against which they have internalized and constructed their professionalism. The next chapter explores the team around the child and the issues and challenges for interdisciplinary working.

Questions for reflective practice

How does social policy impact on your thinking and practice?

What are the essential aspects of social policy that you need to know about?

How will you keep yourself up to date with social policy, government initiatives and the impact of change?

Table 1.5 Milestones of policy and initiatives that have impacted on early childhood in the UK, 1999–2010

Date	Overarching policy	Early childhood education and care	Social work	Health
1999	Sure Start Local Programmes introduced to bring together early education, childcare, health and family support for the benefit of young children and their parents in disadvantaged neighbourhoods. National Family and Parenting Institute established. Family Support Grant set up for projects supporting families and parents. Devolution of powers to National Governments of Northern Ireland, Scotland and Wales. Libraries for All: Social Exclusion in Public Libraries (Department for Culture, Media and Sport).	Sure Start trailblazer areas set up. Sure Start Local Programmes by 2003 to reach one-third of poor children under 4 years old. Early Learning Goals (Qualifications and Curriculum Authority) replaced Desirable Learning Outcomes. Education: Nursery Education and Early Years Development Regulations. Early years education, childcare and playwork framework of nationally accredited qualifications.	Protection of Children Act established a list of people who are considered unsuitable to work with children.	New funds available to the NHS for improving CAMHS via the NHS Modernization Fund. National Healthy Schools Programme (DoH and DfEE) advocates whole school approach to promoting emotional health and well-being. Teenage Pregnancy Strategy in England. Mental Capacity Act.
2000	Children Bill. Millennium Cohort Study following almost 16,000 children. Comprehensive Spending Review increased to £500 million to set up at least 500. Children's Fund for services to children and young people at risk of social exclusion. Learning and Skills Council set up.	Foundation Stage and the Curriculum Guidance for the Foundation Stage (CGFS) introduced. Care Standards Act introduced quality standards. Neighbourhood Nurseries initiative focused on expanding childcare provision to reduce unemployment in disadvantaged areas. National Occupational Standards developed.	Framework for the Assessment of Children in Need and Their Families.	NHS Plan set out a ten-year programme of investment and reform. Included a requirement that health and local authorities work together to produce a local CAMHS strategy. Special Educational Needs (SEN) Code of Practice aimed to provide equality of opportunity and high achievement for all children.
2001	Government's strategy paper 'Tackling child poverty' published. Family services across England and Wales are mapped for the first time by the National Family and Parenting Institute. Children's Tax Credit launched.	Responsibility for regulation of child-minding and daycare for children under 8 transferred to Ofsted, making one regulatory body across England.	Special Educational Needs and Disability Act.	

(Continued)

Table 1.5 Continued

Date	Overarching policy	Early childhood education and care	Social work	Health
2002	2002 Spending Review – £25 million allocated to Parenting Fund; Children at Risk review. Employment Act increased statutory maternity leave to six months' paid leave and a further six months' unpaid leave and introduced two weeks paid paternity leave.	Education Act 2002 – Extended Schools provided childcare, parent-ing support and other services. Interdepartmental Childcare Review established Children's Centres for pre-school children in the 20 per cent most disadvantaged wards. Birth to Three Matters framework. National Literacy and Numeracy Strategies evaluation by Ofsted. Early years sector endorsed founda-tion degree.	Looking After Children System, a planning system for looked after children. Integrated Children's System.	Early Support established. DfEE/DoH: *Practice Guidance for Professionals Working with Disabled Children (Birth to Two) and Families.*
2003	Green paper 'Every Child Matters' (HM Treasury) consultation. Common Assessment Framework (CAF) proposed. Children's Centres programme launched. Rebranding of Early Excellence Centres and Sure Start projects as Children's Centres. Thirty-two established to provide a single place for five key services: early education, child-care, health, family support and help into employment. New Children, Young People and Families Directorate. Children's services (except health and youth justice) brought together under the direction of Minister for Children. Child Tax Credit and Working Tax Credit introduced. DCMS Framework for the Future: Libraries, Learning and Information in the Next Decade – first-ever national public library strategy.	Sure Start programmes also deliver childcare and include Neighbourhood Nurseries. Sure Start launched Investors in Children. Excellence and Enjoyment: a primary National Strategy for schools. Childcare Review announced. Foundation Stage Profile – QDA replaced baseline assessment.	Lord Laming published the report of his inquiry into the death of Victoria Climbié.	Early Support established. DfEE/DoH: *Practice Guidance for Professionals Working with Disabled Children (Birth to Third Birthday) and Their Families.*

2004	Children Act – took forward proposals in Every Child Matters. Every Child Matters: Change for Children. HM Government. Five central outcomes for children: be healthy, stay safe, enjoy and achieve, make a positive contributions, achieve economic well-being. Child Poverty Review.	Choice for parents, the best start for children: a ten-year strategy for childcare. 2004 Spending Review, further funding for Sure Start – target of 2,500 Children's Centres by 2008. The pilot for free early education for 2-year-olds is extended to 12,000 places. Effective Preschool and Primary Education 3–11 Project final report.	'Choosing Health' white paper echoed the importance of parents in improving their children's health. National Service Framework for Children, Young People and Maternity Services set out a Child Centred Approach to Health programme.
2005	Treasury report, *Support for Parents: The Best Start for Children*. Child Trust Fund launched. Transformation Fund. Reports from National Evaluation of Sure Start analysing the early stages of the programme. Children, Young People and Families Grant programme launched. Sure Start Children's Centres practice guidance. National Professional Qualification in Integrated Centre Leadership established in National College of School Leadership. House of Commons, Culture Media and Sport Committee's *Public Libraries: Third Report of Session 2004–05*, emphasized core provision of books.	Childcare Affordability Programme Pilot Review. Social and Emotional Aspects of Learning (SEAL) programme introduced in schools promoting emotional health and well-being and positive behaviour. Extended schools prospectus – to be rolled out nationally by 2010. White paper, 'Higher standards, better schools for all'. Education Act aligned early years inspections with school inspections.	Local authorities implemented the Common Assessment Framework, a form used by any practitioner assessing a child's needs, to simplify the assessment process for parents and professionals and encourage joint working.

(*Continued*)

Table 1.5 Continued

Date	Overarching policy	Early childhood education and care	Social work	Health
2006	1,000 Children's Centres – including 500 Sure Start Local Programmes, 430 Neighbourhood Nurseries and 70 Early Excellence Centres (National Audit Office figures). Funding now provided through local authorities. Children's Trusts bring together social care, health, police, education, districts and other services to ensure integrated, child centered approaches to improve outcomes for children, young people and their families. Parenting support: guidance for local authorities in England. Police and Justice Act enables a local authority or a registered social landlord to enter into a parenting contract with a parent. Transformation Fund. *Working Together to Safeguard Children: A Guide to Inter-Agency Working to Safeguard and Promote the Welfare of Children.* The Children and Young People's Plan (England) – actions and provisions by which local authorities would improve children's and young people's well-being (the five Every Child Matters outcomes for children). Commission on Families and the Wellbeing of Children reports on the relationship between the state and the family.	Childcare Act – first Act to deal solely with early years and childcare. Transition Information Sessions for Parents (Also known as Starting School and Moving On Sessions). Early Learning Partnership projects established to support 1 to 3-year-olds who are at risk of learning delay. Choice for Parents: The Best Start for Children. Education and Inspection Act. Early Years Professional Status. Implementing the Disability Discrimination Act in schools and early years settings.	Children and Adoption Act. Working Together to Safeguard Children. Family Intervention Projects established. 'Care matters' green paper to address problems of children in care and including prevention policies. Reaching Out: An Action Plan on Social Exclusion – focus on families seen not to be benefiting from the general investment in services.	Review of F27 identified priority areas for service providers and commissioners achieving ten-year objectives. £7 million DoH and DFES joint-funded pilots of intensive home visiting to families by health visitors and midwives during pregnancy and the first two years of children's lives. Reaching Out: An Action Plan on Social Exclusion – ten health-led parenting support projects for vulnerable first-time mothers.

2007	Department for Children, Schools and Families (DCSF) created to take lead responsibility overall for children and families. Aiming High for Disabled Children programme. Every Parent Matters – overview of policy relating to parents and parenting (DfES). Comprehensive Spending Review – includes policy review on children and young people. *Aiming High for Children: Supporting Families* report – funding for Children's Centres to support outreach and provide parenting classes for up to 30,000 parents, emphasis on reaching more fathers. Green paper on welfare reform 'In work, better off' proposes measures to get more parents into work including reducing the period for which lone parents are entitled to income support. Paid maternity leave is extended to nine months. DWP publishes *Working for Children*, a strategy to tackle child poverty by getting more parents into work. National standards for leaders of Sure Start Children's Centres.	Governance Guidance for Children's Centres and Extended Schools. Every Parent Matters strategy.	Contact Point – online directory for authorized practitioners in different services to find out who else is working with the same child and deliver faster, more coordinated support. Treasury review of services for children and young people announces a £340 million settlement for disabled children and their families.	Public Service Agreement (PSA) published by Treasury, embedding joint working by DoH and DCSF on child health and highlighting mental health and psychological well-being. DoH review of the role of health visitors, proposing that they should be leading multi-skilled teams. Family Nurse Partnership programme is piloted in ten local authority/PCT areas Strategy on maternity services aims to give women more choice.

(Continued)

Table 1.5 Continued

Date	Overarching policy	Early childhood education and care	Social work	Health
2008	Children's Plan: Building Brighter Futures Next Steps for the Children's Workforce.	Early Years Foundation Stage Statutory framework.	Children and Young Persons Act – delivery of social work services for children and young people.	The final report of the independent CAMHS review.
	Think Family initiative launched, accompanied by a series of Family Pathfinders to test new ways of working across adult and children's services.	DCSF play strategy launched with a commitment of £235 million to improve and develop play facilities.	2020 Children and Young People's Workforce Strategy.	Targeted Mental Health in Schools – pathfinders established, to identify effective ways of delivering mental health support to children aged 5–13.
	Review launched into the impact of the commercial world on children's well-being.	Every Child a Talker: Guidance for Early Language Lead Practitioners.	Staying Safe: Action Plan – response to consultation on the first-ever cross-government strategy.	Child Health Promotion programme emphasizes promotion of psychological well-being through a progressive universal approach starting in pregnancy.
	2020 Children and Young People's Workforce Strategy – to help children and young people develop and succeed across ECM.		Child protection plan within the Integrated Children's System.	Healthy Weight, Healthy Lives – A Cross-Government Strategy for England.
	Launch of the Parent Know-How programme, providing government funding for various helplines and advice websites.		Social Exclusion Task Force's report *Think Family: Improving the Life Chances of Families at Risk*.	Quality Care for All. NHS next stage review final report.
	National Academy for Parenting Practitioners launched.		Social Work Task Force commenced a review of the profession and to advise on a comprehensive reform programme for social work.	Bercow Review of Services for Children and Young People (0–19) with Speech, Language and Communication Needs.
	Child Maintenance Act amended the law relating to child support.			Better Communication. An Action Plan to Improve Services for Children and Young People with Speech, Language and Communication Needs.
				Inclusion Development Programme. Supporting Children with Speech, Language and Communication Needs : Guidance for Practitioners in the Early Years Foundation Stage.

Year				
2009	The Apprenticeships, Skills, Children and Learning Bill gave the Children's Trust Board legal responsibility for preparing, monitoring and implementing the Children and Young People's Plan.	Next Steps for Early Learning and Childcare. Early Education Pilot for Two Year Old Children Evaluation.	Children on child protection registers published every year. Welfare Reform Act – amended the law relating to social security; provision enabling disabled people to be given greater control over the way in which certain public services are provided for them; law relating to child support; provision about the registration of births.	White paper, 'Equity to excellence – liberating the NHS'. CAMHS outcome measure to monitor the impact of professionals' work. Ten-year drug strategy prioritizes families for the first time. Family Nurse Partnership (DSCF/DoH) evaluation report. Healthy Schools' initiative expanded. Health Act – quality and division of NHS services in England. The Operating Framework for the NHS in England 2010/11.
2010	DCSF 'Support for all: the families and relationships green paper' sets out the government's range of measures to support all families. Embedding the play strategy (DSCF) vision for all to have access to free, high-quality space areas in every locality. Child Poverty Act set targets relating to the eradication of child poverty and to make other provision about child poverty. *Starting a Family Revolution: Putting Families in Charge.* The Family Commission for Children. Coalition Government's Comprehensive Spending Review DCMS: *The Modernisation Review of Public Libraries: A Policy Statement.* Cm 7821. London, The Stationery Office. *The Foundation Years: Preventing Poor Children Becoming Poor Adults,* report of The Independent Review on Poverty and Life Chances.	Children, Schools and Families Act. *Making an Impact on Black Children's Achievement* published by National Strategies. Ofsted published *Outstanding Local Authority Children's Services 2009. Breaking the Link in the Early Years Between Disadvantage and Low Achievement* (DCSF). DCSF rebranded as Department of Education by the Coalition Government. Academies Act 2 – 32 schools converted to academy status independent schools. Review of Early Years Foundation Stage. Government proclaims commitment to returning Sure Start to its original purpose of early intervention, increasing its focus on the neediest families.	Social Work Task Force (DCSF) to conduct a 'nuts and bolts' review of the profession and to advise on the shape and content of a comprehensive reform programme for social work.	White paper, National Health Service 2010–2015: from good to great – preventative, people centred and productive.

References

Alexander, C., Duncan, S., and Edwards, R. (eds) (2010), *Teenage Parenthood: What's the Problem?* London: The Tufnell Press.

Allen, G. (2011), *Early Intervention: The Next Steps. An Independent Report to Her Majesty's Government.* London: The Cabinet Office, HM Government.

Anning, A., and Ball, M. (2008), *Improving Services for Young Children from Sure Start to Children's Centre.* London: Sage.

Anning, A., and Edwards, A. (1999), *Promoting Children's Learning from Birth to Five.* Buckingham: Open University Press.

Baldock, P., Fitzgerald, D., and Kay, J. (2009), *Understanding Early Years Policy.* London: Paul Chapman Publishing.

BBC (2009), *The Family,* television programme. British Broadcasting Corporation.

BBC News online newspaper (5 November 2007), Families' future looks brighter. http://news.bbc.co.uk/1/hi/uk/7074760. stm. Accessed 10 January 2010.

Belsky, J., Lowe Vandell, D., Burchinall, M., Clare-Stewart, K., McCarney, K., and Owen, M. (2007), Are there long-term effects of early child care? *Child Development,* 78, 681–701.

Ben-Galim, D., and Lanning, T. (2010), *Strength Against Shocks: Low-Income Families and Debt.* London: Institute for Public Policy Research.

Bourdieu, P. (1990), *The Logic of Practice.* Cambridge: Polity Press.

Broadhead, P., Meleady, C., and Delgado, M. (2008), *Children, Families and Communities.* Maidenhead: McGraw-Hill/OUP.

Brock, A., Dodds, S., Jarvis, P., and Olusoga, Y. (2009), *Perspectives on Play: Learning for Life.* London: Pearson Education.

Bronfenbrenner, U. (1979), *The Ecology of Human Development.* Cambridge, MA: Harvard University Press.

— (1989), Ecological systems theory. *Annals of Child Development,* 6, 187–249.

CAMHS (Children and Mental Health Services) (2008), *Children and Young People in Mind: The Final Report of the National Camhs Review.* Compiled by DCSF and DoH. http://news.bbc.co.uk/1/hi/uk/7074760.stm.

Children's Society (2009), *A Good Childhood.* www.childrenssociety.org.uk/all_about_us/how_we_do_it/the_good_childhood_inquiry/1818.html. Accessed 21 January 2010.

Clarke, K. (2006), Childhood, parenting and early intervention: A critical examination of the Sure Start national programme. *Critical Social Policy,* 26, 699–721.

CPAG (Child Poverty Action Group) (2009a), *Child Wellbeing and Child Poverty: Where the UK Stands in the European Table.* London: Child Poverty Action Group.

— (2009b), *New Child Wellbeing League Table: UK in 24th Place Out of 29 European Countries.* CPAG press release. Accessed 21 April 2009. www.cpag.org.uk/press/2009/210409.htm.

CYPN (2010), (*Children and Young People Now*). www.cypnow.co.uk/Archive/1036354/NCBs-Ennals-throws-down-gauntlet-childrens-services/. Accessed 10 November 2010.

DCSF (Department for Children, Schools and Families) (2007), *Children's Plan: Building Brighter Futures.* London: The Stationery Office.

Department for Children, Schools and Families (2008), *Families in Britain: An Evidence Paper.* London: The Parliamentary Bookshop.

— (2009), *Lamb Inquiry for Special Educational Needs and Parental Confidence.* Nottingham: DCSF Publications.

— (2010), *Support for All: The Families and Relationships Green Paper.* Norwich: The Stationery Office.

Dex, S., and Joshi, H. (eds) (2005), *Children of the 21st Century: From Birth to Nine Months*. Bristol: Policy Press.

DfEE (Department for Education and Employment) (1999), *Sure Start. Making a Difference for Children and Families*. Suffolk: DfEE Publications.

DfES (Department for Education and Skills) (2004), *Every Child Matters: Change in Children in Schools*. London: DfES.

Duncan, S., Edwards, R., and Alexander, C. (2010), *Teenage Parenthood: What's the Problem?* London: The Tufnell Press.

Ennals, P. (2010), Press release of the chief executive of the National Children's Bureau to Children and Young People Now. www.cypnow.co.uk/BigIssues/Details/87746/comprehensive-spending-review/Article/1036354/NCBs-Ennals-throws-down-gauntlet-childrens-services/. Accessed 21 December 2010.

The Family Commission/4Children (2010), *Starting a Family Revolution: Putting Families in Charge. '4Children' Inquiry into Family Life*. www.4children.org.uk/. Accessed 27 October 2010.

Feinstein, L. (2003), Inequality in the early cognitive development of British children in the 1970 cohort. *Economica*, 70, 73–98.

Field, F. (2010), *The Foundation Years: Preventing Poor Children Becoming Poor Adults. The Report of the Independent Review on Poverty and Life Chances*. London: Cabinet Office, HM Government.

Frost, N. (2011), From New Labour to Coalition Policy – two models of childhood. Seminar presentation to CRinCH (Childhood Research into Children), Leeds Metropolitan University. 23.3.11.

Hansen, K., and Joshi, H. (2007), *Millennium Cohort Study. Second Survey: A User's Guide to Initial Findings*. London: Centre for Longitudinal Studies, Institute of Education, University of London.

Hirsch, D. (2007), *Chicken and Egg: Child Poverty and Educational Inequalities*. London: Child Poverty Action Group.

HMSO (2006), *Childcare Act*. London: The Stationery Office.

Hunter, M. (2008), Parents in prison: Don't judge the children. *Learning Support*, 20 (Autumn). Bishops Castle: Brightday Publishing.

James, A., and Prout, A. (1997), *Constructing and Reconstructing Childhood*. London: Falmer Press.

James, C. (2009), *Ten Years of Family Policy 1999–2009*. London: Family and Parenting Institute.

Jones, L., Holmes, R., and Powell, J. (eds) (2006), *Early Childhood Studies: A Multiprofessional Perspective*. Maidenhead: Open University Press.

Laming, W. (2003), *The Victoria Climbié Inquiry Report*. www.victoria-climbie-inquiry.org.uk/.

Lewis, A., and Lindsay, G. (2000), *Researching Children's Perspectives*. Buckingham: Open University Press.

Moss, P. (2006), Structures, understandings and discourses: Possibilities for re-envisioning the early childhood worker. *Contemporary Issues in Early Childhood*, 7, 30–41.

Munro, E. (2011), *The Munro Review of Child Protection—Final Report: A Child-Centred System*. Department for Education. London: The Parliamentary Bookshop.

Nutbrown, C., and Clough, P. (2006), *Inclusion in the Early Years: Cultural Analyses and Enabling Narratives*. London: Sage.

Office for National Statistics (Social Trends web page). www.statistics.gov.uk/socialtrends/. Accessed 10 March 2010.

Pacey, M. (2010), Early education press release. www.early-education.org.uk/press_release_03–12–10.htm. Accessed 21 December 2010.

Raffo, C., Dyson, A., Gunter, H., Hall, D., Jones, L., and Kalambouka, A. (2007), *Education and Poverty: A Critical Review of Theory, Policy and Practice*. York: Joseph Rowntree Foundation and University of Manchester.

Reed, M. (2008), Professional development in reflective practice. In A. Paige-Smith and A. Craft (eds), *Developing Reflective Practice in the Early Years*. Maidenhead: Open University Press/McGraw-Hill .

Seymour, C., and Hairston, C. F. (2001), *Children with Parents in Prison: Child Welfare Policy, Program, and Practice Issues*. Piscataway, NJ: Transaction Publishers.

Smallwood, S., and Wilson, B. (eds) (2007), *Focus on Families*. Basingstoke: Palgrave Macmillan.

Smith, R. (2009), *A Universal Child?* Basingstoke: Palgrave Macmillan.

Storybook Dads (2010), www.storybookdads.co.uk/. Accessed 10 March 2010

Sylva, K., and Pugh, G. (2005), Transforming the early years in England. *Oxford Review of Education*, 31, 11–27.

Sylva, K., Siraj-Blatchford, I., Taggert, B., Sammons, P., Elliot, K., and Melhuish, E. (2004), *The Effective Provision of Preschool Education [EPPE] Project Technical Paper 12 – The Final Report: Effective Preschool Education*. London: DfES and Institute of Education, University of London.

Taggert, B. (2004), Early years education and care: Three agendas (editorial). *British Educational Research Association Journal*, 30, 619–622.

Tickell, C. (2011), *The Early Years Foundation Stage (EYFS) Review. An Independent Report*. London: The Cabinet Office, HM Government.

— (2011), *The Tickell Review (2011) of the Early Years Foundation Stage*. http://www.education.gov.uk/tickellreview. Accessed 10.5.11.

Waldfogel, J., and Washbrook, E. (2010), *Low Income and Early Cognitive Development in the U.K.* www.suttontrust.com/research/low-income-and-early-cognitive-development-in-the-uk/. Accessed 1 October 2010.

Warin, J. (2007), Joined-up services for young children and their families: Papering over the cracks or re-constructing the foundations? *Children and Society*, 21, 87–97.

2

Issues and Challenges for the Interdisciplinary Team in Supporting the Twenty-First-Century Family

Carolynn Rankin and Fiona Butler

Chapter Outline

Introduction

The first chapter in this book looked at the child in the context of the complexities of twenty-first-century family life. This chapter will focus on the practitioners who support the child and considers the complex structural models that have been devised when a range of professionals endeavour to work together to provide services to children and their families. Aspects of theory relating to teams and teamwork will be explored and the challenges associated with working in multi-agency and multi-disciplinary teams discussed. This chapter presents the range of settings and adults that a child may encounter in her early years; this will differ for the individual child according to her family circumstances, health-related issues and particular individual needs and wants as shown by the vignettes provided in Chapter 1. The discussion will draw on the voice of practitioners who work in support of the child, reinforcing the message that teamwork is important. In order to deliver and achieve organizational objectives, practitioners need a functional structure in which to work. Teamwork can be innovative and creative and people working together can help to solve complex problems.

Political directives for teamwork

The UK Government policy under New Labour required a focus on working across professional and organizational boundaries as this was seen as a potential way to help complex societal problems. Partnership working and increased interagency working have been promoted with legislation aimed at increasing these types of cooperation at strategic and operational levels. Glenny and Roaf (2008) refer to a seminal report by Hodgkin and Newell (1996) entitled 'Effective Government Structures for Children', which proposed ways of ensuring that central government is responsive to children's needs. The policy timeline introduced in Chapter 1, p. XX shows a number of examples of this political directive for teamwork. Developments such as the Sure Start programme of interagency efforts to meet the needs of children under 4 years of age and their families provided good early years practice, and the Early Excellence Centres initiative provided a focus for the integration of family support. The Lord Laming report of 2003 (Laming, 2003) highlighted the failure of coordinated working among key agencies, and the Every Child Matters initiative in the same year sought a solution through whole systems reform of interagency working. The Children Act 2004 (Department for Education and Skills, 2004a) indicated a systematic rather than an ad hoc approach to increased partnership working. The act provided a legislative spine for the wider strategy for improving children's lives, covering the universal services which every child accesses and more targeted services for those with additional needs. This new focus on children and families was particularly to improve outcomes for children and young people.

However, this is not such a new idea. In the foreword to *The Team Around the Child* (Siraj-Blatchford et al., 2007), Dame Gillian Pugh reminds us that multi-agency working in the early years is not a new phenomenon, as there is a history of combining the welfare and education of young children. French (2007) provides the historical background to multi-agency working against which current policies have been set. The breadth and overall vision of the new Labour Government agenda beginning in 1997 required a massive paradigm shift on the part of all who worked with children and their families. Multi-agency working was to be encouraged as the most effective way of responding to needs. Young children and their families do not see their needs for early education, health care, literacy support, job or housing advice as separate silos and neither should the professionals working to support them. As French notes:

> All services for children will now be provided through jointly planned, commissioned, financed initiatives in participation and consultation with local parents. This requires a high level of integrated working across agencies, and relies on changed attitudes, the enthusiasm of practitioners, appropriate resources, and effective leadership and management. (2007, p. 64)

Children's Trusts were established as local partnerships which bring together the organizations responsible for services for children, young people and families in a shared commitment to improving children's lives. They were seen as the main catalysts at a local authority level with specific proposals around integrated personnel, integrated processes via a Common Assessment Framework (CAF) and a single database of information on all children. The notion of integrated systems around a single young people's plan and a joint commissioning framework promoted the idea that 'joined-up working' or 'thinking' acknowledged the inter-relatedness of the needs of children, adults and families. This approach spanned the fields of health, education, social services, law enforcement, housing, employment and family support. The political directives encouraging collaboration across professional and organization boundaries called for effective teamwork.

Back to basics – theory of teamwork

Before we look further at how practitioners are required to work together to support the child, let us consider the basic elements of teamwork and why this is an effective way to achieve objectives. In an organizational setting, a team can be regarded as a number of individuals working together to achieve a particular outcome, often tackling difficult, interdependent and complex tasks. Salas et al. (2008) defines a team as a set of two or more individuals that adaptively and dynamically interact through specified roles as they work toward shared and valued goals. Team members can also have different specializations in knowledge and skills, and it is this diversity of expertise that creates the potential for teams to complete work outside the scope of any one individual's capabilities. This is why teams and work groups continue to be such an important asset to organizations.

Belbin (2010) discusses how professionals must fulfil not only their functional roles, but also their roles as team members. Belbin began researching management teams in the 1970s with an interest in finding out why some teams worked successfully and others did not. In researching management team dynamics, each participant undertook a range of psychometric tests so that the effects of attributes such as behaviour and personality could be considered. The research revealed that the differences between success and failure for teams was more dependent on behaviour and not on factors such as intellect. Separate clusters of behaviour were identified by Belbin and his research team. These became known as Team Roles and were defined as 'a tendency to behave, contribute and interrelate with others in a particular way'. A total of nine different Team Roles were identified, indicating the strengths or contributions they provided and the summary descriptions are in Figure 2.1.

Each Team Role was also found to have 'allowable weaknesses', the flipside of the behavioural characteristics allowable in the team because of the strength which goes with it. The 'specialist' role was identified as the final Team Role and the value of an individual with in-depth knowledge of a key area was recognized as an essential team contribution. The allowable weakness for specialists is the tendency to focus narrowly on their own subject of choice and to prioritize this over the team's progress. The Team Roles identified by Belbin are used widely in organizations all over the world based on the premise that by identifying preferred Team Roles, individuals can use their strengths to advantage and try to manage weaknesses in their behaviour.

The social dynamics of effective teamwork are key to achieving the potential benefit for the parent organizations. Salas et al. (2008, p. 41) discuss taskwork competencies that are the knowledge, skills, attitudes and other characteristics used to accomplish individual task performance. However, team members must have individual-level expertise relevant to their own tasks, and also expertise in the social dynamics of teamwork in order to work effectively in an interdependent team. Salas et al. (2008, p. 39) write about the 'wisdom of collectives' as the increased capacity for performance of various types afforded by the interactions of team members. A further level of complexity is provided by an individual's cultural knowledge, acquired knowledge that we use to interpret experience and generate social behaviour, which will have an influence on the social dynamic of the team as cultural knowledge forms values, creates attitudes and influences behaviour (Salas et al., 2008, p. 532). Team building and effective working practices can take time to develop. In our twenty-first-century society there is constant flux and change in organizations and institutions. Organizational restructuring has the potential to damage a team. In a formal structure the job requirements will be clear and common goals shared, but this may only hold until the next reorganization when a team may be dismantled and a new team formed and the team building process needs to start all over again.

Looking at this from a functional viewpoint, teams endeavour to perform their tasks and achieve objectives in a complex, context-rich environment. Teams do not operate in a vacuum and many organizational and environmental factors can have a significant impact on how effectively they function. New forms of organizational structures are evolving to replace the more traditional hierarchical structures; this provides the opportunity and challenge for individuals to play an effective part in a range of settings with a different mix of practitioners.

Belbin® Team Role Summary Descriptions

Team Role Summary Descriptions

Team Role	Contribution	Allowable Weakness
Plant	Creative, imaginative, unorthodox. Solves difficult problems.	Ignores incidentals. Too pre-occupied to communicate effectively.
Resource Investigator	Extrovert, enthusiastic, communicative. Explores opportunities. Develops contacts.	Over-optimistic. Loses interest once initial enthusiasm has passed.
Coordinator	Mature, confident, a good chairperson. Clarifies goals, promotes decision-making, delegates well.	Can be seen as manipulative. Offloads personal work.
Shaper	Challenging, dynamic, thrives on pressure. Has the drive and courage to overcome obstacles.	Prone to provocation. Offends people's feelings.
Monitor Evaluator	Sober, strategic and discerning. Sees all options. Judges accurately.	Lacks drive and ability to inspire others.
Teamworker	Cooperative, mild, perceptive and diplomatic. Listens, builds, averts friction.	Indecisive in crunch situations.
Implementer	Disciplined, reliable, conservative and efficient. Turns ideas into practical actions.	Somewhat inflexible. Slow to respond to new possibilities.
Completer Finisher	Painstaking, conscientious, anxious. Searches out errors and omissions. Polishes and perfects.	Inclined to worry unduly. Reluctant to delegate.
Specialist	Single-minded, self-starting, dedicated. Provides knowledge and skills in rare supply.	Contributes on only a narrow front. Dwells on technicalities.

Figure 2.1 Belbin Team Role summary descriptions

So what makes an effective team in a context-rich environment?

There is an extensive body of literature on the theory, principles, tools and practical know-how about leading, managing and developing effective teams. In the Towards Interprofessional Partnerships (TIPS) research project Brock et al. (2009) found communication, assertive leadership, a supportive culture, individual qualities and organizational issues to be crucial factors for effective team working. Effective teams are characterized by a caring, compassionate approach. Where an atmosphere of openness and trust pervades, there is a sharing of responsibility, accountability and ownership of actions; commitment to the team is strong and strengths and weaknesses are known. The whole team acknowledges and deals with situations of potential conflict. This reinforces the concept of a healthy team in which no members are frightened or, when asking questions, made to feel inadequate because of their status (Brock et al., 2009, p. 20). Bertram et al. (2002, p. 10) argue that successful multi-professional practice requires shared philosophies and agreed working principles:

> A successful team is one that demonstrates professionalism, shared beliefs, common identity and vision and a breadth of experience and skills, and feels secure enough within the management system to take on new activities without fear and to operate within a professional climate which balances openness to new ideas with pragmatic critique. (Bertram et al., 2002, p. 10)

Relaxation of professional boundaries

Certain team processes and behaviour can help teams to perform effectively. A key factor is the need for clear goals and direction and clarity about what needs to be done and who is responsible for doing it. This can be supported by having regular meetings and opportunities to share information and by setting and working to agreed standards. Anticipating problems, having contingency plans and challenging complacency will also create and foster an environment in which team performance has effective outcomes.

> We have actions and targets to meet and we have quarterly planning sessions where I get the whole team together and we look at our actions and outcomes against the five ECM headings. That helps the team to understand why I keep banging on about outcomes, why they are important and make sustainable changes in families lives. It helps them think creatively about why they deliver stuff and the bigger picture. We've just changed the sessions from half day to full day sessions and we now also look at safeguarding across the whole spectrum. And we look at budgeting and resource management. This gives a team focus on what we deliver, why we do what we do, and also makes it not a me and them situation when I'm banging on about the SEF and asking them for the information I need. They're already aware of how they fit into the bigger picture. (Children's Centre Manager, professional background: education)

The settings – where the connections might be made and partnerships developed

Having considered some of the basic teamwork theory, let us look at the variety of settings where children and families might interact with a broad range of professionals and the services they offer. It is important to remember that many twenty-first-century children and their families will carry out their everyday lives without being regarded as having a problem, being at risk or needing particular additional specialist support.

> Obviously working really closely with Children's Centres and family outreach workers there are a lot of vulnerable families and you become aware of issues that may be arising. Also if you have groups in for story time sessions over a period of twelve weeks and you have the same people you build up relationships with them and you do find out what is going on in their lives. (Children's Librarian)

As stated in Chapter 1, a young child may have early childhood education and care experiences at home within the family, and outside her immediate environment, where she may encounter a combination of childminder, private day care, Children's Centre, foundation stage unit, nursery class or special needs school, nursery nurses, early years professionals and teachers. She may visit a health centre or medical practice and require the services of various health professionals such as midwives, health visitors, physiotherapists, paediatrician, dietician or speech and language therapist. The health visitor will introduce her to Bookstart and present her with a complementary book and library card and her parents may take her to meet librarians at their local library, mobile library or the one attached to a nearby Children's Centre. She may come into contact with a social worker or social services throughout her early years or may have one brief connection for a temporary problem. Table 2.1 outlines a range of settings and the professionals a child and her family might meet there. You may be aware of other examples depending on your own experience.

The young child may therefore encounter a range of different professionals who all have particular roles and expertise. These professionals will come together at different points in time to provide support – some are in constant contact with the child and her family, or this may be intermittent when the need or opportunity arises.

What is multi-agency working?

In an earlier section the theory of teamwork and how human interaction can benefit an organization through functional structures that help deliver and achieve organizational objectives were briefly examined. In twenty-first-century society there are many adjectives preceding the word 'team': multi-professional, multi-disciplinary, interdisciplinary, project, senior management, to name but a few. Speck notes that these varied descriptors are 'all

Table 2.1 A range of settings and professionals

Setting	Professionals a child/family might meet in that setting
Baby Café	breast feeding advisor, health visitor
Children's Centre	breast feeding advisor, childcare practitioner, early years professional, family support worker, health visitor, Job Centre Plus advisor, librarian, midwife, outreach team, social worker, speech and language therapist, teacher
crèche	childcare practitioner
Family court	advocate (for child), family liaison officer, guardian ad litem, guardian's solicitor, police officer, social workers, solicitors
Health centre	breastfeeding advisor, dentist, GP/doctor, health visitor, midwife, speech and language therapist,
Home environment	family support worker, GP/doctor health visitor, midwife, social worker, police officer
Home care worker's environment (childminder)	Children's Centre outreach team, home care worker
Hospital	dietician, nurse, paediatricians, play therapist specialists, consultant, doctor, physiotherapist
Library	Children's Centre outreach team, children's librarian, early years librarian
Private integrated child care and education (day care/preschools)	childcare practitioner, early years professional
School	family support worker, learning mentor, school nurse, speech and language therapist, teacher, teaching assistant

attracting different opinions as to their benefits and burdens' (2006, p. 5). The complexity of multi-professional teams for integrated children's services and the dilemmas they face has been described by Anning et al. (2006) and discussed in a management context by Messenger (2009). McInnes (2007, p. 8) notes that many different terms are used when discussing the various ways practitioners work to support children and their families and she refers to Lloyd et al. (2001) in describing this area as a 'terminological quagmire'. Drawing on a review of research and policy, Frost (2005, p. 13) suggested a hierarchy of terms in partnership working:

Level 1: cooperation – services work together toward consistent goals and complementary services while maintaining their independence.
Level 2: collaboration – services plan together and address issues of overlap, duplication and gaps in service provision towards common outcomes.
Level 3: coordination – services work together in a planned and systematic manner towards shared and agreed goals.
Level 4: merger/integration – different services become one organization in order to enhance service delivery.

Whatever the terminology used to describe their working principles and practices, these teams are made up of people from a range of professional backgrounds. The research into practitioners undertaken by Brock et al. (2009, p. 10) found that 'for professionals, a particular knowledge base, set of values, training and standing in the community at large gave them a particular professional identity'.

Atkinson et al. (2005) proposed five models of multi-agency activity based on the findings of a study into multi-agency working involving professionals from the education, social services and health sectors of local authorities:

1. Decision-making groups which provide a forum for different agencies to meet and make decisions;
2. Consultation and training – professionals from one agency provide consultation and/or training in order to enhance the skills and knowledge of another agency;
3. Centre-based delivery – gathering professional expertise in one place in order to deliver a much more coordinated and comprehensive service;
4. Coordinated delivery – similar to centre-based activity but with a coordinator to pull together previously disparate services;
5. Operational-team delivery – professionals from different agencies work together on a day-by-day basis to form a cohesive multi-agency team delivering services directly to service users.

All of these structural models require practitioners to work together to support the child and her family.

Challenges and opportunities in multi-disciplinary teams

The twenty-first-century child may be supported by a range of professionals with different perspectives, knowledge, skills and specialist terminology. Drawing on this diversity of knowledge and skills can be a strength when enabling the most effective interventions for children and families. However, this diversity can also be problematic as different perspectives may mean practitioners can be focused on the family, the mother, the child or a combination of all three (McInnes, 2010, p. 39). As identified in Chapter 1, practitioners may be supporting a very wide range of needs, for example, those contending with poverty and deprivation; looked-after children; children as carers; parents in prison; coping with ill health, mental health or obesity; enduring bereavement; the safeguarding of children from physical and emotional abuse.

Wistow and Hardy (1991) identify five types of obstacle to interagency working:

- structural, for example, lack of coterminosity and fragmented responsibilities across agency oundaries;
- procedural, for example, different operational systems, protocols, procedures and documentation;

- financial, for example, different funding streams and budget cycles;
- professional, for example, different values and roles, professional self-interest, interprofessional competition and competing priorities;
- status and legitimacy, for example, threats to autonomy and domain, and differences between elected and appointed status.

This overview of potential barriers in both working practice and individual perspectives highlights the importance of dialogue between professionals. To be effective this needs to be constant and it is often the informal, chance conversations where real understanding occurs (McInnes, 2010, p. 40). These connections need time so that practitioners have an opportunity to listen and communicate. This flags up the issue of developing trust and understanding. This takes time, a commodity which is at a premium for practitioners in the busy, highly regulated workplace. Effective partnership working takes time to develop and will have a better chance to flourish if space is devoted to planning and staff are fully involved in the process. The real world changes rapidly and the procedures and practices for partnership working will require regular review (Frost, 2005).

Table 2.2 is based on a review of the literature by McInness (2007) and provides an at-a-glance summary of the advantages and disadvantages of interagency working when considered from the differing perspectives of children and families, the professionals and the agencies.

Vision and purpose, roles and responsibilities

For teamwork around the child and her family to be effective there needs to be a common vision and purpose shared by the team members. But key questions are who has the vision, and is the vision shared by all those actively involved in the team? The Children Act (2004), for example, provides a strategic national vision for working with families and children. There need to be clear, realistic, achievable objectives which are understood and accepted by agencies and individual professionals and an acknowledgment that different agencies may have different aims but can still work collaboratively towards supporting the child and her family. In a small-scale study looking at perceptions of the most important factors in facilitating multi-agency working, Watson (2006) suggests that it is particularly important for co-located multi-agency teams to establish a shared vision, with clear and realistic aims and objectives and for team members to have a clear and shared understanding of the roles and responsibilities of members of the team.

> We had a brilliant closure day when we looked at the core offer and the Ofsted requirements – helping staff to look at their own roles and each other's jobs to try to understand each other's roles and responsibilities and where they fit into the bigger picture; trying to get the vision together with the staff; trying to write a joint vision statement. What do you want this centre to be? Trying to fire them up and get them excited about the work that we're doing as a centre. Leading them to move forward and try to lead change in the centre so that it impacts on the families. (Children's Centre manager, professional background: social care)

Table 2.2 Interagency working: Summary of advantages and disadvantages

	Advantages	Disadvantages
Children and families	Effective and focused support. Better access to services Better relationships with services. Improved behaviour/reduced school exclusions. Enhanced social and emotional well-being. High-quality services. Increased cognitive and social development. Rapid and appropriate support. Earlier identification of problems.	Limits choice for families. Increased surveillance of families.
Professionals	High satisfaction and improved quality of working lives. Stimulating and creative work. Less replication of services. Less isolation. Safer practice. Improved awareness of services and families' needs.	Increased workload.
Agencies	Broader perspective. Raised awareness of other agencies. Clarity of role and function. Cost-effective Helps the planning of future development. Holistic approach to commissioning and procurement.	Increased pressure.

Adapted from McInnes, 2007, pp. 20–1.

Creating agreement around a shared vision is not likely to be an easy task, as professionals from separate disciplines are likely to have differing aims and objectives and be starting out from different points in terms of values and culture. Aubrey (2007) notes that although there is the potential to help solve complex societal problems, multi-agency working may require more commitment of time, effort, creative thinking and financial resources than single agencies. Often professionals are directed, and expected, to work in teams.

> The management side of it is a lot more structured and dictatorial and I just find it hard to get my head round. We have all this government strategy stuff for this and this, and organisational and then on top of that we have a local thing. I just think I haven't got time for all of these strategies as well so I just think I'll go out there and do my job and if I'm doing it wrong someone will tell me.
> (Children's Centre manager, professional background: community development)

Children's Centres require a unique form of management due to the complexity of the multi-professional staff team and the variety of support services. Siraj-Blatchford et al.

(2007) suggest that this is why many centre managers show a flair for creativity and innovation.

Communication – the terminological quagmire

Information is often said to be the life blood of organizations and is a vital commodity in its own right. In a classically structured, hierarchical organization, strategic information would flow from the top down, cascaded through management layers. Information from the operational lower tiers would be passed back up the hierarchy by way of reporting on activity and productivity. This is a very simplistic view, but it is worth contrasting with the complex structures now in place to deliver services to children and their families. Poor communication within and between agencies has been cited as a major challenge to successful interdisciplinary working (Atkinson, 2005). Within agencies problems are reported between those working at strategic and operational levels. One example is where, although there may be an agreement at a strategic level for health visitors to pass birth data on to Children's Centres, individual health visitors may decide not to share this information. For interdisciplinary teams to work effectively, clear procedures and systems of communication need to be in place.

> Everyone in the team needs to speak the same language. Since I realized that some of the staff didn't really understand what others were talking about, we have made a real effort not to use jargon and to be a bit more proactive about asking each other what things mean. (Children's Centre manager, professional background: education)

Very practical issues arise concerning the use of specialized terminology regarded as integral to a professional domain. Jargon can be used to reinforce power differences and exclude others (Frost, 2005). Consider the example of the word 'trauma' which means 'major injury' in the health professional world but 'emotional damage' in the social care world. 'Supervision' has a very different connotation for those from an education heritage compared with those from a social services or health background.

> Our teacher thought she was in for a telling off when I organized a safeguarding supervision meeting with her. (Children's Centre manager, professional background: social care)
>
> And the education culture, with all the education speak! I went to a meeting the first week I was here and I didn't understand a word that was said. I remember thinking what on earth am I doing sitting here, I don't understand a word anyone is saying? I think it was the SENCO and she was saying PSED and CLLD and I didn't have a clue what she was going on about. It's now fine and I understand it but it's been a big learning curve joining the education side of life. (Children's Centre manager, professional background: social care)

One of the hallmarks of professionals is that they exhibit command of a specialized body of knowledge. Whitmarsh (2007) points out that tensions in multi-agency working are often caused by misunderstandings about shared language, shared information and mutual practices. She shows how professionals from different disciplines may interpret confidentiality differently. Issues arising from sharing information is one of the commonest causes of tension in multi-agency teams, a key aspect of which is the concept of confidentiality. Whitmarsh notes that ethical codes offer guidance in professional situations but this in itself may raise further issues as the various professionals involved in multi-agency working may all have their own codes, emphasizing different rules, principles and values. Brock et al. (2011) also explored issues arising from the provision of ethical codes to guide professional practice.

The Common Assessment Framework Form

Earlier in this chapter we discussed how sharing information can lead to tensions in multi-disciplinary teams around the child and it will be useful to look at the example of the Common Assessment Form (CAF). Designed to be used for children with additional needs, the CAF was set out in *Every Child Matters: Change for Children* (Department for Education and Skills, 2004b) as a means of averting crises in families by early detection and intervention. In providing a description and critique of the CAF, Walker (2008) explains that the aims included improving joint working and communication between practitioners by embedding a common language of assessment and need. There should be more efficient use of the practitioners' time as they can build on existing information – the picture of a child built up over time could be shared among professionals (with consent). The needs of the child are accessed across three domains: the child's development, parenting capacity and wider family and environmental factors. The CAF contains a simple pre-assessment checklist to help practitioners decide who would benefit from a common assessment, a three-step process (prepare, discuss, deliver) for undertaking a common assessment and a standard form to help practitioners record, and where appropriate, share with others, the findings from the assessment (Walker, 2008, pp. 58–61). The CAF can be led by a trained professional from any discipline. Walker notes this should lead to quicker and better service provision, less repetition and duplication for families as only one worker gathers all the relevant information.

Leadership

Leadership is a central concept in the theory of teamwork, with a leader traditionally having a set of desirable traits and particular skills. A central element in many definitions of leadership, it can be understood as a process of influence based on clear values and beliefs. Leadership requires the capacity to create vision and moral purpose, give direction, provide authority, demonstrate effectiveness and motivate the team. In the TIPS project (Brock et al., 2009) leadership was seen as essential in the process of establishing a healthy team with a strong, shared value base that would enable a team to act promptly and effectively. Rodd describes leadership as 'a process by which one person sets certain standards and expectations and influences the actions of others to behave in what is considered a desirable direction' (Rodd, 2006, p. 11).

> Good leadership will empower staff, I want to know their job and I want everyone to have their own niche, something that they're really interested in – that they have a real passion for. If someone has a special interest it should be encouraged and developed. (Children's Centre manager, professional background: health)
>
> My team are brilliant – we all know that we want to make a real difference for the families and children in our setting and they work really hard to make sure they do. (Children's Centre manager, professional background: education).
>
> I don't really see myself as the leader because we work very much as team and I always encourage people to do what they're good at and what interests them, even if it's not their role. For example our admin worker also does some family support work. (Children's Centre manager, professional background: education).

Effective leadership is required if the challenges of interdisciplinary work are to be overcome. One barrier to interagency working is the lack of clarity about how different line-management systems operate. A major challenge for leaders of Children's Centres, for example, is that of bringing together education, health and social care sectors to form a multi-professional, integrated team to deliver these services (NCSL, 2008). This integration of sectors creates teams whose members have different professional backgrounds and training, practices, levels of pay and terms and conditions of service but who are now expected to plan together and work to a shared vision.

> I don't think a day has gone by over the past year when I haven't drawn on something from my social work, either knowledge or experience. I don't know how people who don't have that skill set manage – I think some managers really struggle with how to best support their family workers because they don't feel confident in that area. If I didn't, I would really struggle with the safeguarding and family support work side. I'm very fortunate in that my line manager (a head teacher) is very supportive and understands that I don't come from an education background so she deals with that side of things. We work well as a team to cover everything we need to. (Children's Centre manager, professional background: social care)

Every Child Matters provided the context for the Children's Workforce Strategy (CWS), which aims to develop a world class workforce to improve outcomes for children. The CWS identified the challenge of creating a graduate workforce, skilled in leadership and management to lead these multi-agency, multi-disciplinary, Children's Centres and identified the need for the development of programmes to foster high calibre leadership in integrated early years settings. The National Professional Qualification for Integrated Centre Leadership (NPQICL) was developed to be such a programme.

Culture – building relationships between practitioners

Culture is a distinctive system of shared beliefs, values and norms that guide the behaviour of its members. Reconciling different professional beliefs and practices is an issue and Atkinson et al. (2005) identify 'agency culture' as a potential challenge to the interdisciplinary team's effective working. Atkinson et al. identified a perception that multi-agency working disrupted, or intruded on, existing agency values and protocols. Specific policy and procedural differences, such as different personnel and referral systems, were also identified as challenges, while different data management systems had implications for sharing information.

Interdisciplinary team working requires professionals to be open and flexible to different ways of working. They need to understand each other's roles and responsibilities. A lack of knowledge concerning each other's roles can lead to misunderstanding and negative stereotypes, but an understanding of each other's roles, philosophies and ideologies can lead to trust and respect between professionals (Frost, 2005).

> There is a culture in social care, whether purposeful or not, I think it's come from having to get through the day and what you deal with, but it is elitist. It's a case of 'We know best and we know what we're doing and we have to do with the hard stuff. So you, the health visitor, can tell me what you like but I'm still going to go off and do this because that's my job and I know best. And it's not you going to go and remove the kids at ten o'clock at night, it's me and so therefore I'm marvellous'. There is definitely a culture of elitism around safeguarding and you buy into it because that's how you get through your day. (Children's Centre manager, professional background: social care)

There may be consequences for effective joint working when preconceived ideas and stereotypes influence team attitudes and practices. The specific roles undertaken by the key professionals will be discussed in detail in subsequent chapters but consider some of the preconceived ideas that may be held about particular areas of work. Health and social work professionals are seen to deal with 'the problems' and are viewed as more interventionist and hence problematic in people's lives. Social workers focus on child protection and when tragedies occur the reasons identified often include a lack of interagency communication and/or poorly supervised staff operating in stressful conditions. Other examples of preconceived ideas about practitioners include speech and language therapists; conventionally associated with children with identified difficulties, they now also play a role in prevention and enrichment and work inclusively to improve the communication environments and skills of early years staff. Children's librarians work hard at breaking through the stereotype by engaging in challenging community outreach work and creative partnerships.

Joint training can be used as an opportunity to develop understanding and awareness between different professionals but everyone needs to 'buy into' this approach.

> The centre staff do quite a lot of training and we always invite the school staff, even though they don't come. We're never invited to join them. (Children's Centre manager, professional background: community development)

A key feature of the NPQICL programme was the attention paid to the distinct features of each profession and how these could be understood and respected. The programme's evaluation found that participants' increased understanding of what motivated colleagues from other professions both generated respect and improved communication (NCSL, 2008).

> When I know what I'm doing, I do a good job. Here, I try to do a good job but there are too many other things. And also managing a team that is very multi-agency so you're not actually directly line-managing people that you can't comment on their practice. People come in and do baby crèches, health sessions and I'm the manager and I want them to do it in a certain way but I don't have any say about it really. They do it their own way. You get that with a lot of organisations that come in – they've all got their own agenda and their own targets to meet and I find that quite hard. (Children's Centre manager, professional background: health)

A key challenge for leaders of multi-disciplinary teams has been identified as the need to support teams in building new and integrated working practices while also retaining and redefining the boundaries of professional identity. (Anning et al., 2006) have recognized the potential disruption to professional identity and proposed that new forms of professional identity need to emerge which can accommodate interdisciplinary policies and practices.

Whalley (2005) proposes a guardianship model of integrated professional working as a response to the challenge of creating partnerships between different professional backgrounds and multi-agency teams within a community. The guardianship model acknowledges the impossibility for the head of a Centre to be fully capable in the professional practice of other agencies. This involves distributing the leadership responsibility for the core domains of Children's Centre work to 'guardians' who act as leaders and advocates for the professional practice of each agency and aspect of the Centre's activity.

> It's a good job to be a leader of a Children's Centre and a good chance to lead a huge multi-disciplinary team – a good experience – it's just that I would like more clearly defined boundaries

around what the job is. When I started off it was like a little tennis ball and it's now like a great big rugby ball and still growing. It's just getting bigger and bigger. Eventually you have to ask where your accountability stops. That's what worries me – is where do my accountabilities stop? I know what my accountabilities are at the moment and it's a hard job, a very skilled job but I don't know what my responsibilities are. They're just getting bigger. (Children's Centre manager, professional background: health)

Issues of dialogue and trust – developing 'communities of practice'

Glenny and Roaf (2008) talk about 'appreciative systems', well-configured communication systems that seem crucial to successful multi-professional practice. 'When professionals have good relationships, they are more likely to make the space and time to have the quality dialogue that allows them to bring their different expertise to the table' (Glenny and Roaf, 2008, p. 96).

Wenger et al. (2002) write about communities of practice being groups of people who share a concern, a set of problems, or a passion about a topic, and who deepen their knowledge and expertise in this way by interacting on an ongoing basis. There is commitment and identification with the group and its expertise. This is based on the premise that knowledge has become the key to success and is simply too valuable a resource to be left to chance. Wenger writes that communities of practice are a natural part of organizational life and can create value in multiple and complex ways both for their members and for the organization. There is both short-term and long-term value. Members can get help with immediate problems as, by including the perspectives of their peers, they devise better solutions and make better decisions. As they are addressing current problems, communities are also building sustained value by developing an ongoing practice that will serve the organization's long-term strategy. The long-term benefit to the individual will be a strong sense of professional identity.

The value communities create includes tangible results such as improved skills in those who become members. Less tangible outcomes may be a sense of trust or an increased ability to innovate. The greatest value may be the relationships communities of practice build among people, the sense of belonging they create, the spirit of enquiry they generate, and the professional confidence they confer to their members. These social networks give rise to trust, reciprocity, and shared understanding. A number of scholars have noted that communities of practice foster both human capital skills (individual skills and professional identity) and social capital which was identified as an asset in Chapter 1.

Taking time to make sense of it all – reflective practice and CPD

Continuing professional development (CPD) is important in any profession, not only to keep abreast of the ongoing policy and latest initiatives addressed in Chapter 1, but also to take on board new practices and knowledge within a particular discipline. CPD is crucial to create effective teamwork for the professionals working around the child. Atkinson (2005) suggests the adoption of a self-critical and reflective approach to an individual's professional identity and work as a key factor for successful multi-agency working. But what is a reflective approach? Moon (1999) says that reflection can be related to learning situations where we are trying to make sense of new material. Reflection can also be associated with situations where there may be no new material but we need to make sense of knowledge and understandings we have already learnt. She uses the term 'cognitive housekeeping' to capture some of the essence of this sorting out of ideas. Some of the outcomes of reflection are the building of theory, self-development, decision making or resolution of uncertainty and empowerment or emancipation. Adams (2010, p. 247) in writing about a busy teaching environment says:

> At the end of the day, many dilemmas are buried under the weight of hosts of other spontaneous judgments. Unless practitioners have a system for recalling these actions and their accompanying decisions, their related values, beliefs and understanding remain embedded.

Through developing a critical, reflective approach to practice, practitioners can become more articulate, secure and able to justify practice in the face of challenge (Adams, 2010). Reflective practice involves critical thinking and enquiry is a highly complex process. Our own values as practitioners will affect how we approach reflective enquiry.

> I always thought of myself as a reflective practitioner but now (post-NPQICL) I know I wasn't really – not like I am now, where I really think things through and analyse my thoughts and actions so that I'm sure I'm doing my best or I know how I could do things better. (Children's Centre manager, professional background: education)

Taking a reflective approach can develop the ability to understand situations and dilemmas faced in working in multi-disciplinary teams. Understanding more about our own values, thoughts and beliefs and becoming confident about presenting these for scrutiny can lead to deeper understanding and potential changes in our working relationships and professional practice. A key issue here, though, is the opportunity to engage in this shared reflective enquiry in a supportive, professional environment. This is where the 'wisdom of collectives' can enhance the social dynamic of the team. Professional development and reflective practice will be discussed further in the next chapter.

Conclusion

This chapter has discussed the basic principles of how teams work and why effective teamwork has many advantages in supporting the child and her family. There are challenges for organizations, agencies and managers in providing structures and systems that enable practitioners to effectively carry out their roles and responsibilities. The New Labour models for integrated working discussed in Chapter 1 will be dismantled by the UK Coalition Government and replaced by a less regulated structure with an emphasis on transparency. Less regulation suggests there is increased space for fostering more optimistic notions of professionalism. Practitioners need to be aware of the specialties and expertise of other professional colleagues working in support of the child. Communities of practice can offer individuals the opportunity to develop a sense of professional identity and the next chapter will further develop the discussion on professionalism.

Questions for reflective practice

Why do you think effective teamwork is so important in supporting the twenty-first-century family? What are the issues and challenges for you in day-to-day work with other professional colleagues? How will you ensure you engage in ongoing critical thinking about these challenges? How will you plan for Continuing Professional Development that enables you to do this?

References

Adams, S. (2010), Putting the bananas to bed! Becoming a reflective teacher. In J. Moyles (ed.), *Beginning Teaching Beginning Learning in Primary Education*, 3rd edition. Buckingham: Open University Press/McGraw-Hill Education, 244–253.

Anning, A., Cottrell, D. M., Frost, N., and Green, J. (2006), *Developing Multi-Professional Teamwork for Integrated Children's Services*. Maidenhead: Open University Press.

Atkinson, M., Doherty, P., and Kinder, K. (2005), Multi-agency working models, challenges and key factors for success. *Journal of Early Childhood Research*, 3, (1), 7–17.

Aubrey, C. (2007), *Leading and Managing in the Early Years*. London: Sage.

Belbin, R. M. (2010), *Team Roles at Work*, 2nd edition. London, Butterworth-Heinemann.

Bertram, T., Pascal, C., Bokhari, C., Gasper, M., Holtermann, S. J., and Nelson, C. (2002), *Early Excellence Centre Pilot Programme Third Annual Evaluation Report, 2001–2002*. Birmingham: Centre for Research in Early Childhood.

Brock, A., Frost, N., Karban, K., and Smith, S. (2009), *Towards Interprofessional Partnerships: A Resource Pack*. Leeds: Leeds Metropolitan University.

Brock, A., Rankin, C., and Swiniarski, L. (2011), Are we doing it by the book? Professional ethics for teachers and librarians in the early years. In A. Campbell and P. Broadhead (eds), *Working with Children and Young People: Ethical Debates and Practices Across Disciplines and Continents*. New International Studies in Applied Ethics. Peter Lang, Chapter 2, 15–36.

Department for Education and Skills (2003), *Every Child Matters*. London: HMSO.

— (2004a), *The Children Act*. London: Department for Education and Skills.

— (2004b), *Every Child Matters: Change for Children*

French, J. (2007), Multi-agency working: The historical background. In I. Siraj-Blatchford, K. Clarke and M. Needham (eds), *The Team Around the Child: Multi-agency Working in the Early Years*. Stoke on Trent: Trentham Books, 47–66.

Frost, N. (2005), *Professionalism, Partnership and Joined-up Thinking: A Research Review of Front-line Working with Children and Families*. Totnes: Research in Practice.

Glenny, G., and Roaf, C. (2008), *Multiprofessional Communication: Making Systems Work for Children*. Maidenhead: Open University Press.

Hodgkin, R., and Newell, P. (1996), *Effective Government Structures for Children: Report of a Gulbenkian Foundation Inquiry*. London: Calouste Gulbenkian Foundation.

Laming, W. (2003), *The Victoria Climbié Inquiry: Report of an Inquiry by Lord Laming*. London: The Stationery Office.

Lloyd, G., Stead, J. and Kendrick, A. (2001), *Hanging On in There. A Study of Inter-Agency Work to Prevent School Exclusion in Three Local Authorities*. London: National Children's Bureau.

McInnes, K. (2007), *A Practitioner's Guide to Interagency Working in Children's Centres: A Review of the Literature*. Barnardo's Policy and Research Unit. www.barnardos.org.uk/cym/a_practitioner_s_guide_to_interagency_working_-_final_report_-_april_2007.pdf.

— (2010), Do we understand each other? Multi-disciplinary working in Children's Centres. In Janet Moyles (ed.), *Beginning Teaching Beginning Learning in Primary Education*, 3rd edition. Buckingham: Open University Press/McGraw-Hill Education, Chapter 3, 33–42.

Messenger, W. (2009), Managing multi agency working. In M. Reed and N. Canning (eds), *Reflective Practice in the Early Years*. London: Sage, Chapter 9, 126–140.

Moon, J. (1999), *Reflection in Learning and Professional Development*. London: Routledge Falmer.

NCSL (National College of School Leadership) (2008), *Realising Leadership: Children's Centre Leaders in Action. The Impact of the National Professional Qualification in Integrated Centre Leadership (NPQICL) on Children's Centre Leaders and Their Centres*. www.ncsl.org.uk.

Rodd, J. (2006), *Leadership in Early Childhood*, 3rd edition. Buckingham: Open University Press.

Salas, E., Goodwin, J., and Burke, C. S. (eds) (2008), *Team Effectiveness in Complex Organizations: Cross-disciplinary Perspectives and Approaches*. London: Routledge.

Siraj-Blatchford, I., Clarke, K., and Needham, M. (eds) (2007), *The Team Around the Child: Multi-agency Working in the Early Years*. Stoke-on-Trent: Trentham Books.

Speck, P. (ed.) (2006), *Teamwork in Palliative Care: Fulfilling or Frustrating*. Oxford: Oxford University Press.

Walker, G. (2008), *Working Together for Children: A Critical Introduction to Multi-Agency Working*. London: Continuum.

Watson, H. (2006), Facilitating effective working in multi-agency co-located teams. *Educational & Child Psychology*, 23, (4), 10–22.

Wenger, E., McDermott, R., and Snyder, W. (2002), *Cultivating Communities of Practice: A Guide to Managing Knowledge*. London: McGraw-Hill.

Whalley, M. (2005), *Leadership and Management in Integrated Children's Centres*. London: Paul Chapman.

Whitmarsh, J. (2007), Negotiating the moral maze: Developing ethical literacy in multi-agency settings. In I. Siraj-Blatchford, K. Clarke and M. Needham (eds), *The Team Around the Child: Multi-agency Working in the Early Years*. Stoke-on-Trent: Trentham Books, 87–103.

Wistow, G., and Hardy, B. (1991), Joint management in community care. *Journal of Management in Medicine*, 5, (4), 44–8.

3

Perspectives on Professionalism
Avril Brock

Chapter Outline

Introduction

What factors contribute to a theory of professionalism and how can it be defined for those working with young children? This chapter explores the contemporary issues surrounding professionalism and professionalization for the diverse professionals working with young children in the UK in the early twenty-first century. How have policy, theory and research impacted professionals' knowledge and practice and against which they have internalized and constructed their professionalism? This chapter presents an argument for the different professionals working in the team around the young child. The aim is to provide a unified concept of professionalism that will enhance the interdisciplinary way of working through promoting agreement regarding principles of professional practice. The formation of professional relationships can be supported when team members gain an understanding of each other's professional background and notions of professionalism. For those working with young children, this chapter advocates a collective perspective on professionalism which can generate closer working relationships. A conceptual framework of seven key dimensions – knowledge, education and training, skills, autonomy, values, ethics and reward – is presented as a model for unifying the 'team around the child's' perspective on professionalism.

Professionalism – what is it?

At the heart of this book is the debate about professionalism, a contentious issue for many professions during the last quarter century. This debate has merited the attention of several disciplines – sociology, philosophy, history, management and education. It is recognized as a complex changing phenomenon located in specific cultural and historical situations (Friedson, 1994, 2001). It 'defies common agreement as to its meaning' despite widespread use of the term 'professionalism' in the media and everyday discourse (Hoyle and John, 1995, p. 1). This lack of consensus occurs because its use varies both pragmatically and conceptually within a complex society, and there has been much debate about what constitutes 'the professions' and how they should be defined. To 'professionalize' is to make an occupation a profession. Does this imply that with the right conditions, any occupation could become a profession? Occupations seek recognition as professions, as this should lead to enhanced esteem, status, remuneration and power. So it is important in contemporary society for occupations to be established as professions, as there are implications for both career and personal success.

The terms 'profession' and 'professional' are often applied to a variety of occupations 'with elusive and continual reinterpretation of the concepts' (Helsby, 1996, p. 135). To 'be a professional' is a phrase often in use in the contemporary workplace and may relate to competence and punctiliousness. Professionalism can be 'attitudinal' – there may be professional and unprofessional garage mechanics, just as there are professional and unprofessional teachers, lawyers and doctors. Professionalism is related to proficiency – the knowledge, skill, competence or character of a highly trained individual, as opposed to one of amateur status or capability. There is a distinction between 'being a professional', which includes issues of pay, status, reward and public recognition, and 'behaving professionally', which implies dedication, commitment, standards of behaviour and a strong service ethic. Components of pay, recognition and reward depict 'professionalization', while characteristics of ethics, standards and commitment represent 'professionalism' (Osgood, 2006). A definition of professionalism is complex; for Friedman (2007, p. 126) it is 'like a ball of knotted string' and in 'order to untangle the string, all of the other knots must be opened'. The next sections of this chapter attempt to unravel some of the complicated knots through examining the varied definitions, perspectives, dimensions and traits of professionalism.

Challenges to professionalization

Many occupational groups have faced challenges to their authority, legitimacy and inevitably their professionalization. Those already deemed to be 'professionals' resist attempts by others, whom they might deem to be less qualified, to join their high status 'fellowship'. Traditionally professions have been a group of prestigious occupations with particular ideologies and identified by education, professional training and status. The three historically 'learned' professions of medicine, law and the clergy originated at European medieval universities and had an elite, gentlemanly status (Friedson, 1994). These origins gave rise to political influence and an economic elite in relation to the market and class system. Since the Second World War and the shift to mass education in universities, the range of careers demanding professional status increased to include accountants, veterinary surgeons and architects (Bacon et al., 2000). However, there has been an ongoing and complex struggle by some contemporary professionals to negotiate their professional status with employers, governments, administrators and other professionals, clients and the general public (Frost, 2001). Engineers, pharmacists, social workers, schoolteachers and librarians were among those who have struggled to gain status as professionals. This has also been the case for the various 'professions' within the health service – occupational therapists, physiotherapists and nurses who have all fought to 'professionalize' and gain public recognition. The challenges for professionalization have been particularly contentious for the caring professions of education, nursing and social work, where there is still a greater concentration of women.

The main challenges for professionals have come from the government through reorganization, decreased autonomy, increased bureaucracy, financial controls and target setting. According to Friedson (2001) there is a tension between government that tends to be concerned with efficiency and professionals who care mainly about providing the highest-quality service. He explores the concept of professionalism as a form of social organization where workers can organize and control their knowledge and service more freely without directives from management, as state policy often undermines the individual professional institutions. In Perkin's (2002) opinion the questioning of the status of the professions in England was concurrent with the growth of the welfare state. There was contention as the professions argued for the importance of their distinct, specialist knowledge and expertise, but their 'self-protective autonomy' was perceived by the state as their having too much power without sufficient accountability. Perkin believes there are new conceptions of professionalism developing through openness between the professions and government that create a balance between autonomy and accountability. Is this different for the diverse professions – do educators, health workers and social workers believe that they have their professional attributes recognized and their needs met?

voices of professionals

~~ssionals working with young children should have a voice in shaping policy with their expertise and knowledge sought and respected. The voices of those working in the field therefore need to be elicited to create a fuller definition of professionalism. Definitions of professionalism may vary between policymakers and practitioners as they inhabit different spheres. It is therefore important that the voices of the diverse professionals are elicited for *their* perspectives on their professionalism. Any definition of professionalism should include the experiences and views of the professionals themselves to determine the qualities, dimensions and scope of professional practice to improve *being* professional (Osgood, 2006). There is therefore a need for a further analysis of the discourse of professionalism to be constructed and reconstructed within professional occupational groups (Evetts, 2009). The contributors in this book promote this discourse and attempt to establish common threads that will unify their professionalism in their collective and collaborative teamwork with young children, even though their knowledge, skills and values may differ. The chapters are written by lecturers who are situated in universities and colleges connected to the northern cities of Leeds and Bradford. They have sought the voices of practitioners working with young children and families. As a preface to their chapters, here are some varied perspectives on professionalism – a speech by a health-care executive, a radio interview with a social worker and a research interview with a teacher.

Perspectives from health care

Sir Nigel Crisp was the chief executive at Department of Health and NHS from 2000 to 2006. In his opening remarks to the Royal College of Physicians Working Party on Medical Professionalism (2005) he observes how professionalism is a much used and misused word today that might simply be regarded as the pedantic opposite of 'amateur' or simply denotes a high standard.

A health executive's perspective on professionalism

In medicine, professionalism means that a patient can expect a high standard of care from individuals and teams even in the most difficult circumstances. This implies professionalism of two kinds, for example, from the NHS:

- individual professionalism through which individuals and teams care for patients as well as relating to their families and their carers;
- institutional professionalism whereby systems are in place to encourage and support individuals and teams and to assure standards.

I am building a picture of professionalism which goes wider than treating patients effectively. I am thinking in terms of building and maintaining relationships, trust, understanding, honesty, confidentiality and in fact humanity (Crisp, 2005).

Crisp (2005) questions how to instil, maintain and measure professionalism in a way that is comprehensible and usable in an environment of increasingly complex systems where considerable public money is invested. He believes ongoing questioning of professionalism can safeguard the standards of a profession and be informed by the needs and wishes of patients and the public. In Coles's (2006) opinion, professional practice generally (and medical practice in particular) is characterized by complexity, uncertainty and unpredictability. Professional practitioners use their judgement and wisdom, developed in their own practice and through their contacts with fellow practitioners and with clients. Further perspectives from health and social care professionals will be presented in Chapter 6.

Perspectives from social work

In recent years in the UK, social workers have often seemed to find themselves under attack from government, the media and the public as some high-profile cases of child neglect hit the headlines. Social workers generally enter the profession with a vocation and a vision of meeting children's and their families' needs, but have funding restraints, reduction in autonomy over work processes, the lack of time to build relationships with clients/service users and case overloads made their professional roles increasingly difficult?

A social worker's perspective on professional role, status and values

I remember a young woman whom I will call Kelly who had a distressed background and was in a violent domestic situation when she had three of her children removed. There was no hope of rehabilitation as the situation was so bleak and dire at that time. The children were eventually adopted. Kelly was very distressed and she became pregnant again and it could have been predicted that this child would also be removed. She was a quite courageous woman who decided she did want to be a mother, and decided to make some changes to her life. She left her violent partner, accepting help from a whole range of services – midwife, health visitor, family support worker, social worker, housing, education, parents' groups and together – and it was teamwork, really important in child protection – we were able to see her making progress to such an extent that she was able to keep that baby with her. I suppose good news doesn't sell newspapers. There are thousands of good works going on and numerous good news stories – little moments in everyday practice that have had massive impacts on people. We've had children return to us and say thanks for removing me from that abusive family. (Extracted from an interview from On Broadcasting House, 28.2.10)

Social workers are specialists in the social, emotional and financial needs of families and play an essential role in protecting and supporting children and young people from harm and they are in vulnerable circumstances. The government established the Social Work Force in 2008 to conduct a review of the profession and to advise on a comprehensive reform programme for social work. Recommendations included a reform of initial training, greater leadership, a national career structure and a strong national voice for the social work profession led by a college of social work. However, Lavalette (2010) questions whether more professionalism is the answer to the crisis in social work and if the Royal College will represent the voice of those working in the field. Chapter 7 explores issues of professionalism from a social-work perspective.

Perspectives from early childhood education and care

Policy change has inevitably impacted educators' professional knowledge and practice and the way in which they have internalized and constructed their professionalism. An emphasis on educational achievement has often produced conflicts for early years educators. In the 1990s the need for evidence-based policy on outcomes-based education through testing, target setting, publication, benchmarking, reporting and inspection led to a statutory schooling discourse and an emphasis on young children's school readiness and achievement in the basics of literacy and numeracy (Anning, 2008). Many teachers of young children found that the outcome-driven curriculum did not adequately reflect the complexity of children's learning. They considered that their teaching expertise, professional knowledge and therefore their professional autonomy and values were being confronted and undermined by the government. The introduction of the Foundation Stage in 2000 was broadly welcomed by practitioners because it emphasized the role and value of play. The following interview with a reception class teacher took place in 2001.

An early years teacher's perspective on autonomy

In general I don't feel that teaching is seen as such a highly viewed profession as it used to be, because I think you get slated in the press and the government seem to criticize you all the time, so in that way I don't think there is a very good perception really. But I feel, in my school, I feel that I deal with things professionally and I treat it as a profession … I'm particularly glad about being committed to early years – it was one of the reasons that I applied for the job here. I just felt I wanted a more positive environment, so when I knew the head had a commitment to early years that was really important to me. I like the flexibility and the learning through doing and playing that the Foundation Stage offers. I've now got much more confidence in my teaching and what I'm doing is right. If Ofsted arrived tomorrow I feel confident enough to justify what I'm doing and I believe it's what the government are telling me to do, so I'm quite happy. But then if I was in Key Stage 1 or Key Stage 2, I might feel differently. Redundant.

The introduction of the Foundation Stage and its curriculum guidance was 'a major step towards the professionalization and potentially enhanced status of early years teachers' (Hargreaves and Hopper, 2006, p. 181). In 2008 the Curriculum Guidance for the Foundation Stage (QCA/DfES, 2000) was replaced by the Early Years Foundation Stage (DCSF, 2007). However there seemed to be different perspectives from researchers and practitioners regarding its suitability for the education and care of young children. In Moss's (2007) opinion the documents were highly prescriptive technical manuals with 'no democratic space' and so undermined the professional knowledge of practitioners. What are the perspectives of early years educators today – do they feel they have autonomy to use their professional expertise in their work with young children? This will be explored in the next two chapters.

Professional boundaries

There are complex issues surrounding the relationships between the professional, the employer, the state and the client. There may be dilemmas, challenges and tensions for the professionals through the changing relationships, boundaries and power relationships. The title of multi-professional 'indicates a degree of interagency and interdisciplinary cooperation' and 'shared cultural belonging where meanings, values and understandings can be explored' (Powell in Jones et al., 2005, p. 78). The 'new professional' has to be multi-skilled, flexible and able to work in teams with other professionals. However, while effective communication is essential for coherent provision and collaborative interprofessional practice, professional dialogue can be problematic. Research by Anning and Edwards (1999) and Anning (2002) stresses that an overview of everyone's work is difficult and there are sometimes tensions between staff from different disciplines and backgrounds. This indicates the dilemmas for practitioners and Anning (2002) proposes that professionals' changing identities require skilful management to ensure real integration of services and so improve provision.

Undoubtedly there are problems with partnership and joined-up thinking, and as Frost (2005) finds in his research through front-line working with children and families, co-location does not solve all the problems. Warin (2007, p. 90) is also concerned that there are 'cracks below the rhetoric of seamlessness'. Anning's (2005, p. 20) research indicates a tension between the rhetoric and the actual reality in the 'mantras of joined-up services and multi-agency teamwork'. Furthermore, early childhood professionals have been informed that they 'are fortunate to have been given so much public money' and they are expected to get on and make 'joined-up thinking work' (Anning, 2005, p. 43). Will this result in, as Lane (2006, p. 341) claims, professional boundaries becoming 'blurred, reordered and reconstituted'? Is it not more important for the diverse professionals working in the team around the young child to celebrate each other's expertise and determine where the commonalities and differences are situated?

odern professional realizes her/his professionalism through discourses with new
ιd through forming new 'crosscutting interrelationships' (Barnett, 2008, p. 206).
fe promotes contrasting and alternative discourses, as the concepts of 'profession',
ιalism' and 'professional life' are challenged by those of marketability, standards,
performance management, quality assurance and client satisfaction (Barnett, 2008). The
conscientious professional attempts to handle these multiple discourses within a personal
context of professional identity, values, autonomy and ethics. Professionals need creative and
articulate responses if they are to hold on to their sense of professionalism (Power, 2008).
A unified concept of professionalism could enhance the interdisciplinary way of working
through promoting agreement of principles of professional practice. A collective perspective
on professionalism for those working with young children can enhance provision of high-
quality services. In this way, an ethos of professionalism will foster a collaborative environment and generate closer working relationships for the benefit of young children and their
families.

Dimensions and traits – a model of professionalism

The concept and practice of professionalism is complex as it is not one, but a cluster of related
concepts. My (Brock, 2006, 2009) research (Box 3.1) contributes to a model of professionalism (Table 3.1) formulated from the analysis of a group of early years educators' critical
issues. The significance of this model is that it establishes a construction of professionalism
that acknowledges the complexity of the work and the interconnections across the different
domains in the field of ECEC. This framework is presented through a case study of my six-
year longitudinal research with early years educators and demonstrates how seven dimensions of professionalism were generated from the respondents' voices.

Professionalism has been explored across several disciplines and theorists have formed
different models: social relationship (Sims et al., 1993); process (Friedson, 1994); functional
(Hoyle and John, 1995); post-modern (Goodson, 2003); activist (Sachs, 2003) and occupational (Evetts, 2009). A literature search across the fields of philosophy, sociology and education revealed common traits of specialized knowledge and skills gained through education;
regulation through mandatory, systematic training; values, standards and codes of ethics. My
analysis of the research findings generated a conceptual framework of professionalism for
those working in the field of early years education and care. It comprises seven key dimensions of knowledge, education and training, skills, autonomy, values, ethics and reward.

Knowledge

Professional knowledge is generally considered to be formed from theory and research that is
acquired through a lengthy period of professional study. This specialized body of knowledge

that other people are not necessarily able to comprehend gives professionals their u[n]
expertise.

Education and training

Admission to a profession is controlled by qualification gained in higher education, after
attaining prerequisite skills and knowledge. This is integrated with relevant experience and
practical application through specialized training.

Skills

The professional education or training leads to the acquisition of a high degree of skill and
competence to cope effectively with complex tasks, to problem-solve and to use judgement in
new situations. Professionals use these skills to provide a service and form effective working
relationships with stakeholders, clients and other professional groups.

Autonomy

Professionals traditionally had control over their own qualifications, professional responsibilities and discretionary judgement. As more external accountability and governmental
regulations affect the majority of occupations and professions, autonomy has become eroded
for some professionals.

Values

Professionals often have strong feelings for a specific ideology and related professional
values, dedicated to upholding their sense of worth, expertise and knowledge of what
is good for society. The professional traditionally guarantees to perform her utmost
to meet the demands of the job appropriately, employing core professional skills and
values.

Ethics

Professions should be morally accountable occupations with an ethical responsibility, and
often a code of conduct to always act in the client's best interests. The ethical relationship
with the client involves trust and confidentiality. Integrity is important for a profession to
balance new situations with the group needs of its members and those of the society for
which it works.

Reward

Professionals participate in a process of deferred gratification, undertaking a lengthy period
of study and training, with the ambition to be rewarded by high prestige and a high level of
remuneration. There may also be rewards connected to power, influence and social status.
Many professionals have a vocation for an occupation that brings satisfaction, enjoyment and
a commitment to others.

Box 3.1 Eliciting early years educators' thinking: How do they define and sustain their professionalism?

The study

Professionalism has been an ongoing contentious issue in the field of early childhood education and care for many years. Policy has not always acknowledged the professional knowledge or professional status of those working with young children, yet how they themselves perceive their professional roles is crucial to how they operate as professionals. The study provided a sample of early years educators (EYEs) with opportunity to voice their interests and issues. The focus of the research was on how this sample, in a particular set of contexts and at a particular time, defined and sustained their professionalism. It elicited their professional thinking in order to contribute to a model of professionalism. The data was collected at two points in time:

Phase 1 2001–2002: Main study gathering data with a sample of 12

Phase 2 2007–2008: Follow-up study with 9 of the original sample

Policy change has inevitably impacted on educators' professional knowledge and practice and the way in which they have internalized and constructed their professionalism. This empirical research was stimulated by the concerns of EYEs who attended in-service modules in the late 1990s and felt challenged by policy-driven educational change. During the interim between the data collection sets a plethora of initiatives and policy documents had been introduced and the sample had been variously affected by these demands, resulting in the restructuring of settings and changes in role.

The methodology

The objective of the research was to explore 12 early years educators' perspectives on their critical issues, the complexities of their roles, their professional knowledge base and the impact of policy change on their practice. The methodology was interpretative/exploratory and elicited their thinking about their professionalism. The respondents in this study were accountable for curriculum and pedagogy; management of staff, families and children; and the interpretation of social policy within their settings. The sample was a group of early years professionals from across three local authorities who had been recommended by local authority managers and university lecturers. They had diverse roles of teachers, nursery nurses, head teachers, managers and lecturers. They were diverse in gender, ethnicity, age, and length of service and worked in nursery schools, Foundation Stage units, reception classes, independent schools, Sure Start settings, workplace nurseries, college and university.

The data collection techniques included personal/professional timelines, continuing professional development questionnaires, semi-structured interviews, reflective-video-dialogues and a focus group meeting. The range of techniques aimed to elicit the respondents' thinking in diverse ways and so gain a breadth of perspectives. The continuing professional development questionnaires provided factual data about the respondents' training, qualifications, experience and work situations. The timelines afforded factual personal and professional aspects that impacted upon their work and values. The data from the semi-structured interviews, video-reflective-dialogues and focus-group meeting elicited data about their professional knowledge, critical issues and the impact of policy change on their practice.

WINMAX (1998) and MAXQDA (2007), computer-assisted quality data analysis software, was used in Phase 1 and Phase 2 to code, sort and analyse the data. This facilitated an efficient and reliable analysis of the data through a comparison of qualitative and quantitative interpretations.

The findings

The findings revealed insights into perceptions and practice in the early years regarding knowledge domains, values and practice, contributing to a model of early years professionalism (Table 3.1). This model is a conceptual framework of seven key dimensions: knowledge, education and training, skills, autonomy, values, ethics and reward which have been developed from both the research findings and a literature review across the fields of philosophy, sociology and education. The data analysis gave rise to the collective traits of their professionalism which were located within the seven overarching dimensions. Thus the dimensions and traits were derived from the early years educators' perspectives and they were consistent across both the data sets. The sample had a collective resonance which was demonstrated through the generic issues they raised and which underpinned their professionalism. The model can only summarize the complexity of these dimensions and traits. The seven dimensions have equal status as all are necessary for a holistic model of early years professionalism. They are interdependent as the dimensions are complex and may share common elements. While a number of traits are specific to ECEC, the majority are probably generic for the varied professionals working with young children. The model provides a starting point for heightening awareness and establishing a discourse of what professionalism entails.

Table 3.1 A model of professionalism derived from early years educators' perspectives

The Seven Dimensions of Professionalism	The Dimensional Traits
Knowledge	Knowledge gained through study of varying theoretical frameworks including child development; how children think and learn; curriculum and pedagogy. Knowledge gained through experience of working with young children and their families. Knowledge gained through experience of children's social and cultural backgrounds and their individual needs. Knowledge of local and national policy and implications for practice.
Education and Training	Qualifications gained through FE and HE and apprenticeship through working with young children, applying knowledge to practical experience. Self-directed continuing professional development to further develop knowledge and expertise. Appropriate training with regard to young children's learning and development. Training to deliver flexible curriculum and high level of pedagogic knowledge.

(Continued)

Table 3.1 Continued

The Seven Dimensions of Professionalism	The Dimensional Traits
Skills	Planning curriculum and teaching particularly through a play-based pedagogy.
	Observing and assessing young children's learning and development.
	Monitoring and evaluating effectiveness to inform practice and provision; able to critique, reflect and articulate understanding and application.
	Multi-disciplinary skills that encompass the demands of the role.
	Effective teamwork with different professionals, creating an inclusive ethos for children and families.
	Ability to make judgements regarding appropriate practice and dealing with problems.
	Effective communication of aims and expectations to stakeholders: families, colleagues, advisors, governors, Ofsted.
Autonomy	Recognition of specific professional knowledge and expertise regarding young children's learning and development.
	Autonomy over professional responsibilities and allowed to use discretionary judgement.
	Able to provide what they see as appropriate curriculum and pedagogy for their particular groups of young children; stronger voice and consultation in the shaping of relevant policy and practice that affects young children's education and care.
	Recognition of professionalism, promoting status and value for the field of ECEC.
	Vocational aspects of working with young children recognized and endorsed.
Values	Sharing of a similar ideology based on appropriate knowledge, education and experience.
	Strong belief in teaching and learning through a play-based curriculum.
	Beliefs in principles for appropriate provision that meets children's and families' needs.
	Commitment to professional values and vocation built on moral and social purposes.
	Public service and accountability to the community and client group of children and families.
	Creating an environment of trust and mutual respect inherent in professional role.
Ethics	Ethical principles and engaging with values regarding young children's education and care.
	High level of commitment to professional role and to the client group of parents, carers and children.
	Collaborative and collective behaviour with colleagues in the setting and other professionals.
	Inclusiveness while valuing diversity in working relationships with children, families and communities.
	Self-regulating code of ethics applied to everyday working practice.
Reward	Personal satisfaction, interest and enjoyment in working with young children.
	Forming strong and supportive relationships with young children and their families.
	Strong commitment for the professional role and to own professionalism.
	Being valued and gaining acclaim for professional expertise from colleagues and policymakers.
	Financial remuneration through appropriate salary.

The importance of the research is that it elicited voices to contribute to the contemporary debate of professionalism. The sample demonstrated a collective understanding of the complexity of professionalism which crossed the different domains in their field of early childhood care and education. It can be seen in the following extracts that, while these early years educators take different things from the model, they are in agreement as to its usefulness in creating a collective perspective on professionalism for the many and varied practitioners in the field.

> A clear code of professionalism does indeed need to underpin the 'competencies' required by early years practitioners and leaders. (Children's Centre manager)
> I think this is a comprehensive and balanced breakdown of the components of early years professionalism. The disparity between the vast majority of practitioners and teachers is vast – does it have an influence on professional status? We are expecting people to deliver quality provision using complex skills yet many cannot see any way of getting adequate pay and some of the best leave early on. (Children's Centre teacher)
> The seven dimensions are all good words. I like knowledge; autonomy and values; education and ethics are important. I normally have a problem with skills because it is overused and is also often used instead of education which has been reduced to a set of skills and outcomes model, however early years educators do need a lot of skills but combined with education. Autonomy is part of being a professional and educators should have a stronger voice in shaping early years policy. Values – ideology is an interesting word often used pejoratively. It is annoying that curriculum and educational policy is often portrayed as being value neutral; many people don't think there is anything political about the documents yet there is. (Lecturer in higher education)

The model provides a starting point for establishing a discourse of what professionalism entails for those working in early childhood education and care. At times government initiatives in the UK have lacked the voices of professionals working in the field and they themselves might not always engage in professional discourse or address their critical issues at policy level as their roles are so all-encompassing. The ability to reflect on and evaluate one's professional role and its practical application is key to professionalism (Hughes and Menmuir, 2002). The model of professionalism could provide a stimulus for professional discourse for practitioners across the varied disciplines. Reflecting on the dimensions and traits as defined in the model can be a valuable strategy in professionals' continuing professional development.

Professional development and reflective practice

Continuing professional development is essential for practitioners who have to continually respond to the ever-changing social context. The model of professionalism was trialled with students from a range of disciplines – social work, health care, education and probation services – who were studying Master's degree courses. A core module entitled Personal, Professional, Reflective Practice focused on developing these traits:

- ability to examine personal style and performance through a process of reflective thinking and practice;
- engagement in reflective thinking and varied writing processes;
- ability to reflect on concepts of professionalism and relate these to their academic and professional thinking and practice.

The students were expected to engage in a variety of writing exercises and reflective synopses of personal and professional development, which included diaries, autobiographies, timelines, digital portfolios and critical incidents. These were presented during informal seminar discussions and debates and then contributed to the final assessment of a portfolio of analytical reflections. While students may commence the writing and the compilation of the portfolio with trepidation, the tutor has the advantage of knowing through experience that the students will develop reflective, insightful and interesting contributions. The following examples are from three of the students who reflected on their professionalism:

> The more experience I gain the more I feel like a professional. This year I feel more in control and although I am still learning, I now feel I have a lot of knowledge. I feel more confident as a professional and feel I have more to give as a member of the staff. This year I have run staff meetings, discussed assessment and helped present a conference. The reflections on my actions (Schön, 1983) and my experiences as an NQT have all built my personal sense of professionalism more than when I just had knowledge; therefore experience was essential to my sense of professionalism … I carried out some research with the teachers at my school and a key dimension for them was their autonomy. An important trait for all of us, which was not particularly emphasised in Brock's research, was passion gained through being a caregiver and having a love and enthusiasm for teaching. The teachers wrote about: 'enjoying helping people and supporting children'; 'playing a part in children's lives'; 'the occasions when children do something wonderful'; 'providing a fundamental role for future society'; 'relationships with children'. Professionalism cannot be seen without passion and I believe it to be a most important trait in its own right as a dimension. A further dimension not included is that of creativity which I believe is central to being a professional in the early years education. Creativity helps inform the professional I am today. As a staff we have created a culture of professionalism that may not exist in other schools and it is characterised by passion, autonomy and creativity. I have always known how valuable reflective practice is to teaching as a profession, but it is only through completing this portfolio that I have truly recognised the value of reflection to inform my professional practice. (Early years teacher)

> Looking at research like that of Brock helps me understand the difference between being professional in the way you work and actually being a professional. Considering the seven dimensions, I would class my role as needing professional status. Knowledge, education, training and skills speak for themselves but autonomy, values, ethics and rewards that Brock illustrates really illustrates the depth of being an early years practitioner for me, emphasising the work that other professions might not consider. Creating an awareness of the work involved in early years settings is important

as I consider my role to be highly skilled and knowledgeable in order to work in a multi-disciplir team as I do. Although it does not yet have the status of teaching, it is now being recognised a profession. Professionalism is a concept I have come across frequently in my studies, but I v unclear about how it applied to me and to early years practitioners and I did not class myself a professional. As my knowledge and understanding has developed I have changed my perceptio and believe the term should be applicable to me as I have knowledge, experience and professional qualifications. Early years practitioners have a right to the status of being professional. Without key pieces of research such as Brock (2006) and Moyles (2001) I would not have viewed my current working role in a professional light. (Practitioner in a private day nursery)

My current job is working with children with disabilities. A lot of people find it surprising that this job is enjoyable; this may be due to the fact that the care sector is often forgotten about (Folbre, 2008). Dyeson (2005) states that home care workers often come across emergencies and possibly stressful situations, so that people in this job must be of a certain personality. There is socially a negative view of the home care worker and many people still do not regard this job as a profession (Healy, 2008). However it is clear from my job description that there is a personal, proud view of the work being done, and when you are aiding the blind, elderly and disabled (Boris and Klein, 2006) it is difficult to look down on the work done and not describe it as a profession. (Home care worker)

Critical reflection has become a key facet of professional life. Insight is gained by respecting the reflective and reflexive processes to cast light upon and enlighten that which needs examination (Bolton, 2005). In this way thoughts can be clarified, new comprehensions evoked, practice re-evaluated and solutions determined. The model of professionalism was used in the Master's class sessions to promote discussion and it was one of several options of focus for the student's portfolio assignment. The three students had different professional roles – two of which would still be challenged as being worthy of the title of profession – and they elected to explore the concept of professionalism from their own personal professional perspective and so demonstrated the depth of their critical thinking and reflection.

Conclusion

The model of professionalism provides a starting point to heighten awareness of what professionalism entails for those who work with young children and their families. A collective conception of professionalism could create unification for these diverse professionals. This will not only be an interesting and challenging exercise, but aims to be beneficial for future working partnerships in the interdisciplinary team. Wenger's 'communities of practice' (2005) requires those who operate in multi-disciplinary teams to work together to achieve common goals – 'straddling' the professional boundaries through reflection on and exchange of perspectives and interpreting not only the repertoire of practice but engendering collaborative perspectives. Dialogues reflecting on the dimensions and traits encompassed in the model of professionalism could promote the embrace of a collective professionalism. In this way, connectivity is valued, professional boundaries are diffused and individual professional identity, knowledge base and values become clarified. In the following chapters the contributors present their professional identities through engaging with the dimensions and traits presented in this chapter.

Questions for reflective practice

Do you feel that professionals should be aware of each other's skills and expertise? How can you disseminate your professional knowledge to other colleagues?

What are the key issues in your own professionalism – are they reflected in this chapter?

How do the seven dimensions of professionalism relate to your position? Consider past experiences, current situation and future aspirations.

References

Anning, A. (2002), Investigating the impact of working in integrated service delivery settings on early years practitioners' professional knowledge and practice: Strategies for dealing with controversial issues. Paper presented at the British Educational Research Association Annual Conference, 12–14 September, Exeter: University of Exeter.

— (2005), Investigating the impact of working in multi-agency service delivery settings in the UK on early years practitioners' beliefs and practices. *Journal of Early Childhood Research*, 3, 19–50.

— (2008), The co-construction of an early childhood curriculum. In A. Anning, J. Cullen and M. Fleer (eds), *Early Childhood Education*. London: Sage, 57–68.

Anning, A., and Edwards, A. (1999), *Promoting Children's Learning from Birth to Five*. Buckingham: Open University Press.

Bacon, W., Groundwater-Smith, S., Nash, C., and Sachs, J. (2000), Legitimating professionalism? Paper presented at the British Educational Research Association Annual Conference, 7/10 September, Cardiff University, Wales.

Barnett, R. (2008), Critical professionalism in an age of uncertainty. In B. Cunningham (ed.), *Exploring Professionalism*. London: Bedford Way Papers, 190–208.

Bolton, G. (2005), *Reflective Practice: Writing and Professionals' Development*. London: Sage.

Boris, E., and Klein, J. (2006), Organizing home care: Low waged workers in the welfare state. *Politics and Society*, 34, 81–106.

Brock, A. (2006), Eliciting early years educators' thinking: How do they define and sustain their professionalism? Paper presented to the European Early Childhood Education Research Association Conference, 30 August–2 September, University of Iceland, Reykjaviik.

— (2009), Seven dimensions of professionalism for early years education and care: A model of professionalism for interdisciplinary practice? British Educational Research Association Annual Conference, 2–5 September, University of Manchester, Manchester, England.

Coles, C. (2006), Uncertainty in a world of regulation. *Advances in Psychiatric Treatment*, 12, 397–401.

Crisp, N. (2005), *Royal College of Physicians Working Parties: Medical Professionalism*. www.rcplondon.ac.uk/wp/medprof/medprof_prog_050520.asp. Accessed 19 November 2009.

DCSF (Department for Children, Schools and Families) (2007), *The Early Years Foundation Stage*. Nottingham: DfES Publications.

Dyeson, T. D. (2005), The myriad roles of the home care social worker. *Home Health Care Management and Practice*, 17, (5), 398–400.

Evetts, J. (2009), New professionalism and new public management: Changes, continuities and consequences. *Comparative Sociology*, 8, 247–266.

Folbre, N. (2008), Reforming care. *Politics and Society*, 36, (3), 373–87.

Forster, N. (2000), A case study of women academics' views on equal opportunities, career prospects and work family conflicts in a British university. *Women in Management Review*, 15, 316–27.

Friedman, R. (2007), Listening to children in the early years. In M. Wild and H. Mitchell (eds), *Early Childhood Studies: Reflective Reader*. Exeter: Learning Matters, 81–94.

Friedson, E. (1994), *Professionalism Reborn: Theory, Prophecy and Policy*. Oxford: Polity Press.

— (2001), *Professionalism: The Third Logic*. Cambridge: Polity Press.

Frost, N. (2001), Professionalism, change and the politics of lifelong learning. *Studies in Continuing Education*, 23, 5–17.

— (2005), Professionalism, partnership and joined-up thinking. Dartington: Research in Practice.

Goodson, I. (2003), *Professional Knowledge, Professional Lives: Studies in Education and Change*. London: Open University Press.

Hargreaves, L., and Hopper, B. (2006), Early years, low status? Early years teachers' perceptions of their occupational status. *Early Years: An International Journal of Research and Development*, 26, 171–86.

Healy, L. (2008), Social work as a human rights profession. *International Social Work*, 51, (6), 735–48.

Helsby, G. (1996), Professionalism in English secondary schools. *Journal of Education for Teaching*, 22, 135–48.

Hoyle, E., and John, P. D. (1995), *Professional Knowledge and Professional Practice*. London: Cassell.

Hughes, A., and Menmuir, J. (2002), Being a student on a part-time early years degree. *Early Years Journal of International Research and Development*, 22, 147–61.

Lane, K. (2006), The plasticity of professional boundaries: A case study of collaborative care in maternity services. *Health Sociology Review*, 15, (4), 341–52.

Lavalette, M. (2010), A (royal?) college – is more professionalism the answer to the crisis of social work? *Social Work Action Network*. www.socialworkfuture.org/index.php/contributions/29-the-cms/54-a-royal-college-is-more-professionalism-the-answer-to-the-crisis-of-social-work-michael-lavalette?84e4966ffb2a94832870f77fe3157220=5fc1f0493b50f0d4b9fb68002ef59899. Accessed 22 January 2010.

Moss, P. (2007), Bringing politics into the nursery: Early childhood education as a democratic practice. *European Early Childhood Education Research Journal*, 15, (1), 5–20.

Moyles, J. (2001), Passion, paradox and professionalism in early years education. *Early Years: Journal of International Research and Development*, 21, 81–95.

On Broadcasting House (2010) British Broadcasting Corporation (BBC). Broadcast 28.2.10.

Osgood, J. (2006), Deconstructing professionalism in early childhood education: Resisting the regulatory gaze. *Contemporary Issues in Early Childhood*, 7, 5–14.

Perkin, H. (2002), *The Rise of the Professional Society: England Since 1880*, 3rd edition. London: Routledge.

Powell, J. (2005), Multiprofessional perspectives. In L. Jones, R. Holmes and J. Powell (eds), *Early Childhood Studies: A Multiprofessional Perspective*. Maidenhead: Open University Press, Chapter 6, 77–89.

Power, S. (2008), The imaginative professional. In B. Cunningham (ed.), *Exploring Professionalism*. London: Bedford Way Papers, 144–160.

QCA and DfES (2000), *Curriculum Guidance for the Foundation Stage*. London: Department of Education and Employment.

Sachs, J. (2003), *The Activist Teaching Profession*. London: Open University Press.

Schön, D. (1983), *The Reflective Practitioner. How Professionals Think in Action*. London: Temple Smith.

Sims, D., Fine, S., and Gabriel, Y. (eds) (1993), *Organising and Organisations*. London: Sage.

Warin, J. (2007), Joined-up services for young children and their families: Papering over the cracks or re-constructing the foundations? *Children and Society*, 21, 87–97.

Wenger, E. (2005), *Communities of Practice: Learning, Meaning and Identity*. Cambridge: Cambridge University Press.

Part II
Meet the Key Professionals

4

The Early Years Professional and the Children's Centre: At the Hub of the 'Big Society'?

Pam Jarvis and Wendy Holland

Chapter Outline

Introduction

This chapter was written in the period between the election of the Coalition Government on 11 May 2010 and the publication of the Review of Public Services in October 2010. As such, some amount of intelligent guesswork has had to be applied to the likely position of early years professionals (EYPs) from 2011 onwards. We feel that our vision constructs the most positive developmental pathway for this very new professional role, and that any other possible trajectory would be likely to have the effect of crushing potential; as such we very much hope that this will not become a chapter that outlines 'what could have been'.

We will initially outline the background and current position of the early years professional and Children's Centre projects, moving on to briefly describe how EYPs are currently trained, and the professional knowledge, key skills, values and ethics that they need to embrace in order to move forward to successful validation. We close with some points for reflection and discussion relating to the potential future of the role within English early years practice.

Early years professional status (EYPS) and the Sure Start Children's Centre: What is the background and current position of these projects?

As the twenty-first century dawned, a number of reports (e.g. Laming, 2003, and Ofsted reports of some day-care settings, for example, Ward, 2005) had indicated that we were seriously failing the very young in our society. The Every Child Matters (2003) agenda was produced, and all the agencies involved in the care of children and families were consequently required to 'sit up and listen', revise old practices and, most importantly, put the child at the centre of their vision.

In October 2005, the Early Education Advisory Group (EEAG) in England agreed that the core organization and management of early years care and education services needed to be reviewed and reshaped. Their focus was to produce a leading practitioner role that, while encompassing many of the features of the existing nursery teacher role, also embraced the multi-agency practitioner leadership of a child care and education team in the new Children's Centres, which had begun to provide a complex range services for children aged from birth to 5 years and their families. The other aspect that the Advisory Group wished to address was that services for children under three were, at that time most frequently led by staff who, while frequently possessing high levels of practitioner competence and dedication, had not received education and training at university (or Higher Education/HE) level. Many recent high-profile early years research projects, in particular, the British-based Effective Provision of Pre-School Education (EPPE) project (Sylva et al., 2003) had produced findings indicating that outcomes for children, particularly those from a background of disadvantage, were improved when practice in the setting was led by a graduate. The result was a new impetus for 'professionalism' within early years, and those who had been campaigning for years for just such a change rejoiced in the fact that a government had for once put aside the 'top-down' approach to education, and realized the necessity for high-quality educare for the youngest in our society.

The role of the early years professional developed from this basis, under the administration of the Children's Workforce Development Council (CWDC), a QUANGO created in 2005 by the New Labour Government. The EYPS project represented an attempt to retain the best concepts and structures of early years practice in England and develop it from this basis into a more flexible model for the twenty-first century, with some features drawn from the role of the 'pedagogue', which has a long record of success in Scandinavian countries.

The initial requirements for the envisioned new professional were stated as follows:

- An in-depth understanding of child development from birth to 12;
- A focus on how children develop and learn; the role of the adult in supporting learning – about natural science, the arts (dance, music, visual, drama and literature), mathematics, music;
- Observing, assessing, evaluating and planning learning opportunities, for individual children and groups of children;
- Working effectively with the most vulnerable children, including children with special educational needs and disabilities;
- Working with parents; working within a multi-agency team, with an understanding of the contribution of other professional disciplines;
- The ability to listen, to reflect, to critically analyse and to apply in practice, with an emphasis on practitioners as evidence based practitioner researchers;
- An understanding of the broader social and economic issues that impact on children and families. (Early Education Advisory Group, 2005, online)

The focus on the wider age range was dropped during the later planning stage of the project in favour of a more concentrated focus on the highly developmentally significant years from birth to 5 years. In its final incarnation, EYPS was shaped into a graduate leadership role for early years settings in England. The resulting training programme was piloted by the CWDC in 2006, and its first full year of national operation commenced in January 2007.

Training providers were advised by the CWDC that EYPs would lead practice within settings providing collective care for children aged from birth to 5 years. The stated intention was that a graduate led workforce would raise standards, skills, experience, commitment and effective leadership of practice across the full range of the early years provision.

Early years professional status was introduced as a qualification that was to be equivalent to qualified teacher status (QTS). However, in practice, when teachers and EYPs began to operate within the same environments, some role confusion arose. The professional standards required for each status are related and equally stringent, but they are not identical. In particular, the focus for early years teachers is upon children between the ages of 3 and 7 years, while EYPs focus on children aged between birth and 5 years. Teacher training also emphasizes the delivery of specified learning outcomes to children, while EYP training focuses upon a child-led agenda, which requires more theoretical child development content. One of the early solutions introduced by Children's Centre management was to employ teachers under the proviso that they would enter the short pathway training programme (see below) to gain EYP Status; most recently we are being told that some EYPs are now being employed under the proviso that they will gain qualified teacher status (early years) through the Graduate Teacher programme. Such solutions have, by and large, only added to the confusion, which has fed forward into government policy making (see below).

The stated New Labour Government target was that there was to be at least one EYP leading practice in all Children's Centres offering day care by 2010 (two in areas of disadvantage), and at least one EYP in every full day care setting by 2015. When the role was created, it was stated that EYPs were intended to: 'lead and transform practice by modelling skills and behaviours that promote good outcomes for children' (CWDC, 2006, Online). The EYP programme was, at its inception, tightly bound to the Sure Start Children's Centre initiative, and to the Early Years Foundation Stage (EYFS) statutory guidelines.

The British Sure Start project (1998) was modelled upon the US Head Start initiative, which began in 1965 (Head Start, 2010). Sure Start was introduced in the 1998 Comprehensive Spending Review, with the New Labour Government's announcement that it would set up 250 Sure Start Local Programmes in disadvantaged areas around the country. In 2000, the number of Sure Start projects expanded to 524. In what was designated 'Phase One' of the Children's Centres programme (2004–2006), 800 existing settings were given the status of 'Children's Centres'. In 'Phase Two' (2006–2008), funding was made available to open many more Children's Centres, taking the overall numbers to 2,500. Most of these additional settings were newly created. By 2010, at the end of 'Phase Three', it was intended that there should be 3,500 Centres nationwide (Children, Schools and Families Committee, 2010, online).

The New Labour Government did not however mention the EYP role in this 2010 report, stating instead that 'The involvement of early years qualified teachers is essential to the ambitions of Children's Centres to provide the highest quality early years experiences.... [T]he requirement for early years qualified teacher posts should be increased to achieve this if necessary'. Two months later, they were voted out of office and a new Conservative Liberal Coalition took over, proposing in their manifesto:

> We will take Sure Start back to its original purpose of early intervention, increase its focus on the neediest families, and better involve organisations with a track record of supporting families. We will investigate ways of ensuring that providers are paid in part by the results they achieve. We will refocus funding from Sure Start peripatetic outreach services, and from the Department of Health budget, to pay for 4,200 extra Sure Start health visitors. (Cabinet Office, 2010, p. 19)

As such, the 4,000 individuals (CWDC figures, March 2011 online) who have qualified as EYPs across the nation over the past three years – a role which requires graduate status, and a rigorous validation process – have not only been ignored by the outgoing government that created and funded the status, but have also been subsequently sidelined by the incoming Coalition Government, which has stated an intention to revert to a purely health oriented model of services for young children and their families. The new government currently proposes to accomplish this by funding the training of a nearly identical number of new health visitors to those existing EYPs whose expensive training has already been funded by the state!

'Children and Young People Now' reported that, as of 1 March 2010, the New Labour Government target of 3,500 Children's Centres was likely to be reached within the following month, but that

> The future is likely to see a merging of centres in regions to remove ineffective, inefficient and unnecessary supply, based on new target criteria. In this environment Phase Three centres are vulnerable. ... some concerns have been raised over whether third phase centres are in locations that best meet the needs of local families. (Watson, 2010)

On 6 July 2010, the new Department for Education (which had been the Department for Children, Schools and Families under the New Labour Government) announced a full review of the EYFS:

> Children's Minister Sarah Teather today asked Dame Clare Tickell, Chief Executive of Action for Children, to carry out a review of the Early Years Foundation Stage (EYFS) so that it is less bureaucratic and more focused on young children's learning and development.
>
> Ministers are concerned that the EYFS framework is currently too rigid and puts too many burdens on the Early Years workforce, which has led to some of the workforce saying they are spending less time with children, and more time ticking boxes. (DFE, 2010, online)

The report was published in the spring of 2011 (Tickell, 2011) and is also discussed in Chapter 1.

The national situation is therefore clearly in a state of major upheaval at the moment, which has placed those who train EYPs in a difficult position when requested to provide information and advice relating to the programme. We are currently trying to support the candidates still in the national training process in the best ways that we can. It is proposed by the authors of this chapter that the whole Sure Start and EYP project can hardly be seen to be 'working for the child' at the time of writing, amidst such confusion. This chapter will nevertheless attempt to take a positive direction, constructing some theorized future roles for EYPs, based on the experiences of EYPs currently working with children and families, and with an eye to likely developments within the new political landscape.

How can I become an early years professional?

The current EYPS training pathways are:

- **The four-month part-time validation pathway** for graduates currently employed in a leading role in a Children's Centre, or in a private, voluntary or independent childcare/education setting dealing with the full birth-to-five age range;
- **The six-month part-time professional development (short) pathway** for graduates who are currently employed in a senior role in a Children's Centre, or in a private, voluntary or independent childcare/education setting, dealing with at least part of the birth-to-five age range;

fifteen-month part-time professional development (long) pathway for candidates who currently employed in a Children's Centre, or in a private, voluntary or independent childcare/ ication setting dealing with at least part of the birth-to-five age range *and* have an HND or ndation Degree in a child care/early years education-related discipline *or* an ordinary or hon- s degree in a non-childcare/early years education-related subject. Non-graduate candidates are funded by the CWDC to undertake 60 credits of Stage 6 study in early years or early childhood studies across the duration of the programme.

- **The twelve-month full-time professional development (full) pathway** for graduates who have limited, or no experience of working with children in the birth-to-five age range, but who can demonstrate at interview that they have a strong ambition to develop or change their career in order to work in a leadership role in an early years setting, and are in a position to undertake a year's unpaid intensive professional development, both practical and academic, in order to accomplish this.

Between 2007 and 2010, all pathways had financial support packages provided by the CWDC; this was variously allocated between employer and candidate depending on the pathway taken. There were no course fees to pay, and up to £4000 supply cover costs were available to settings that released an employee for EYPS training. Candidates on the full pathway were entitled to a personal bursary of £5000. It is expected that this system of operation will be subject to change in the *Public Services Review* due to be published in October 2010.

All EYPS candidates are additionally required to have achieved both English and maths GCSEs at grade 'C' or above, provide a Criminal Records Bureau enhanced clearance and a medical history that indicates that they are in sufficiently good physical and mental health to work with young children.

Within an EYPS 'validation' process, candidates must demonstrate their competence in areas covered by the 39 EYPS standards, which are both knowledge- and practice-based, and cover leading practice with babies and children in the birth-to-five age range. The validation process is highly detailed, comprised of written tasks adding up to approximately 6000 words and a five-and-a-half-hour exploratory visit to the candidate's practice environment by an assessor who has not previously been involved in training the candidate concerned.

What professional knowledge and key skills does the EYP need, and what are the values and ethics underlying EYPs' practice?

Professional knowledge

So what kind of professional knowledge do EYPs require? Detailed and specialist knowledge of theoretical child development is a given (an area that is often only summarily addressed in education studies degrees). That knowledge needs to be up to date too, taking in the latest research into brain development, attachment, linguistic development, social and emotional competencies. If the EYP is to bear witness on a daily basis to what children are experiencing, and to plan for and support play-based learning, they need to be able i schema, various types of play, the non-verbal cues from pre-lingual infants to the u matical utterances of 2- and 3-year-olds, or the child with English as an addition guage. They need to be able to accurately assess a child's levels of well-being and knov confidence what his/her next steps should be. EYPs are introduced within their train... the international approaches to early childhood care and education, in particular, the role of the pedagogue, seen in the Reggio Emilia preschools in Northern Italy, the preschools (*barnkammare*) in Sweden, experiential education in Belgium and the bicultural programme of Te Whariki in New Zealand, to name but a few, and be able to critically compare such approaches to England's Early Years Foundation Stage. Clear ongoing knowledge of the UK latest approaches to early educare is essential, covering principles, themes and commitments, its statutory regulations and practice guidance, importantly including safeguarding/child protection and legal responsibilities. They must also be aware of myriad other local and government initiatives, for example, Bookstart and ICAN (the speech development initiative), which underpin daily practice.

The EYP needs to consider the wider landscape too, in terms of the influences of family and community upon the child's self-esteem and development. Working with parents and carers is seen as pivotal to the EYP's role. This was an area that was previously approached with varying degrees of commitment and success in primary schools. The EYP is also required to demonstrate a deep knowledge of and professional approach to multi-agency working, and knowledge and tolerance of agendas different to and sometimes in conflict with their own.

Focus on EYPs: Reflections of an experienced assessor

'Verity' has over 25 years of experience as an early years teacher, and ten years of experience as a teacher trainer and QTS assessor. She has assessed EYPS candidates in every assessment period since the national programme began. Here are some of her reflections on her experiences:

It was obvious to those involved in the training of those first assessors of the EYPS, that successful candidates would need extensive knowledge, a vast range of complex skills, the ability to lead practice and make autonomous decisions, be secure in their personal and professional value systems, with a clear code of ethics in working with young children. The monetary reward for such a catalogue of abilities even then was under debate, and this debate continues. What was not in doubt was the rigour with which each candidate would be assessed. Some assessors of long standing compared the process to that involved in assessing deputy heads and head teachers, and judged that the EYPS validation process is more complex than the current assessment of NQTs. The EYP, this proclaimed, would be a person of authority with serious responsibilities for cascading and maintaining effective early years practice.

I have witnessed some outstanding practice, for example, where EYP candidates have been at the forefront of inventive and creative uses of outdoor spaces. They have also pushed for changes, some quite radical, in established routines for set 'playtimes' which favour staffing needs rather than the needs of children, or what I call 'weather resistant' attitudes on the part of staff who fail to see the pleasure rain, puddles, wind and snow can have for children, if appropriately dressed.

Often the EYP candidate will have been a longstanding member of staff who had naturally been following the ethos and principles underpinning the EYPS. There are so many examples: A 'kindness tree' where children decided as a group themselves who had done a 'kind' act that day, and deserved a place on the special tree; an EYP's very effective behaviour management strategy; a setting where difference and diversity were totally accepted. In this particular instance, the setting had a young amputee who was quite forgetful. During the tour, I heard several children call out 'everybody – look for Peter's leg – he's lost it again'. In another setting, children sat down to lunch still in 'role' as a fairy, a doctor and a fireman, showing how flexible rules allow for growth and continuity of play.

EYP candidates, on the whole, have clearly demonstrated a child centred approach, understanding that children being 'creative' doesn't mean the formation of a production line of the same greetings card, or miles of scrunched up tissue paper pasted onto card cut outs, so 'adulterated', a child doesn't recognize his or her own handiwork. Praise and encouragement given for that first tentative attempt at marks on a paper or in the sand or chalked on the ground outside, has demonstrated some real understanding of how children develop and learn. In the best practice, EYPs have achieved all this, through diplomacy and a real wish to be part of a team of practitioners who strive for excellence.

Key skills

So, what key skills must underpin this bank of contemporary, professional knowledge? Effectively relating knowledge to practice is an essential characteristic of the EYP role. Unlike 'teaching', this pedagogic role has less to do with the transmission of knowledge, but rather providing an enabling environment that allows the child to discover autonomously for him or herself, or with some support from sustained shared thinking, take that leap in understanding that is then internalized and owned through active learning. This learning needs close observation, whether participant or non-participant. The role of observation has gained in importance, and it is an area in which the EYP is expected to model and lead practice. Planning for children's interests is again an aspect of the EYP's role that requires complex skills. It is much easier to plan within an existing framework, where themes or subject knowledge can be planned and resourced for several weeks in advance, planning that is definitely adult led, where children have very little input. Planning using a mainly child-led approach requires a great deal of mental agility, subject knowledge and flexibility, where EYPs cannot be too precious about their own adult-led activities. This kind of planning also requires strong teamwork, with the EYP showing effective organization and good interpersonal skills in pulling together the observations and ideas of the rest of an often diverse early years team, to provide a more personalized learning journey for each child. It is the EYP's responsibility to inform parents and those agencies that can provide help and assistance, or in the case of a child being at risk of harm, having clear knowledge of the appropriate procedures. It is also the responsibility of the EYP to ensure that staff in the centre engage in

Figure 4.1 Learning through play

suitable continuing professional development and to lead the policymaking, taking the ideas of staff on board, so they have knowledge and ownership of the eventual policies.

The above outline of the wide-ranging, hugely flexible EYP role takes as read that there must be the potential for a high degree of autonomy and multi-agency engagement.

Focus on EYPs: The Children's Centre as community 'hub'

'Lesley' is an experienced early years teacher and manager of a Phase Two Children's Centre. She received her EYPS in 2008, not long after her return from several years teaching young children within an African village environment. She reflects:

I think (multi-agency working) will grow and be much more vast than people realize … with the integrated working in Children's Centres. We've taken on our Children's Centre workers; one has come from social care and one has come from health; both of them have nursery nurse qualifications. So as we're pulling in from health as new posts become available, it's an understanding of children's development that's going to be the base line and you're going to be able to move, I think, between health and education. So it'll open it up further [but] we've got to get Children's Centres established; we've got to

> get multi-agency working, really working; you know we've really got to be working together. I do think hopefully all the edges will be blurred; there will be crossover and you will get people, for example, who might be on such as a health support team who could perhaps go and do some stuff down at [the nursery associated with the Children's Centre]. So you do get this flow and sharing of practice, which has got to benefit the children if [we] have got more knowledge in different aspects. We are here for the parents and support how they make their social network and we have workers that can do outreach and stuff. The working with parents would be essential wouldn't it, in Children's Centres, because that's the main thing; it just takes time doesn't it? You've just got to give things time for word to get out and somebody to try it. What is happening slowly is the conversations are not about who's fallen out on the estate, although you do get a little bit of that. Conversations are about the children when the children are playing. We are here for the parents and support how they make their social network and we have workers that can do outreach and stuff, but the conversations – just when you hear people talking about their children and enjoying their children; we give the community a chance to be a community instead of just a word. So they know each other, know their neighbours. That whole sense of community which I think in this country we are losing and that is the social fabric that's missing, isn't it? That's where a lot of the problems are coming from. This is about parents and children in the local community outside those doors there.

Values and ethics

What values and ethics, then, do the above examples of professional knowledge, skills and autonomy presuppose? For the EYP it is difficult to separate personal and professional values and ethics for both help to form professional identity, aspects of which could be altruism, dedication and personal commitment to children and their families. At the centre of their value and ethics system has to be their concept of the child. This will be a child 'rich' in possibilities and potential, the awesome young researcher, investigator of their environment, the carer of friends, the negotiator, the innovator, the visionary. This does not necessarily cohere with current government perceptions of children and childhood, or with the aspects of the Every Child Matters agenda that sees the child as human capital (Alderson, 2008). The ongoing tension between education and care is at the root of the issues surrounding the status of EYPs and the relationship of their role to those of other professionals working with children in the birth-to-five age range and their parents and families. The push for an agenda of social inclusion without the necessary ongoing resources to carry it out effectively, especially personnel, has been an ongoing issue for all who work within the Children's Centre environment; the current drive to cut public spending has a huge potential to further exacerbate this state of affairs.

Focus on EYPs: The crucial importance of the early years

'Sunita' is the owner/manager of a well-established small day-care setting. She has a particular interest in working with children with English as an additional language, children with special needs and children in unique family circumstances. She gained early years professional status in mid 2007, and has since gained experience as a setting-based EYPS trainer, and subsequently as a peripatetic mentor and assessor, contracted by her local EYPS training provider. She proposes:

One of the areas they [the government] really do need to look at is the skill sets that EYPs have, and why they are so important and so significant for children under 5 years. I think a lot of EYPs do look at the holistic development of the children; they do look at the routine of the day and use it, and exploit the learning opportunities. You know, fostering independence is a huge part of early years child care and I think sometimes that's lost if you take too much of a 'teacher's' perspective. If children haven't had their self-esteem, their self-confidence and their independence nurtured from a young age, the transition to school becomes a lot harder. We need the right people in place working with the under-fives who understand we need children with a good self-esteem; self-starters who have the confidence to move forward in life, because those skills that you are giving children will hopefully help them overcome several things, not just the transition to school. Hopefully they'll stand up in the gun cultures that they then might be living in, and hopefully they'll have the confidence to say 'I know what the right path is and this is what I'm gonna do.' You see a lot of young people; they're led into these things, you know; it's probably only 10 per cent that really want to commit, do all the bad things and the other 90 per cent are following like sheep. Children need a good set of ethics and that doesn't come about from sitting down and doing worksheets, it comes about from fostering independence, improving self-esteem, self-worth, independent problem solving.

And the reward for all this? EYPs are as yet not fully unionized and there are no national pay scales. Consequently, remuneration is still derisory when one considers the knowledge and skills integral to the status, and pay has become more of an issue as EYPs embed themselves into the professional landscape of early years educare in this country. This is partly the result of serious lack of direction from the previous government, and concerns over what the intentions of the new government will be. But EYPs frequently answer the question, 'Was gaining the status worth all the effort it requires?' with a resounding 'Yes'. They talk of intrinsic job satisfaction, of having the privilege of witnessing the development of children from as young as a few months until their fifth year, and the fact that no other professionals have access to such a range of stages in a child's development. They explain how vital they consider their role to be. Where EYPs have been allowed to have real autonomy, they have transformed the early years provision and practice they lead and support, through building solid and respectful cross-agency relationships with colleagues, parents and families and successful interagency working. The writers of this chapter urge the Coalition Government to realize and value the potential for change and stability they have in Children's Centres and EYPs who could be charged with building and consolidating relationships between children, families, agencies and communities.

Points for reflection and discussion

A document published by UNICEF clearly recognizes the value of EYPs' specialist training to work with children in the birth-to-three stage of development. It is presented not just as an issue for early years practice in England, but also for other European nations:

> Benchmark 6 reinforces the training dimension of 'high quality care' by stipulating that a minimum of 50 per cent of staff in early education centres, including classroom assistants and all advisers and teachers, should have a minimum of three years tertiary education, with specialist qualifications in early childhood studies or a related field. … This benchmark … has had to be interpreted somewhat liberally in order to admit … countries such as France, Ireland, and the UK, where a primary school teaching qualification, with no special training in the developmental needs of preschool children, is all that is required. (UNICEF *Child Care Transition* report, 2008, pp. 25–6)

The EYP is inevitably linked to the arena of the Sure Start Children's Centre, and the support of children in such an early stage of life creates the need to deeply engage with parents, families and communities, and to liaise across professional boundaries with health workers, social services and, in the later stages of early childhood development, with nursery teachers. It will always be a complex role, straddling education, health and care, and we are as yet still in the embedding stage for the profession.

Governments that plan in five-year cycles are always pressing for quick results. However, this is a very short time within the development of individual human beings, families and communities. The US project Head Start gives us a powerful reason why the Sure Start project, and the role of EYPs within it should continue to be nationally supported, particularly within the most disadvantaged areas of the country. More than 40 years of research undertaken by the High/Scope Perry Pre-School study indicated that there had been a huge financial saving for society created by Head Start. In the early 1960s, under the Kennedy Government, the Head Start programme of centres for disadvantaged families and young children was planned to provide a community 'hub' for families of young children who lived within ghetto areas in several large US cities. Parents were offered the chance to engage in training and education while their children were cared for by professional childcare and education staff. Some of the training offered to the adults related to parenting and 'life management' skills. The project was initially deemed a failure, because during its early years of operation, there was no significant rise in the IQs of children whose families were supported through the Head Start family centres.

By the late 1970s, however, unexpected 'sleeper' results began to emerge. A significant percentage of the first generation of children whose families had experienced the Head Start programme avoided getting into trouble with the law, and did not become teenage parents at the rate of contemporaries whose families had not been supported by Head Start in their earliest years of life. By the 1980s it became clear that the Head Start cohort were more likely to graduate from high school, gain employment and set up stable families of their own than their non-Head Start contemporaries. By the early 2000s the project reported an overall saving of '$258,888 per participant, on an investment of $15,166 per participant: $17.07 per dollar invested'. In particular, it was proposed that 93 per cent of this return was 'due to the large programme effect of reduced crime rates for programme males' (Schweinhart et al., 2005, pp. xvi–xvii). This figure of course does not take in any projected reduction of costs with regard to the offspring of the Head Start children who had higher chances of being raised in stable families by socially and emotionally stable parents, or of the third 'grandchild generation' who will now be entering the world.

Conclusion

The current government should be urged to look across the Atlantic when they are considering the fate of the Sure Start and early years professional training projects. It is very easy to make a quick saving on early years when national resources are stretched by leaving families in difficulty to fend for themselves, but several years hence, even greater expenditure is needed to deal with the problems that condemning small children to poverty, poor parenting and broken communities create. In the words of the African proverb made famous by Hillary Clinton (2006), 'it takes a village to raise a child'. If we can show children that their community cares for them, then they will be far more likely to grow up to care for their community; to truly embrace David Cameron's concept of 'the Big Society'. The EYP role has been designed to sit at the hub of such communities, and as such, we would urge those with the power to allocate funds to keep faith with the project, particularly within disadvantaged areas, allowing EYPs to blossom into the pivotal task that awaits them in the troubled local communities of post-Thatcherist, post-credit-crunch Britain.

Questions for reflective practice

Early years professionals and early years teachers need to have their own sphere of leadership. How do you think policy should shape these?

The government needs early years leaders who are trained at the postgraduate level – how might pay scales be reconciled with this in the current political and economical climate?

At the time of publication, policy for Children's Centres is still evolving. How would you shape policy for Children's Centres in different areas of the UK and why?

Further reading, resources and/or websites

Anning, A., and Ball, M. (2008), *Improving Services for Young Children: From Sure Start to Children's Centres*. London: Sage.

Broadhead, P., Meleady, C., and Delgardo, J. (2007), *Children, Families and Communities: Creating and Sustaining Integrated Services* (Education in an Urbanised Society). Milton Keynes: Open University Press.

Jarvis, P., George, J., and Holland, W. (2010), *The Early Years Professional's Complete Companion*. Harlow: Pearson Educational.

Trodd, G., and Goodliff, G. (eds) (2010), *The Achieving EYPS Series*. www.learningmatters.co.uk/series. asp?mySeriesName=Achieving%20EYPS.

Aspect EYP Zone: www.aspect.org.uk/eyp/2010/04/chasing-answers-on-early-years-professional-status-eyps/.

Department for Education: www.education.gov.uk/.

Early Years Educator: www.earlyyearseducator.co.uk/.

Nursery World: www.nurseryworld.co.uk/.

Together for Children: www.childrens-centres.org/default.aspx.

References

Alderson, P. (2008), *Young Children's Rights*, 2nd edition. London: Jessica Kingsley Publishing.

Cabinet Office (2010), *The Coalition: Our Programme for Government*. www.programmeforgovernment.hmg.gov.uk/files/2010/05/coalition-programme.pdf. Accessed 1 July 2010.

Children, Schools and Families Committee (2010), *Fifth Parliamentary Report – Sure Start Children's Centres*. www.publications.parliament.uk/pa/cm200910/cmselect/cmchilsch/130/13002.htm. Accessed 24 July 2010.

Clinton, H. (2006), *It Takes a Village*. New York: Simon and Schuster.

CWDC (2006), *Early Years Home Page*. www.cwdcouncil.org.uk/projects/earlyyears.htm. Accessed 2 April 2008.

— (2011), http://www.cwdcouncil.org.uk/eyps. Accessed 6 May 2011

DCSF (2010), *The History of Sure Start*. www.dcsf.gov.uk/everychildmatters/earlyyears/surestart/surestartchildrenscentres/history/history/. Accessed 31 July 2010.

Department for Education (2010), *Review of Early Years Foundation Stage*. www.education.gov.uk/news/news/eyfs-review. Accessed 24 July 2010.

DfES (2003), *Every Child Matters Green Paper*. London: The Stationery Office.

Early Education Advisory Group (EEAG) (2005), Annex 3, Paper 05/5/9, Item M. www.tda.gov.uk/upload/resources/doc/b/boardoct05_early_years_teachers_c.doc. Accessed 2 April 2008.

Head Start Association (2010), *Basic Head Start Facts*. www.nhsa.org/files/static_page_files/399A3EB7–1D09–3519-AD-B004D2DAFA33DD/BasicHeadStartFacts.pdf. Accessed 31 July 2010.

Laming, W. (2003), *The Victoria Climbié Report*. http://image.guardian.co.uk/sys-files/Society/documents/2003/01/28/climbiereport.pdf. Accessed 26 July 2010.

Schweinhart, L., Montie, J., Xiang, Z., Barnett, W. S., Belfield, C., and Nores, M. (2005), *Lifetime Effects: The High/Scope Perry Preschool Study Through Age 40*. Yipsilanti: High/Scope Press.

Sylva, K., Siraj-Blatchford, I., Taggert, B., Sammons, P., Elliot, K., and Melhuish, E. (2003), *The Effective Provision of Pre-School Education (EPPE) Project (2008) 1998 – Ongoing*. http://k1.ioe.ac.uk/schools/ecpe/eppe/. Accessed 29 March 2008.

Tickell, C. (2011), *The Early Years Foundation Stage (EYFS) Review. An Independent Report* . London: The Cabinet Office, HM Government.

UNICEF (2008), *The Child Care Transition: A League Table of Early Childhood Education and Care in Economically Advanced Countries*. www.Unicef-Irc.Org/Publications/Pdf/Rc8_Eng.Pdf. Accessed 6 July 2009.

Ward, L. (2005), *Ofsted Finds Problems with Morning Nursery Care: The Guardian Online*. www.guardian.co.uk/society/2005/dec/06/childrensservices.politics. Accessed 25 July 2010.

Watson, R. (2010), *Children's Centres Could Be Closed to Boost Efficiency. Children and Young People Now*. www.cypnow.co.uk/news/ByDiscipline/Childcare-and-Early-Years/987320/Childrens-centres-closed-boost-efficiency/. Accessed 25 July 2010.

5

The Early Years Teacher: Working Across the Birth-to-Seven Age Range

Pat Broadhead

Chapter Outline

Introduction

This chapter considers the early years teacher's activity and professionalism across the birth-to-seven age range. It examines the role in relation to younger and older children with particular reference to playful learning. The chapter locates the teacher's role amid the extensive and ongoing changes in schools relating to Every Child Matters and sets the extended schools agenda as the context for changing professionalism. It then reflects on future directions for early years teachers and teaching.

The decision to focus this chapter on the birth-to-seven age range may seem unusual within the English educational context. Traditionally, teachers have worked with 3- and 4-year-olds in nursery classes attached to primary schools and with this age range in nursery schools located within and funded by the local authority. Within the maintained schools sector they have of course also worked with 4- and 5-year-olds in reception classes and with 5-, 6- and 7-year-olds in Year 1 and Year 2 classes. The reception class is something of an anomaly, being neither nursery nor 'school'. They emerged in primary schools with no nursery class to accommodate preschool-aged children when the Nursery Education Grant was targeted at 4-year-olds in the mid 1980s, but now all English schools have a reception class unless, as in a small but increasing number of cases, they have combined their nursery and reception classes into an early years unit, led by a teacher for children aged from 3 to 5 years.

The teacher's role in the early years

The Early Years Foundation Stage (EYFS) statutory guidance (DfES, 2007) states in Appendix 2, Point 6 that 'teacher involvement, due to their specific training and expertise, can have a significant impact on children's learning. Therefore, the teaching and learning in each class or group of pupils aged 3 and over in maintained schools and nursery schools must be led by a teacher'.

This aspect was also emphasized in the EPPE and REPEY studies which showed that Level 6 qualifications (e.g., trained teachers) correlated with high quality in the provision (Sammons, 2010; Siraj-Blatchford et al., 2002; Taggart et al., 2000). The required staff–pupil ratios identified in the EYFS statutory guidance are also influenced by whether or not a qualified teacher or early years professional (both of which professions require Level 6 qualifications) is present for both nursery and reception classes. The guidance uses the phrase 'working directly with the children' to presumably distinguish those who are working directly with children from those who are only distantly connected to the children. This quote is ambiguous in its use of the phrase 'led by a teacher' because this can be interpreted as the reception teacher 'leading' the nursery provision while only being present occasionally. In Point 10 the statutory guidance states that a teacher must be present except for non-contact breaks for children aged 3 and older in nursery classes and nursery schools. There is no teacher-to-pupil ratio guidance for reception classes other than that for infant classes where the ratio remains at 30:1 (DfES, 2007, Appendix 2, Point 11). To summarize, then, teachers have traditionally been located with children aged 3 to 7 in school and nursery school settings and now there are clear, legal requirements for their presence across the birth-to-seven age range.

The remit of the teacher in relation to children under 3 years of age has been most substantially influenced by the phased opening of a considerable number of Children's Centres with an intention under the previous Labour Government to provide 3,500 by 2010. This Labour Government required that a teacher must be present in every Children's Centre that offered integrated early learning and care and in all Centres located in the 30-per-cent most disadvantaged areas. The minimum requirement was for a part-time teacher, but this would become a full-time appointment within two years of designation; some local authorities appointed full-time teachers from the designation. Under the Coalition Government the teacher related requirement for Children's Centres remain unclear at the time of publication.

It is widely recognized that the teacher's role in a Children's Centre is a complex one, requiring teachers to lead on curriculum planning and assessment across sometimes quite large teams, to have a capacity for integrated working with a range of other professionals and to play a significant role with parents, some of whom may be living with financial disadvantage and related family difficulties. They are expected to work with childminders and with the voluntary sector and also to support the family outreach worker if this person is planning to work with groups. An influential document, the DCSF's *Working Together to Safeguard Children,* offers explicit guidance for the role, based on the assumption that centres have appointed a full-time teacher who is working some of the time with children and the remainder of the time with staff, parents and providers in the wider community. Clearly there is a policy context influencing the development of the teacher's role and presence across the early years and although birth-to-three age range has never traditionally been their domain in England, this is changing with the advent of Children's Centres.

The chapter will address the seven dimensions of professionalism through a focus on and discussion of two aspects of the teacher's role. The first aspect concerns the well-established role and responsibilities relating to the curriculum and its relationship with children's learning through the medium of play. The curriculum and learning aspect is of particular interest because early years teachers are constantly beset by the ideological tensions arising from the ideological conflict between the play-orientated curriculum and the transmissive curriculum, the latter dominating educational settings since the development of the National Curriculum in 1988. Nowhere is this more manifest and more problematic than in the 'anomalous' reception class where the play-orientated nursery ethos meets or indeed clashes with the transmissive, teacher-dominated ethos which tends to prevail in school, driven by testing, league tables and a policy climate that puts teacher direction before children's interests.

The second aspect of the teacher's role addresses the more recent developments of the role towards a need for multi-disciplinary working. Early years teachers, particularly in nursery classes and nursery schools, have always worked more closely with parents and other professionals than have their primary school counterparts, but this aspect of their role is now more widely acknowledged in policy, particularly in relation to Children's Centres, as discussed above. The policy changes in schools arising from the Every Child Matters agenda (Broadhead and Martin, 2009; Walker, 2008) are impacting in a range of ways and not least in those Children's Centres attached to and aligned with both primary and secondary schools.

Knowledge: What are teachers learning?

Piagetian theory has been hugely influential in the training and development of early years teachers over the years and still, I would argue, substantially influences the ideological ethos of today. Piaget's theoretical frames are highly complex and were subsequently subject to critique through the writings of Donaldson (1978) and others. Nevertheless, it was Piaget's work that substantially informed the Plowden Report (CACE, 1967) and that brought into English teacher education in the 1960s and 1970s the concept of the 'active child' who comes to understand the wider world through exploration and experimentation. Piaget's constructs of *accommodation and assimilation* formed the basis of the educational theory of many early years teachers of my generation, enabling them to develop a concept of the *thinking child* as opposed to the *child as empty vessel* waiting to be filled by the knowing adult. Interpreting Piagetian theory pedagogically (not a word we used in the 1960s, 1970s, 1980s or 1990s) was a huge challenge and indeed Piaget was not overly concerned with teaching but rather with deepening understanding of learning processes. However, interpretations of his work gave rise to the centrality of play as important for active learning in educational settings and the emergence of this idea in early years teachers' repertoires revealed the influence not only of Piaget but also that of the other great innovators such as Froebel and Montessori. Play became the 'thing' and the playful classrooms and playgrounds of the early years during the 1970s and 1980s drew many visitors to our shores from around the world to see what was deemed to be innovative practice. The child as active, curious, exploratory learner also influenced the practices of the primary schools during the 1970s, these practices subsequently being termed 'progressive' and eventually dismissed and diminished by the legislative policy of the late 1980s and 1990s. However, the concept of the developing, active child has never disappeared from our theorizations of learning and has remained influential, if diminished in more recent times, in the professional development and learning of the early years teacher during initial teacher education.

While Piaget is not forgotten, and most certainly not dismissed, more recently, Vygotskyan theory has been embedded within the theorizing of emerging teachers. It is important, however, not to see Piagetian and Vygotskyan theory as in any way contradictory (Bruner, 1996). Vygotsky's work located the child more firmly as a learner within a community of learners (Rogoff, 1994; Wenger, 1998), as learning from expert others, both adults and other children, and of using the objects and materials around them to change themselves internally and to change their own view of how the world works. Play is a more central tenet of Vygotskyan theory, and his work, perhaps more substantially than Piaget's, has brought clearer pedagogical responsibilities for the educator in terms of how the environment is structured and the kinds of resources that might be provided, how the adult operates within that environment and whether and when the adult might engage with the child in playful activity to support learning. While Piaget's work established constructs of 'starting from the child', Vygotsky's work led to clearer illustrations of the adult's role as a playful pedagogue and moved our thinking more firmly towards better understanding of the adult's responsibilities as observer, narrator, facilitator, engager and pedagogue – a much broader conceptualization than that of 'assessor', which is also, of course, a key and necessary role in support of children's learning in an educational setting.

We came to see how understanding children's learning was a central tenet in the development of early years teachers' skills and professionalism within the emerging constructs of socio-cultural theory (Edwards, 2003). It must also be acknowledged that the term 'child centred' has never been unproblematic and theorizing following Vygotsky might be seen to decentre the individual child, 'viewing the child as existing through its relations with others and always in a particular context' (Dahlberg et al., 1999, p. 43).

More recent texts illustrate the extent to which children define their culture and identity through play and learning (Brooker, 2002) and how these experiences are linked with the efficacy of learning processes and with the creation of an effective learning environment. We have always known that home and school are inextricably linked for the young child; the Plowden report (CACE, 1967) was perhaps the first piece of influential government policy to make this very evident in England, but recent studies also now show the extent to which the home experiences, born of home and local community cultures, might find voice in the classroom with supportive adults. Bronfenbrenner's (1979) nested ecological model of the child at home, in the community and in the educational setting helps us to interconnect the diverse cultural dimensions of early transitions across a range of settings familiar to the young child and to recognize the simultaneous influences on learning and work discussed by Anning et al. (2004). Carr (2000), Fleer (1995) and others have moved theoretical frames forward to conceive of the co-constructed curriculum (between adult and child) as the basis of a high-quality experience and sound pedagogical practice (Wood, 2010a; Wood, 2010b). But we do need to be aware that, however we construct childhood and hence how we conceive of early education, we are engaging with 'cultural constructions' and the cultures of teachers and learners are not always the same (Woodhead, 1996, p. 6).

These theoretical and conceptual developments have been mirrored to some extent in developments in the EYFS (DfES, 2007), which addresses the birth-to-five age range. Related publications (DCSF, 2009a; 2009b) have sought to build on and more firmly embed the high profile of play in relation to learning within the early years curriculum, to acknowledge playful and child-initiated experiences as central to the young child's experience in educational settings and to explore the educator's role as facilitator and as bringer of new understandings to the child's world. As we await a planned review of the EYFS, it does seem that playful approaches are once more well established in nursery settings but may still be diminished in reception settings and in the experiences of children in the first and second years of the primary school.

Education and training

Teaching has been an all-graduate profession since the early 1970s; prior to this time, a teacher could qualify with a Certificate in Education and without a degree. Qualified Teacher Status, was awarded by the GTC (General Teaching Council), although at the time of writing there is talk of returning it to the newly developed Department of Education under the 2010 Coalition Government. Routes for early years teachers have usually covered either the three-to-7 age range or had, usually, minimal coverage within a predominantly primary 5–11 route. Initial teacher education courses must address two phases of education. As noted above, teachers have not always worked in nursery classes attached to primary schools; in the past, legislation has been sufficiently vague so as to 'allow' nursery nurses to work alone or for the reception class teacher to be designated as 'overseeing the nursery' but as stated above, the legislation for their presence, while now clearer, is also becoming somewhat merged with the role of the early years professional in relation to children under 5 years of age.

It has been recognized that current initial teacher education training models may not significantly prepare beginning teachers for the extended management role of their work in Children's Centres nor for working with children from birth to 3 years (Siraj-Blatchford et al., 2002). The recent Select Committee report on the training of teachers (House of Commons, 2010) makes two clear statements (Paragraph 35):

> The Department must develop its policies in relation to early years provision in line with the findings from a range of studies, many of which it funded, showing the critical importance of qualified teachers in early years settings. We call on the Department to provide a clear statement on the respective roles of qualified teachers and Early Years Professionals in early years settings. (House of Commons, 2010)

The role of the early years professional is the subject of Chapter 4 but the recommendation of the Select Committee shows the continuing concerns and confusions relating to the respective roles and responsibilities of these two groups of workers. The second key recommendation of the Select Committee comes in paragraph 36:

> For too long, early years provision has been associated with the least skilled and lowest status section of the children's workforce. We recommend that the Training and Development Agency for Schools be given a remit to oversee initial teacher training programmes that train teachers in relation to the birth-to-five age group. The standards for Qualified Teacher Status should be modified as necessary to support such birth-to-five training. (House of Commons, 2010)

The Select Committee was an all-party group of MPs. Therefore the recent change of government is not an opportunity to disregard these important statements, both of which could have significant implications for the future development of the early years teacher's roles and responsibilities.

The standards for teacher education are highly generic and there were intellectual tussles when they were being established to retain a reference to the developing child, initially driven by Piagetian theory around stages of development, but then more substantially by social constructivist theories of the child within the community of learners as an active meaning maker through playful and self-selected activities. The emphasis of the standards on core and foundation subjects, deriving from a highly prescriptive National Curriculum, drove the focus away from the child as learner and also away from playful learning as an integral part of teacher education, and many student teachers were not exposed to any depth of teaching and thinking in relation to these aspects. The introduction of the EYFS was a concerted attempt to reintroduce learning and development as integral features of an early years curriculum and recent publications (DCSF, 2009a; 2009b) have sought to more substantially open the policy debate and early years practice to socio-constructivist views of learning and to debates around playful learning and playful pedagogies as essential initial training experiences for the early years teacher.

It is interesting to note that the TDA does not know how many early years teachers are being trained at any one time because their figures relate only to the training of primary and secondary teachers. Early years trained teachers are subsumed within the primary figures.

Skills: Becoming a skilful professional in a multi-disciplinary world

The early years teacher working in nursery classes, nursery schools and more recently Children's Centres has always needed to be a team player and for this, a capacity for interprofessional communication has been central. This particular skill is a key element as the 'team around the child' extends under the influence of the Every Child Matters agenda. The Sure Start Children's Centre initiative, currently in place, grew out of initiatives under the previous Labour Government designed to target and ultimately reduce the numbers of children under 5 years of age living in poverty. Early Excellence Centres were the forerunners of the Children's Centres and were complemented in some areas of the country by the Neighbourhood Nurseries Initiative, all of which targeted economically deprived communities by supporting return to work and training for parents but which did not necessarily have teachers on site. The Education Act of 2002 gave powers to local authorities to prepare the way for Extended Schools which would provide core services including childcare on site, before and after school provision and parenting support. This often resulted in Children's Centres being located on primary school sites and in some cases on secondary school sites as the secondary school sector began to take the lead in the move towards twenty-first-century schools as extended, community-based services designed to improve learning experiences by recognizing and responding to the holistic needs of children and young people, especially those living in poverty.

These initiatives, on the face of it, would seem to lead ever further away from the role of the early years teacher who may seemingly become swallowed up in much bigger organizational structures. However, in working with younger children, it is often the early years teacher (not, of course, just the teacher; other professionals are involved and affected) who comes to better understand the holistic nature of the learning process and who can see at first hand, if they are trained to recognize it, the detrimental impact of poverty on learning, the impact of language delay on learning and the impact of difficult family circumstances on children's learning. It is often in such circumstances as these that the therapeutic powers of play are increasingly acknowledged and that early years teachers can come to welcome and value the professional knowledge of others involved with the families such as play therapists, speech therapists, family outreach workers, children and family social workers, and more recently, early years professionals. These teams around the child are interconnected only by their respective capacities to reach out and relate to other professionals and there is a wealth of literature to show that these skills are of a high order and result from professional development and related reflective experiences (Siraj-Blatchford et al., 2007).

The early years teacher has also, traditionally, become skilled at understanding the child within the wider sphere of influences upon the child as individual and as learner – how their culture, religion, ethnicity, social class and family constitution might influence the children's identity, development and learning. Understanding the extent to which children's early learning experiences are culturally situated and the links with and importance of good relationships between parents, teachers and the wider community members is a highly skilled activity and is substantially influenced by prevailing cultural norms (New, 1999). In her article New describes the extended cultural prioritizing that is given to the family within the wider community in many Italian towns and cities, including Reggio Emilia (Edwards et al., 1998), which is perhaps one of the best-known initiatives internationally and which has been in development for more than 25 years. Because of the cultural embeddedness of family life, home–school links are forged in natural ways and bring Bronfenbrenner's ecological model, discussed earlier, very much to life. In many English schools, parents are kept at the door as a norm and such embeddedness is therefore culturally more challenging to achieve. As New points out, culture reflects the choices that adults make and the early years teacher needs to develop the intent and the skill to connect the adults in the children's lives outside their early years setting or classroom with their experiences within the classroom.

Autonomy and values: Preserving and sustaining a professional value system and professional autonomy in an ever-changing world

The coherence of the early years has been constantly beset by the artificial distinctions drawn between care and education and nowhere has this confused and confounded more than across the early years. Some readers may remember the attempts to introduce the term 'educare' to address this artificial divide which arose from previous policy initiatives. Its roots were laudable and re-emphasized the artificiality of the split in the conceptualization of a child's life. Pugh (1992) and others have long campaigned for a coordinated policy manifest at all levels of policymaking in recognition of the fact that the multiplicity of terms in use 'such as "day care", "child care" and "nursery education" remain common without an adequate alternative (educare may carry the meaning but is a clumsy term …)' (Pugh, 1992, p. 43). The previous Labour Government's establishment of a Department for Children, Schools and Families was an innovative culmination of the recognition that care and education needed to be irrevocably interconnected as a fundamental of the human experience. Under the new Coalition Government, we have returned to the Department of Education. However, as noted above, we have absorbed the term 'pedagogy' into the teacher's professional lexicon and Brannen and Moss remind us that in Europe the term is used to relate to the 'education of the whole person: body, mind, feelings, spirit, creativity, and crucially the relationship of the individual to others' (Brannen and Moss, 2003, p. 63).

If the ethos of the school has required it (and many have) Year 1 and Year 2 teachers have often been required or expected to neglect the need for nurturing and warm relationships that creates a climate for learning among younger children. As Broadhead and Martin point out (2009, p. 46), in the climate of testing, league tables and punitive Ofsted inspection, 'schools gradually distanced themselves from the affective to focus on the cognitive. With an emphasis on subject knowledge acquisition, especially in relation to testing and with particular subjects having primacy and dominance, a pedagogy of child/student direction based on personal interests and agendas gradually disappeared; there was not time for it'.

These developments created an emphasis on transmissive teaching rather than transformative learning (O'Sullivan, 1999). Within the early years there must be a concern for the care and protection of children, and equally, the support for them to reach their intellectual potential (Moss, 2006). The following three, brief case studies, aim to explore the two remaining professional dimensions, ethics and reward, within the broader context of three teachers' experiences in a changing world of playful learning and multi-professional expansion.

Three case studies: Considering ethics and reward for an early years teacher

This section presents three case studies, one from an experienced teacher newly appointed to a Children's Centre, one from a teacher in a nursery setting who has moved into Year 1, and one from a teacher in an early years unit. All three teachers find themselves with professional and ethical dilemmas relating to wider expectations versus what they believe is best for children. As their individual ethics of practice are challenged, so too is the extent to which they find intrinsic reward in their work. These quotes are summarized from more extensive discussions with the individuals to try and convey their professional journeys within the wider context of changing policies and ethos. The case studies are, of course, anonymous as they address especially sensitive issues.

Case Study 1

When I was first appointed to work in a Children's Centre, it was horrendous. It was clear that other staff were asking what they needed a teacher for; they felt 'they already did it as child carers and knew what they were doing'. It was clear the managers didn't know what to do with us; they had no understanding of our role. It's taken a long time and a lot of unpicking and an awful lot of tears, discussions and arguments to get this far – I'd say about six years from the time the first Children's Centre opened. We had to negotiate our terms and conditions and this is still being negotiated even now. In our Authority we had a separate early years advisory team who supported schools, centres and the private sector and they could pull together the work. Other Authorities put their advisors actually in the Centres as the teacher but they have worked across several Centres which must be incredibly difficult to have any impact in any one place. They've been more concerned with data collection than, for example, curriculum development. In our Authority, the advisors connect the teachers in the Centres with the voluntary and private sector providers and support the development of training sessions across the different 'Reach Areas' – a Reach Area is the area around the Centre and might have up to a 1000 children within it and a wide range of providers. The Centre teacher is expected to receive and analyse the data for the Foundation Stage Profile across the schools in the area and from this, to determine what kind of training needs there are among the providers across the area. Teachers are also expected to talk to the outreach worker about courses for parents like how you can support language development for your child. There were six of us when we were first appointed and it did begin to change and get better over time; we met as a support group for years because it was so difficult at first; we used to meet in the pub. We began to shape the job and think about the different expectations of the managers; there was no guidance at first. As more teachers came on board we set up a support network and provided written guidance and then I joined the advisory service myself. (Children's Centre teacher)

Comment: Despite the early dip in confidence and the sense of isolation, this teacher was able to come together with others to address their intent to once again bring intrinsic reward to their work, to re-establish a professional identity in these new arenas of practice and to operate once again in ways they believed were best for children. The centre teacher's job is complex and wide ranging, going well beyond the remit of the traditional class teacher. By coming together they not only reaffirmed their new identities as teachers but gradually influenced for the better the emerging support networks for those teachers who were to follow. Being in the vanguard of a new initiative requires strategies for emotional, ethical and intellectual survival; coming through periods of difficulty can result in more extensive professional knowledge and a capacity to improve integrated approaches.

Case Study 2

I have worked in a nursery for many years with a very experienced nursery nurse. The head teacher was very supportive of play and really understood how important it was especially for children in this area where there are high levels of disadvantage; many parents live on low income. When the EYFS was implemented we were really pleased because we felt it really encouraged a play based curriculum; we felt we were being given permission to play. We built our curriculum around observations of the children so that we really began to understand what their interests were and how we could develop these interests with a more flexible learning environment. We got very excited about what the children were doing and the quality of the play we were seeing. We were recording it with pictures and learning journals and sharing these with the parents and they were becoming really interested. The two Year 1 teachers also began to take an interest in what we were doing and they began trying out some of the ideas, with the head's support. Then the head left and I was moved by the new head to the Year 1 class. It was made very clear to me that playful approaches have no place in Year 1 and that they were seen as undermining the SATs scores. I am not happy with this; it's been very difficult to come to terms with it all. I've thought about leaving but I need to work. (Nursery teacher)

Comment: From a stable and professionally developing teaching environment we see this teacher subject to management changes which consequently diminish her professional confidence and feelings of reward from work and which subsequently also create huge ethical challenges in terms of whether or not to operate with young children in ways that she finds unethical. There is a clear split for her between a period when she felt professionally autonomous and able – over time and with much reflection and discussion – to create a playful but challenging learning environment for the nursery children and a period of disempowerment and autocracy and what she now experiences as inappropriateness in her curriculum provision. This shows the extent to which individual teachers can be subject to the louder and more powerful voices of authority, and can have their own professional knowledge and skills discounted in a changed policy environment.

Case Study 3

The unit has children in it from 3 to 5 years; we have the reception children in here also, and they go straight from us to Year 1/2 mixed class. We've been looking at ways of making the play much more open ended and flexible and have developed the outside area in all sorts of ways. We get lots of visitors coming to look at what we've been doing and they comment on the levels of concentration and absorption in the children's play. We have seen the children, especially the older ones, develop some incredibly complex play scenarios and make some amazing designs with the materials. They certainly do things that no adult would ever think of suggesting and their capacity for problem solving just grows and grows as they get older. They come in as uncertain 3-year-olds and just learn from one another as the months go by. The school staff have said in the past that the children are resilient and confident when they go into Year 1/2 and in general, have really good language skills. We do plan group times with the reception children, some literacy and numeracy activities, but try to plan it for the beginnings and ends of sessions so they have extended play periods in the mornings and the afternoons. Just recently and for a range of reasons, there have been pressures on us to undertake more group learning times with the reception children and also, some pressures to extend that to the younger children. I am in discussion with colleagues at the moment and not really happy about this. I can't decide whether to just cave in, be pragmatic and get on with it. Basically we have some staff in school who just can't see what we are trying to do here around play and learning nor can they seem to see what we have done. They don't understand that confidence as learners and resilience come from our playful environment. I'm not sure what will happen now. (Early years teacher)

Comment: There are some similarities here with the experiences of the nursery teacher quoted above although the situation does not as yet sound as ethically confrontational. There seems to be some potential for compromise, but a shift from the previous position of professional autonomy is evident. This teacher clearly understands that other teachers in the school do not share her own levels of professional knowledge about the relationship between play and learning and the importance of self-direction and choice for children. But there is also the pragmatic, reflective consideration of how far one can actually go in seeking to protect a particular approach to, and the children's experiences of, teaching and learning. Compromise is far from submission, but these are not simple decisions when children's well-being seems to be at stake.

Conclusion

This chapter has sought to outline the changing contexts for and the challenges for early years teachers in the recent and current policy climates in keeping with the seven areas of professionalism upon which this book is focused. These professionals have worked amid, and been subject to, changing theoretical shifts in our wider understanding of teaching and learning and seemingly worked hard to protect playful approaches and to deepen their own understanding of why playful approaches are best for children. They have been variously supported in the development of this professional knowledge and related skills set depending on policy measures which in turn influence both their initial and ongoing development opportunities. Their levels of autonomy, their sense of personal value and reward and their self-belief as ethical practitioners are also significantly influenced by policy measures, whether from government, from the local authority or within their own settings. The case studies suggest that these teachers feel at their best when they are able to be reflective and autonomous and feel at their worst when isolated and intellectually stifled. None of this is perhaps surprising and we must, of course, be fair and acknowledge that teachers, just like other professionals, have shortcomings. The teacher's role has traditionally been class based; to move towards more integrated approaches requires professional shifts of thinking, of identity and, as perhaps illustrated in the final case study, of compromise. But just where to compromise and where to stand firm is perhaps the biggest ethical challenge that a teacher might face in a constantly changing educational world.

Questions for reflective practice

What knowledge and skills does the early years teacher need to sustain a challenging and playful learning environment?

In what ways can the child's home and community culture find space in the early years setting?

Bearing in mind the case studies, what ethical challenges do you feel you are currently confronting in your professional practice?

Further reading, resources and/or websites

Barker, R. (ed.) (2008), *Making Sense of Every Child Matters: Multi-Professional Practice Guidelines*. London: Policy Press.

Broadhead, P., Howard, J., and Wood, E. (2010), *Play and Learning in the Early Years: From Research to Practice*. London: Sage.

Walker, G. (2008), *Working Together for the Child: A Critical Introduction to Multi-Agency Working*. London: Continuum.

www.bbc.co.uk/schools/teachers/.

www.early-education.org.uk/.

www.tactyc.co.uk.

References

Anning, A., Cullen, J., and Fleer, M. (2004), *Early Childhood Education, Society and Culture*. London: Sage.

Brannen, J., and Moss, P. (2003), *Rethinking Children's Care*. Buckingham: Open University Press.

Broadhead, P. and Martin, D. (2009), Education and every child matters. Chapter 3 of R. Barker (ed.), *Making Sense of Every Child Matters; Multi-Professional Practice Guidance*. Bristol: Policy Press, 45–58.

Bronfenbrenner, U. (1979), *The Ecology of Human Development*. Cambridge, MA: Harvard University Press.

Brooker, L. (2002), *Starting School: Young Children Learning Cultures*. Buckingham: Open University Press.

Bruner, J. (1996), *Celebrating Divergence: Piaget and Vygotsky*. Keynote address to the joint meetings of the Growing Minds Conference and the Vygotsky-Piaget Conference. Geneva, 15 September.

CACE (Central Advisory Council for England) (1967), *Children and Their Primary Schools. The Plowden Report*. London: HMSO.

Carr, M. (2000), *Assessment in Early Childhood Settings: Learning Stories*. London: Paul Chapman.

Dahlberg, G., Moss, P., and Pence, A. (1999), *Beyond Quality in Early Childhood Education and Care: Postmodern Perspectives*. London: RoutledgeFalmer.

DCSF (Department for Children, Schools and Families) (2009a), Evangelou, M., Sylva, K., Wild, M., Glenny, G., and Kyriacou, M. *Early Years Learning and Development: Literature Review*. London: DCSF

— (2009b), *Learning, Playing and Interacting: Good Practice in the Early Years Foundation Stage*. London: DCSF.

DfES (Department for Education and Skills) (2007), *The Early Years Foundation Stage*. London: QCA.

Donaldson, M. (1978), *Children's Minds*. London: Fontana Press.

Edwards, C., Gandini, L., and Forman, G. (1998), *The Hundred Languages of Children; The Reggio Emilia Approach – Advanced Reflections*. Westport, CT: Ablex Publishing Corporation.

Edwards, S. (2003), New directions: Charting the paths for the socio-cultural theory in early childhood education and curriculum. *Contemporary Issues in Early Childhood*, 4, (3), 251–66.

Fleer, M. (ed.) (1995), *DAP Centrism: Challenging Developmentally Appropriate Practice*. Watson, ACT: Australian Early Childhood Association.

House of Commons (2010), Children, Schools and Families Committee. *Training of Teachers*. HC275–11. Norwich: The Stationery Office.

Moss, P. (2006), Farewell to childcare? *National Institute Economic Review*, no. 195.

New, R. (1999), What should children learn; making choices and taking chances? *Early Childhood Research and Practice*, 1, (2), 1–12.

O'Sullivan, E. (1999), *Transformative Learning: Educational Vision for the 21st Century*. London: Zed Books.

Pugh, G. (ed.) (1992), *Contemporary Issues in the Early Years: Working Collaboratively for Children*. London: Paul Chapman Publishing.

Rogoff, B. (1994), Developing understanding of the idea of communities of learners. *Mind, Culture and Activity*, 1, (4), 75–91.

Sammons P. (2010), Does pre-school make a difference? Identifying the impact of preschool on children's cognitive and social behavioural development at different ages. In K. Sylva, E. Melhuish, P. Sammons, I. Siraj-Blatchford and B. Taggart (eds), *Early Childhood Matters. Evidence from the Effective Pre-school and Primary Education Project*. London: Routledge, 92–113.

Siraj-Blatchford, I., Clarke, K., and Needham, M. (eds) (2007), *The Team Around the Child: Multi-agency Working in the Early Years*. Stoke on Trent: Trentham Books.

Siraj-Blatchford, I., Sylva, K., Muttock, S., Gliden, R., and Bell, D. (2002), *Researching effective pedagogy in the early years (REPEY)*. DfES Research Report 256. London: DfES.

Taggart, B., Sylva, K., Siraj-Blatchford, I., Melhuish, E., Sammons, P., and Walker-Hall, J. (2000), *The Effective Provision of Pre-school Education Project (EPPE): Technical Paper 5 – Characteristics of Centres in the EPPE Study: Interviews*. London: Institute of Education, University of London.

Walker, G. (2008), *Working Together for Children: A Critical Introduction to Multi-Agency Working*. London: Continuum.

Wenger, E. (1998), *Communities of Practice: Learning, Meaning and Identity*. Cambridge: Cambridge University Press.

Wood, E. (2010a), Developing integrated pedagogical approaches to play and learning. In P. Broadhead, J. Howard and E. Wood (eds), *Play and Learning in the Early Years*. London: Sage, 9–26.

— (2010b), Reconceptualising the play-pedagogy relationship: From control to complexity. In S. Edwards and L. Brooker (eds), *Rethinking Play*. Maidenhead: Open University Press.

Woodhead, M. (1996), *In Search of the Rainbow: Pathways to Quality in Large Scale Programmes for Young Disadvantaged Children*. The Hague: Bernard Van Leer Foundation.

6

Health and Social Care Professionals: A Holistic Approach

Kate Karban and Sue Smith

Chapter Outline

Introduction

This chapter is intended to explore the contributions of health and social care professionals to the early years interprofessional team. In particular, we will consider the diverse professional contributions and preparation for professionals working in the early years, such as physiotherapists and nurses who have a generic training but may not have a specific early years identity or specialist qualification. In addition, this chapter will refer to the roles of other professionals such as dieticians and speech and language therapists, with the latter's roles considered in Chapter 8.

The first part of the chapter examines the current political and social background to early years practice and health and social care. A second section focuses on the different roles of health and social care professionals. Two case scenarios are used to illuminate the seven dimensions of professionalism (Brock, 2009) and give the opportunity for the readers to analyse and discuss key issues for themselves.

The discussion and case examples draw on our experience of designing and delivering an interprofessional curriculum for pre-registration health and social care students, with additional material developed in collaboration with local multi-disciplinary health and social care teams (Brock et al., 2009). Our work has also been rooted in our own professional disciplines of physiotherapy and social work with extensive practice experience and research across a range of settings including services for children and families.

Background

The political and social context

New Labour ideology acknowledged the interconnectedness of social and economic problems. The idea was that 'joined-up working' or 'thinking' acknowledged the interrelatedness of the needs of children, adults and families spanning the fields of health, education, social services, law enforcement, housing, employment and family support. The aim was to reshape services: joined-up working would make them more flexible, more responsive to local demographics and priorities, more efficient by reducing overlap of treatments, diagnoses and records, and ultimately more effective.

In particular, joined-up working was a central tenet of New Labour policy for reducing poverty and social exclusion where 'interventions' were to be negotiated with local communities to support them in escaping the poverty trap. This can be seen in the development of the Sure Start programmes in the 1990s. These aimed to support families with young children, bringing together health and social care services with a range of family support and child care services (Glass, 1999).

The impact of the Baby Peter case

One essential perspective on the importance of working together for the individual health and social care professionals is offered by the Baby Peter (P) case. Despite being the subject of a multi-agency child protection plan in December 2006, Baby P died on 3 August 2007 at the age of 17 months. At one level, inquiries (CQC, 2009) have drawn attention to the complex organizational relationships, including four NHS Trusts as well as social services and the police, the lack of awareness of child protection procedures, poor recording systems and inadequate governance. However, other key themes highlight the lack of communication between the professionals involved, including staff not completing paperwork adequately, non-attendance at multi-agency meetings, insufficient and confusing information as well as delays in making referrals and limited sharing of information. Additionally, Baby P's growth charts were poorly documented: there was an absence of bone and skeletal scan information and neither the social worker nor the health visitor was able to attend vital health assessments, leaving a serious gap in the information available at the clinic. In some instances, the lack of teamwork was noted, leaving individuals unable to seek other information or expertise and limiting opportunity for shared learning and contributing to a climate of professional isolation. While a range of actions have now been put in place to address these many issues, it is important to draw out the lessons from this and other similar events. These have relevance for the everyday practices of all health and social care professionals working together to support young children and their families and for reducing the risk of further tragedies.

Evidence indicates that families recognize and value effective communication, shared knowledge across the team and positive multi-agency teamwork (Brock et al., 2009). The benefits of mutual team support were also identified by service users who themselves appreciated the supportive environment provided by a team that was seen to work well together. These views are also reflected in service users' views (Atkinson et al., 2007), which included recognition of the need for more appropriate referrals and more focused support.

Promoting user participation

Bearing in mind some of the key drivers for health and social care in the twenty-first century, the updated National Plan (DoH, 2009) describes practical measures to meet the increased prevalence of lifestyle diseases. The vision is for an NHS that is organized around the real needs of service users whether at home, in a community setting, or in hospital. The increasing use of concepts such as co-production, based on '… more active involvement and decision-making by the person using a service …' (Needham and Carr, 2009), is also relevant here. Co-production can be seen as closely aligned with the health agenda in moving '… from a service that does things to and for its patients to one which is patient led, where the service works with patients to support them with their health needs' (DoH, 2005, p. 3).

Needham and Carr (2009) identify challenges associated with this agenda in respect of the need to emphasize collective and community level co-production rather than the focus remaining at an individual level. Additionally there are issues regarding the involvement of marginalized communities and the need to offer support to these groups to enhance their capacity for involvement. Co-production also offers fundamental challenges for health and social care professionals. It requires them to initiate, enable and model co-production and, more significantly, to adjust to the shift required to meet this agenda in terms of their professional identity, organizational practice and culture (Dunston et al., 2009, p. 49) in order to change relationships between the providers and recipients of care.

In parallel, there is a renewed focus on health promotion with people taking increasing personal responsibility for improving their own and their children's health and taking advantage of new opportunities to become more physically active and eat healthily. Promoting good health will require professionals to develop their understanding of the evidence base and use strategies to motivate individuals to make lifestyle changes. They will need to work together to deliver interventions consistently and need professionals to adjust their own behaviours (which may stem from their own professional and personal experiences), shifting from a 'cure all', we say/you do, interventionist approach to one based on collaboration and empowerment.

Health inequalities

Another dimension to consider is a wider perspective on health inequalities and the social determinants of health, recognizing that socio-economic status is associated with a range of outcomes for children with far-reaching consequences extending into adult life (Marmot, 2010). These include the impact of disadvantage on physical, emotional and intellectual development in early childhood, which is seen to influence children's readiness for school, decrease educational attainment as well as affect health (Dyson et al., 2009). Despite more than £10 billion being spent on improving the health of under-fives in England since 1998, the Audit Commission's report *Giving Children a Healthy Start* (2010) found health care for under-fives had not improved over the past decade. The findings do show some improvements in certain aspects of young children's health, including fewer deaths in infancy and signs of slowing obesity rates. However the gap between the health of children in disadvantaged areas and those in more affluent areas has widened. For example, as stated in Chapter 1, children with high cognitive scores at 22 months, but with parents of low socio-economic status, have been found to do less well than those with low scores and parents of higher socio-economic status (Feinstein, 2003). Issues of maternal health and prenatal care are also relevant here with disadvantaged mothers being more likely to deliver low birth weight babies who in turn are at greater risk of infant mortality and poor educational outcomes (Jefferis et al., 2002).

Notwithstanding the emphasis on personal responsibility and the co-production of health, a shared awareness of the wider issues, particularly recognizing the impact of poverty and inequality on children's health and well-being, is essential for all professionals to be able to respond to the needs of families at a community as well as an individual level (Baldwin, 2009). While acknowledging the important role and success of Sure Start centres in disadvantaged

Figure 6.1 A healthcare professional supporting families

areas which offer health and child care services to millions of families, the Audit Commission recommends that local bodies should coordinate policies and targets for a more coherent approach to working together to improve health for young children. This should include the needs of disabled children where there is a need to improve communication with families and coordination between professionals in different services (DSCF, 2009).

There is clearly further work to be done in developing effective approaches to working with families to improve children's health. On the positive side there are examples of success with multi-agency working being seen to be associated with better outcomes for patients and children and lower levels of stress for staff (Sloper, 2004) and as offering a useful way of addressing physical and mental health issues and health promotion programmes (NFER, 2004).

Health and social care professions in the early years

Education for practice

This section explores how the education of professionals may impact on their behaviour and practice. All health and social care professionals undergo a generic training and education in order to achieve qualified status. Nurses, physiotherapists and speech and language therapists, for example, are generally prepared for practice across a broad range of settings and service user groups, drawing on a profession-specific blend of knowledge, skills and values and the expectation that these will be applied and developed more specifically in response to particular areas of work. In each of these roles there is an expectation that interventions are targeted to meet specific needs; services are accessed by a process of referral and may be seen as 'problem focused', requiring a process based on a cycle of assessment/diagnosis, planning and treatment/intervention and evaluation. That said, it is, important to acknowledge that professional bodies do encourage the development of a holistic perspective. Students are formally assessed to be fit for practice against criteria which take into account their interprofessional communication skills, understanding of the whole person and the ability to work effectively with different agencies in a range of settings. Universities have also been encouraged to develop interprofessional modules and foundation degrees for potential and current practitioners. These programmes address policy issues, service goals, user needs and effective team working. The development of practice-informed curricula uses a relationship-based reflection model which allows participants to reflect on their own interprofessional experiences. This has a natural synergy with Brock et al.'s qualitative study (2009) on interprofessional team practice.

Targeted or universal practice – how does this impact the way early years workers are viewed by others and each other?

By comparison, those trained specifically for work with children, such as early years teachers or child care workers working with children and families, receive an in-depth preparation for child development and other relevant subjects. Their practice is more likely to be involved in the delivery of a universal rather than a targeted service in which they are concerned with meeting the needs of any child and his or her family, rather than one where difficulties have necessarily been identified. At the policy level, Marmot (2010) recommends the principle of *proportionate universalism*, whereby, rather than focusing on the most disadvantaged to be effective, action must be universal but with a scale and intensity proportionate to the level of disadvantage (2010, p. 15). Such an approach might contribute to an overarching framework for early years interprofessional working, recognizing a continuum of interventions rather than a simplistic binary distinction between targeted and universal interventions.

While it is important not to oversimplify this discussion, it is worth considering the implications of these differences. One possibility is that this may contribute to the creation of a different 'public' image whereby early years professionals are seen as able to do no wrong because they are delivering a universal service. However, it seems likely that the recent emergence of evidence of abuse by staff in nursery settings (the Vanessa George case) may begin to challenge such an image and raise demands for further safeguards and regulation. The report into the investigation of serial sexual abuse by Vanessa George at a nursery in Plymouth stated that all nurseries would be wise to reflect on their policies and practice, as well as the culture within their settings, to ensure such events did not happen again (Plymouth Safeguarding Children Board, 2010). At a general level, the GSCC Codes of Practice (2002) apply to all social care workers and provide best practice guidance and the intention is that social care workers will be also be required to register at some future date. By comparison, the other health and social work professions deal with 'the problems' and may be viewed as more interventionist and hence problematic in people's lives. There may also be consequences for effective joint working as these stereotypes can influence team attitudes and practices.

The physical location for practice can vary with some professionals being primarily based in children's or early years centres or schools while others spend a large part of their working day on visits to families in their homes. This may assist in creating a full picture of home and family circumstances and making a full assessment under the Common Assessment Framework (CAF), potentially creating more leverage for successful outcomes. However, there may be a greater vulnerability associated with working in this way if professionals' diverse experiences and assessment findings contribute to tensions between colleagues. Individual treatment notes and poorly integrated planning and documentation for integrated education and treatment may also create tensions between staff used to a particular way of working or recording assessment findings. Diverse professional allegiances may also be reflected in differential pay, conditions and status with a range of consequences impacting team morale and practice. While such dichotomies are not helpful, they may need to be carefully examined in order that more nuanced ways of understanding and practising can be elicited.

New roles and new challenges

The introduction of new roles may also create new challenges. One example can be found in the development of Family Nurse Partnerships that were initially piloted in ten areas in England beginning in 2007 and have since been extended to a further 20 sites. The scheme offers intensive home visiting to young first-time parents, from early pregnancy until the child reaches the age of 2 years. Drawing on the successful evidence from a similar programme in the United States of America, family nurses work to build supportive relationships and offer guidance on pregnancy, child development and parenting. Initial findings from the first year evaluation (Barnes et al., 2008) indicate that the service has been well received by parents, including fathers, and that breastfeeding rates have improved, while smoking rates have decreased. Interestingly, parents' feedback indicated they valued the involvement of the family nurse compared to their previous experience of universal maternity services. However, the evaluation did highlight some concern as to how the scheme was aligned alongside other services. There appeared to be a lack of understanding from local Children's Centres and a need for greater levels of partnership working with midwifery services in response to the charge of elitism from other professionals. This example illuminates the need for early years workers to appreciate a whole-system perspective, recognizing the range of professional roles and agencies that may be involved. Additionally the scheme appears to emphasize the value of building relationships with parents in their home environment and provides a holistic approach to supporting families.

Another example of a new approach to interprofessional working can be found in the Barnsley Team Around the Child (TAC) programme that offers a structure in which practitioners can support children, young people and families. TAC is not dependent on the context or the number of people; for example, for one child the TAC could be small, comprising a parent, teacher and special education needs coordinator (SENCO), whereas for another child, it might include, at the very least, an occupational therapist, a physiotherapist, a speech and language therapist, a health visitor and the family itself.

This preliminary discussion suggests that the task of preparing health and social care professionals for working in early years interprofessional teams requires careful consideration as to how the core uniprofessional curriculum, containing profession-specific knowledge and competence, can be articulated with an understanding of practice that includes recognizing and valuing transferable frameworks and skills and enabling the newly qualified professional to effectively practise within the new environment. This also needs to be located within an understanding of practice as complex and uncertain, requiring professionals to be reflexive and critically reflective in their response to the various challenges that will be presented (Smith and Karban, 2008). Brechin (2000) offers a helpful perspective based on two guiding principles: that of 'respecting others as equals' and 'an open and not-knowing approach.' She sees these as informing the development of relationships based on negotiation that are central to practice, rather than autonomous professionals acting independently.

Dimensions of professionalism

An outline of some of the key implications of Brock's seven areas of professionalism on health and social care practice with early years provision follows. Two authentic scenarios will be used to illustrate how these dimensions, which underpin professionalism (knowledge, education and training, skills, ethics, rewards, autonomy and values), can be considered and applied in the reality of practice. These two scenarios illustrate examples of issues which impact the experience of all the key players: the child, the family and the staff. The aim is for readers to understand how consideration of all the different issues should be viewed as beneficial for practice and not as a source of angst which engenders competition, professional tribalism or tension, in turn reducing the quality of the service provision.

The first scenario (Table 6.1) should be read now and the information which explains and contextualizes some of the terminology about the dimensions of professionalism can be used to help the reader answer the discussion questions. The second scenario (Table 6.2) raises different issues about the scope and challenges of professional practice in an early years setting.

Table 6.1 Scenario 1

Setting	Nursery school		
Individuals	Physiotherapist, based at local health centre, visits school once a week. He has been qualified for 6 months and new to early years work.	Child B: Age 4. Well integrated into class. Likes school. Has mild cerebral palsy, respiratory and swallowing problems, normal IQ, standing and exercise tolerance; compromised because of increased tone in the lower limbs.	Teacher and classroom assistant. Experienced female teacher. New classroom assistant who is returning to work after bringing up her family.
Main aims of individual	Main aim is to advise child, mother and school staff on how best to reduce tone in legs in order to improve child's function and mobility.	Keen to improve functional mobility. Likes football and participation in active sports.	Keen for child to maintain academic progress and remain integrated with his peer group in a classroom setting.
Constraints to collaboration	Thinks teacher and teaching assistant don't understand the importance of physiotherapy. The physiotherapist wants to take child from classroom on a daily basis to stretch legs and reduce tone. Too distracting for child to do this in the classroom.	Enjoys his physiotherapy, but likes to be with his friends in the classroom. Fluctuating concentration. Picks upon his mother's anxiety about his future physical function and how this will change as he matures.	Teacher concerned child is missing key activities. Feels that the rehabilitation in the treatment room away from the classroom is artificial and takes child away from peers. Classroom assistant is anxious about the physiotherapy, cannot see its relevance and finds it difficult to encourage B to repeat his exercises. Feels she does not fully understand child's physical and educational needs.

Scenario 1

> ### Discussion questions for scenario 1
>
> - Reflect on Brock's seven dimensions of professionalism and consider if all the issues raised by B's care could be linked to this model.
> - How might the conflicting views impact the child?
> - How might the professionals feel about their identity when challenged by this kind of situation?
> - In view of child B's associated medical needs, which other professionals might be involved in his care?
> - Is B's physical fitness as important as his educational progress? Think about how the different professional values are impacting child B.
> - Look at the constraints to collaboration. How would you generate a workable solution?

Applying the seven dimensions of professionalism to the case scenario

Brock's knowledge dimension specifically relates to professional contributions made by each of the professional areas being considered in this chapter, including issues relating to the content of curricula for professional practice. For example, all health and social care pre-registration students acquire core, subject-specific knowledge necessary to reach the standard of professional qualification. For physiotherapists, for example, this will be detailed knowledge required by their professional body about anatomy, physiology, different treatment interventions and specialist areas, such as cardiothoracic physiotherapy. However, there are a range of core skills and knowledge which all health and social care students need to learn and which are often taught in shared learning sessions, cross-course modules or through integrated interprofessional learning programmes. One example is the knowledge underpinning effective communication, teamworking skills and ethics.

The education and training dimension relates to the *process* of education and training as the preparation for professional practice, addressing both the uniprofessional and the interprofessional curriculum. Profession specific education is supported by a whole infrastructure of standards and regulations. Course standards are high, have to be endorsed by the Health Professions Council, are rigorously monitored through approved universities and are bound to professional body standards for practice. Often professional training programmes will not offer specific early years placements, viewing the skills needed to be useful here as transferable between clinical/practice placements and classroom sessions. So, for example, physiotherapy training will address issues across the life span, in acute and primary health care settings, leading to practice in situations as varied as hospital clinics, inpatient services and community-based services (CSP, 2002), but they may not necessarily have an early years focused practice placement pre-qualification. Speech and language therapists also have a similar profession-specific training (RCSLT, 2006) only some of which focuses on the communication problems of children. Expertise is usually developed at the postgraduate level through a rotation scheme covering different clinical and practice areas. For example, health visitors will be registered nurses who have undergone further post-registration training in community nursing. It is worth recognizing the increasing complexity of education in this area. There are many nursery and Children's Centre workers with no professional qualifications who are improving their skills by undertaking vocational training and foundation degrees which include health and social issues in their curricula. This can only enhance the holistic approach.

Future challenges for the education of future health and social care professionals include using teaching methods that develop students' communication and investigation skills to facilitate the transfer of profession-specific skills to different working areas and effective teamwork (e.g. problem based learning rather than traditional didactic methods) (Engel, 1991). It is also important to include the contributions of service users and carers in the curricula to provide real life accounts of their experiences. Shared with students first-hand, these can provide learning triggers offering a potent stimulus for learning. They are highly valued by students and are seen to increase students' confidence in dealing with problems and in communicating (Dammers et al., 2008). Additionally, increasing attention towards co-production of health and welfare requires a rethinking of current practices. Dunston et al. (2009) point out that there is a need to re-imagine the identity, role and practice of the health professional as currently there is '... little recognition of the deep entrenchment and ongoing reproduction of expert based identities and practices within health professional education pedagogy' (2009, p. 49).

The skills dimension requires a collegiate approach to other professionals and an insight into the limits of one's own professional knowledge. All practitioners want to use their skills when intervening for the benefit of the child. However, it is possible that each has only a partial view of what is best for the child at the centre of the practice. Professional action and interventions can be misinterpreted by other professionals. Individual professionals can be so confident in the appropriateness of their own knowledge and skills that they can become entrenched and less open to negotiation. This may be particularly the case if the process of education and training has been primarily uniprofessional and based within clear-cut professional frameworks to guide and inform practice. In this scenario it is possible that the newly qualified physiotherapist is anxious to demonstrate his professional competence, feeling unsure about the room for manoeuvre in the work with child B. In comparison the experienced teacher is very familiar with her role, although less sure of her contribution to the new 'joined-up working' agenda. She is recognized for her skills in classroom management and her success in establishing high standards at this stage in the National Curriculum. Liaison with other professionals and recognition of one's own skill limitations also need to be considered as part of the holistic approach as, for example, in Case Scenario 1, where the physiotherapist needs to include others to form a clearer picture of the care required.

Likewise, different professional value bases and staff members' level of autonomy can impact their ability to work effectively in a team. Management structures, independent working, accountability, working hours and pay levels can impact an individual's sense of worth and value in the workplace and thus influence his or her behaviour and actions.

The rewards dimension leads to particular challenges associated with teamwork in relation to rewards in terms of pay, status and job satisfaction. These differential rewards, when accompanied by 'flexible' working practices, contribute to the blurring of boundaries between different professional roles and may have the potential to leave some workers feeling devalued. For example, in practice this might occur when a classroom assistant is left to take responsibility in the absence of the teacher. In another situation, a lower paid family support worker with in-depth knowledge of a family's circumstances might feel excluded from a multi-agency discussion while other professionally qualified staff dominate the discussion.

This first scenario elucidates three themes: skills, autonomy and values are brought into sharp relief as each practitioner contributes his or her individual perspective on the process and outcomes that will be most beneficial for child B. For the physiotherapist this is focused on the current and future physical mobility of child B, recognizing that this will have far reaching implications for his wider well-being, depending on his level of disability. The teacher's concerns are focused on B's academic development, seeing that his ability to progress normally alongside his peers will influence his educational development and achievements. This includes the belief that educational success will assist B in overcoming his physical limitations. While the classroom assistant concurs with this, she is also mindful that B is just a little boy who gets tired at school, particularly with the added stress of the physiotherapy regime. On occasions this can lead her to find excuses for not encouraging him to repeat his exercises. At the heart of the scenario is child B and his mother, a single parent, who can feel overwhelmed by the advice she is offered by the various professionals involved.

Another level of analysis can be found if less tangible issues, including gender and status, are considered. The male physiotherapist offers a valuable role model for child B and he naturally talks to the child about football and TV programmes of interest.

Now read the second scenario below in Table 6.2. Are there issues that are similar to the professional dimensions evident in the first case?

Scenario 2

A health visitor has concerns about a child and what is happening at home. She is trying to coordinate with the Children's Centre.

Table 6.2 Scenario 2

Setting	Community-based Children's Centre	
Individuals	2-year-old child with one older half-brother who is 9. Mother is expecting another baby. Lives with both parents and mother's younger brother. Home is chaotic; neither parent nor mother's brother is in work and mother's pregnancy leaves her lacking energy to care for child C. Child C is described by mother as naughty. Child C is slow in meeting her developmental milestones and appears to be finding it difficult to be around other children in the Children's Centre. She attends two sessions a week. Mother's brother has been in trouble with the police and has also caused a disturbance with neighbours, leading to ASBO.	Health visitor (HV) has recently moved into this area, having qualified five years ago. She has a lot of experience in working with children with disabilities. She is based at the local health centre. Children's Centre (CC) worker has worked with Sure Start for a number of years and is very committed to working with families and involving parents in the centre. She has known the family for a number of years.
Main aims of individual/family	Mother would like child to attend the Children's Centre every day so that she can rest and 'get some peace'. This is backed up by child's father. When child is at home, she appears to be left in front of the TV and has few toys or activities.	HV would like to see more parent–child interaction and is concerned about the relationship between child C and her mother. At times child C appears listless. CC workers would like to engage mum in sessions at the centre and provide her with support. They are concerned that mother is vulnerable and that father and brother dominate the household
Constraints to collaboration	Mother is positive about the Children's Centre sessions for her child but is wary of the HV.	Anxious about child's development and well-being and is uneasy about the family dynamics. Feels that child's needs are being lost in the family and that mother is too overwhelmed with new pregnancy to focus on child. Feels that more sessions at centre would help provide stimulation. Considering referral to child development centre but not optimistic about the benefits of involving mother in parenting support group and sees this as a distraction from a focus on child's needs. CC workers feels that the HV does not yet understand the community and the range of social issues that affect most families. Would like to involve mother in mum's parenting support group and also father in new community group for dads. They have asked the HV to encourage this but are not sure that this is happening.

Consider the scenario in Table 6.2 and try to address some of the discussion questions in the light of what you already know about professional dimensions and how they might underpin professional practice and behaviours.

Discussion questions for Scenario 2

- How do these different perspectives relate to the different dimensions of professionalism?
- How might this situation develop if a collaborative way forward is not found? How would you generate a workable solution?
- What other dynamics might influence this situation? Which other agencies or professionals might be a helpful resource in this situation?

Conclusion

This chapter has outlined the contribution of health and social care professionals in their work with children. We have aimed to show, via a discussion of the political and social context and case studies, how individuals who have a clear understanding of their professional values, knowledge skills and behaviours, can enhance the quality of care for children and their families.

It is recognized that applying a holistic and critically reflective approach to professional practice can be difficult in circumstances where both the team's structure and the individual cases are complex and multifaceted. However this is the only way to ensure the needs of the children and families remain at the heart of practice.

Questions for reflective practice

Can you identify any recent policy changes which have directly impacted your day-to-day practice? Reflect on the ways that change has recently positively impacted your interdisciplinary team work. Reflect on some practical strategies that could strengthen teamwork in your area? Which do you think might be the most successful and why?

Further reading, resources and/or websites

Brock, A., Frost, N., Karban, K., and Smith, S. (2009), *Towards Interprofessional Partnerships*. This learning resource pack contains learning resources, a DVD of staff interviews and tips to improve interprofessional working in the health and social care workplace. Available from Sue Smith, Leeds Metropolitan University. E mail: s.v.smith@leedsmet.ac.uk.
The Children's Workforce Development Council has developed a tool that allows organizations to explore where they are in the journey towards integration. This can be viewed at www.cwdcouncil.org.uk/implementing-integrated-working.

The Victoria Climbié Data Corpus Online. A learning resource which includes all the transcriptions from the 68 days of oral evidence made available to the project by the Department for Education and Skills and testimony from 168 witnesses. The Climbié Corpus project has created a mechanism for extracting relevant subsets of this otherwise huge data set which can be used for teaching health and social work professionals. http://victoriaclimbie.hud. ac.uk/.

References

Atkinson, M., Jones, M., and Lamont, E. (2007), *Multi-agency Working and Its Implications for Practice: A Review of the Literature*. Reading : Centre for British Teachers.

Audit Commission Review (2010), *Giving Children a Healthy Start*. London: Audit Commission.

Baldwin, N. (2009), Laying the foundations for good health in childhood. In P. Bywaters, E. McCleod and L. Napier (eds), *Social Work and Global Health Inequalities, Practice and Policy Developments*. Bristol: Policy Press.

Barnes, J., Ball, M., Meadows, P., McLeish, J., and Belsky, J. (2008), *Nurse-Family Partnership Programme: First Year Pilot Sites Implementation in England*. Research Report DCSF-RW051. London: Birkbeck, University of London, Institute for Study of Children, Families and Social Issues.

Brechin, A. (2000), Introducing critical practice. In A. Brechin, H. Brown and M. Eby (eds), *Critical Practice in Health and Social Care*. London: Sage/Open University, 25–47.

Brock, A. (2009), Seven dimensions of professionalism for early years education and care: A model of professionalism for interdisciplinary practice? Paper presented at the British Educational Research Association Annual Conference, 2–5 September 2009, University of Manchester, Manchester, England.

Brock, A., Frost, N., Karban, K., and Smith S. (2009), *Towards Interprofessional Partnerships: A Resource Pack*. Leeds: Leeds Metropolitan University, Institute for Enterprise.

Children's Workforce Development Council (2009), *What Is Integrated Working?* www.cwdcouncil.org.uk/implementing-integrated-working. Accessed 2 July 2009.

CQC (Care Quality Commission) (2009), Review of the investigation and action taken by health bodies in response to the care of Baby London : Quality Care Commission.

CSP (Chartered Society of Physiotherapy) (2002), *Curriculum Framework for Qualifying Programmes in Physiotherapy*. London: CSP.

Dammers J., Spencer, J., and Thomas, M. (2008), Using real patients in problem-based learning: Students' comments on the value of using real, as opposed to paper cases, in a problem-based learning module in general practice. *Medical Education*, 35, (1), 27–34.

Department for Children, Schools and Families (2009), *Parental Experience of Services for Disabled Children*. Research Report DCSF-RR147.

DfES (Department for Education and Skills) (2004), *Every Child Matters: Change for Children*. London: HMSO.

DoH (Department of Health) (2005), *Creating a Patient-led NHS. Delivering the NHS Improvement Plan*. London: Department of Health.

— (2009), NHS 2010–2015: From Good to Great. Preventative, People-centred, Productive. HMSO. http://www.dh.gov.uk/en/Publicationsandstatistics/Publications/PublicationsPolicyAndGuidance/DH_109876.

Dunston, R., Lee, A., Boud, D., Brodie, P., and Chiarella, M. (2009), Co-production and health system reform – from re-imagining to re-making. *The Australian Journal of Public Administration*, 68, (1), 39–52.

Dyson, A., Hertzman, C., Roberts, H., Tunstill, J., and Vaghri, Z. (2009), Childhood development, education and health inequalities. Report of Task Group 1, Submission to the Marmot Review. www.ucl.ac.uk/ gheg/marmotreview/ consultation/early_years_and_education_report.

Engel, C. E. (1991), Not just a method but a way of learning. In D. Boud and G. Feletti (eds), *The Challenge of Problem-Based Learning*. London: Kogan Page, 23–33.

Feinstein, L. (2003), Inequality in the early cognitive development of British children in the 1970 cohort. *Economica*, 70, 3–97.

Frost, N., and Parton, N. (2009), *Understanding Children's Social Care*. London: Sage.

General Social Care Council (GSCC) (2002), Codes of Practice. London : General Social Care Council. http://www.gscc.org.uk/page/35/Codes+of+practice.html.

Glass, N. (1999), Origins of the Sure Start Programme. *Children and Society*, 13, (4), 257–264.

Jefferis, B., Power, C., and Hertzman, C. (2002), Birth weight, childhood socioeconomic environment, and cognitive development in the 1958 British birth cohort study. *British Medical Journal*, 325: 305–8.

Karban, K., and Smith, S. (2009), Developing critical reflection within an inter-professional learning programme. Chapter 13. In H. Bradbury, N. Frost, S. Kilminster and M. Zukas (eds), *Beyond Reflective Practice*. London: Routledge. 170–181.

Laming, W. (2003) *The Victoria Climbié Inquiry*. London: HMSO.

Marmot, M. (2010) *Fair Society, Healthy Lives – The Marmot Review. Strategic Review of Health Inequalities in England post-2010*. The Marmot Review. www.ucl.ac.uk/marmotreview. Accessed 21 May 2010.

Needham, C., and Carr, S. (2009), SCIE Research briefing 31: Co-production: An emerging evidence base for adult social care transformation. www.scie.org.uk/publications/briefings/briefing31/index.asp. Accessed 21 May 2010.

NFER (National Foundation for Educational Research) (2004), *On Track: A Qualitative Study of the Early Impacts of Services*. DfES Research Report RR473. Norwich: HM Stationery Office.

Plymouth Safeguarding Children Board (2010), *Serious Case Review Overview Report: Executive Summary in Respect of Nursery Z* . www.plymouth.gov.uk/serious_case_review_nursery_z.pdf. Accessed 20 December 2010.

RCSLT (Royal College of Speech and Language Therapists) (2006), *National Standards for Practice-based Learning*. London: RCSLT

Robinson, M., Atkinson, M., and Downing, D. (2008), *Supporting Theory Building in Integrated Services Research*. London: NFER.

Sloper, S. (2004), Facilitators and barriers for coordinated multi-agency services. *Child Care, Health and Development*, 30, (6), 571–580.

Smith, S., and Karban, K. (2008), Tutor experiences of developing an interprofessional learning (IPL) programme in higher education: Recognising a parallel process. *Response*, 4, 1. ISSN – 1752-0991. www.derby.ac.uk/response/6d.asp?aid=15.

7

The Social Worker: Protecting the World's Most Vulnerable Children

David Saltiel

Introduction

Social work is a complex, demanding and emotionally challenging profession. The work involves caring for vulnerable people in great personal crisis but also exerting an element of social control through the use of legal powers. Unlike a number of early years services social work services are not universal but targeted at those in greatest need. Professional training and codes of practice emphasize that social workers must work to a set of clear values that protect the most vulnerable. They need an understanding of the nature of discrimination and inequality in our society.

Social workers require a complex variety of skills and specialist knowledge and often need to use them in volatile situations with distressed service users. Some of the issues this creates are explored through a case scenario. One of the key areas of knowledge is having an understanding of social as well as individual models of human behaviour so that what people do is seen in its social context.

In recent years there has been a loss of confidence in many welfare services. Social work has been criticized for its failures to protect children and some of the particular difficulties in this area are discussed.

Working together to protect children

As a social work educator I have been involved in a collaborative working project which brings together students training for a range of caring professions. The focus for discussion in this project is a case study which I would like to use in this chapter to help illustrate what social workers do and how they work alongside other professionals working with children.

Case Study

As the social worker on duty in your office you are asked to visit a family where the mother has been hospitalized for a drug overdose, leaving her two children in the care of their father, who has said he can only look after them for today.

When you arrive you meet the father, Rob, his stepson Liam (8) and his daughter Amy (6). Amy's mother has a history of alcohol abuse and has also been prescribed medication for 'stress' and depression. The most recent episode of heavy drinking was sparked by her father being hospitalized for a heart attack. She was unable to look after the children during this time and they had to fend for themselves. There is clearly a family history of neglect and of volatile, sometimes violent, adult relationships which have put the children at risk.

They cannot stay with their maternal grandparents as the children's mother alleges that her father has sexually abused her in the past.

Rob decides to offer to take the children for a while to come and live with him and his girlfriend, who has never met them. Liam does not want to go but Amy says she does. It emerges that Rob may have been violent to the children's mother and has physically punished Liam in a way that Rob admits was over the top. Rob is a soldier. He is on leave and due to return to his regiment in a week's time.

One of the most widely accepted definitions of social work is that drawn up by the International Federation of Social Work (IFSW) and quoted in many social work texts (e.g., Payne, 2006, p. 28):

> The social work profession promotes social change, problem solving in human relationships and the empowerment and liberation of people to enhance well-being.

Utilising theories of human behaviour and social systems, social work intervenes at the points where people interact with their environments. Principles of human rights and social justice are fundamental to social work.

Bearing this definition in mind, how might our social worker approach the task of ensuring the safety and welfare of these children? Her knowledge base would need to include an understanding of the developmental needs of two young children and how these might be best met under these less than optimal circumstances. She would need an understanding of the risks associated with parental drug and alcohol abuse. She would need to know what resources were available to provide care for the children if they could not remain within their family and what procedures she would need to follow to access these resources. She would need to understand the legal position: what powers and responsibilities does she have? What are the family members' rights and responsibilities?

But as well as this mix of theoretical and practical knowledge, our social worker would also need the skills to engage with some distressed children and adults and be guided by a set of values that emphasizes the importance of listening carefully to everyone's wishes and feelings and ensuring that those of the most vulnerable people are not marginalized. She would need to hear their stories, try to make sense of the situation from their perspectives – perspectives that may be in conflict with one another – and make some judgements about what needs to happen next.

And she would need to think about who else might need to be involved in resolving the situation: what other professionals have areas of expertise that would be helpful to this family?

Ask yourself: what other agencies might be involved in this case?

You might have included local authority social workers, a family centre from the voluntary sector, the GP, the police, a community mental health team, a child and adolescent mental health team, a specialist domestic abuse unit, a specialist alcohol abuse agency, the children's school, the hospital social work team and so on. Some of these agencies are, as a result of government policies, themselves composed of various professionals such as the mental health team which would include psychiatrists, social workers, psychiatric nurses and so on.

From this ordinary example of everyday family breakdown, sadly familiar to many caring professionals, we can see that our social worker needs a grasp of a complex range of knowledge, skills and values and needs to apply them to a situation where people are feeling angry, upset and frightened and where some people may be at risk of harm.

When the government of the day decided to upgrade the basic social work qualification from a two-year diploma to a three-year degree, it specified five areas that were to be core to the curriculum:

- Human growth, development, mental health and disability
- Assessment, planning, intervention and review

- Communication skills with children, adults and those with particular communication needs
- Law
- Partnership working and information sharing across professional disciplines and agencies (Department of Health, 2002)

We can see how a case such as the one above will involve all those key areas of knowledge and skills.

And we might decide that, concise as it is, the IFSW definition needs some additions. It does not, for example, take enough account of the need to use legal powers to control situations in order to protect the vulnerable (Horner, 2009) or of the need to work alongside other agencies and professionals (Morris, 2008) and we might ask how easy is it to decide what we mean by 'rights' and 'justice' when people are in bitter conflict over intimate issues in their lives?

In its review of social work for the twenty-first century, the Scottish Executive suggested that social work activity takes place in four tiers ranging from Tier 1, where social workers work alongside more universal services to develop community-based prevention, to Tier 4, where work is focused on people with complex problems characterized by high levels of risk and need and interventions are likely to be statutory. While universal services such as schools will focus on the lower tiers, social workers are likely to concentrate on the upper tiers where needs and risks are high and specialist intervention may be needed from social workers armed with statutory powers to control peoples' behaviour as well as to care for them (Scottish Executive, 2006).

So another key element of any definition of social work is that while social workers work alongside universal services, the specialist services they provide are not universal; they are targeted at those with the greatest need and may need to be provided with some degree of compulsion. While the social worker in our case study will try to work with everyone in the family, she may need to use some legal powers to ensure the children are safeguarded properly and she is almost certainly going to have to access some services that are only available to those with the greatest need. At the same time she will be working with other professionals including providers of universal services such as schools and health clinics, who have extremely valuable contributions to make.

We might now summarize the key aspects of social work practice as:

- Working with human relationships to achieve change
- Working in complex situations where needs and risks are high
- Working closely with other professionals
- Working with the legal powers to provide targeted services, sometimes using compulsion

Of course other professions might be characterized in similar ways; so what (if anything!) makes social work unique?

Knowledge and values

Social work's origins lie in nineteenth-century philanthropy and were based on firm moral visions about how to restore a society after communal bonds had, it seemed to many, been broken by industrialization and urbanization, threatening a breakdown in social order. Some have seen this social morality as a secularized version of religious principles that emphasize the importance of charity and caring. Others have emphasized the way social work developed in response to fears that poverty and other social forces created a threat to the social order. This balance between care and social control is a constant feature of social work activities. It is one reason why it is so important that clear values and ethics exist to govern the way we treat others and the way we are ourselves accountable for what we do. But these values and ethics change over time in response to changing social conditions.

Thompson (2000) distinguishes between what he calls traditional and emancipatory values. The former, associated with the work of Felix Biestek, emphasize the principles that should underpin the relationship between worker and client. These include: respecting and valuing individuals, enabling clients to discuss their feelings through attentive and non-judgemental listening, helping people to help themselves by making their own decisions and respecting confidentiality. The humanistic ideas of Carl Rogers (cited in Payne, 2005) – congruence or genuineness, empathy and unconditional positive regard for others – are also key to these 'traditional' or 'person-centred' values. Unconditional positive regard and being non-judgemental are ideas that cause much misunderstanding among students. If people have intrinsic worth as individuals, their *persons* should be valued, but that does not mean we do not make judgements about what they do and take steps to protect them or others. Morrison (2007) cites research showing that empathy, understanding and attunement to the other's needs are highly valued by clients and more important in achieving change than any particular method of intervention. Rather than dismissing such traditional values as outmoded relics of an era when one-to-one casework was seen as the main method of social work, we should appreciate that such a skilled, purposeful and ethical approach to interpersonal relationships is essential in engaging and supporting clients, whatever interventions we choose. Whatever our social worker may think of the past and present actions of the parents in the case study, her ability to listen to their narratives in a genuine and empathetic way may help them to change and enable her to support them – though she might also need to take steps to protect the children if necessary.

But such individualistic values are not enough and Thompson argues that more 'emancipatory' values are necessary too. Social workers should understand the profound, multidimensional impact on people's lives of inequalities based on social class, gender, ethnicity, disability, age, sexual orientation and so on, the processes of marginalization, stigmatization and labelling that affect the identities and opportunities of people in vulnerable groups, the nature of organizations – including those that employ social workers – that can and have contributed to inequality and discrimination rather than alleviating it. So values of empowerment, social justice, working in partnership with clients, of taking an anti-discriminatory position (Thompson, 2006) are important in complementing, not replacing, the older values.

Such values are not unique to social work, but it might be argued that they have a uniquely important role in the profession because social workers provide selective services targeted at the most vulnerable and marginalized people in society and social workers' knowledge base is explicitly based on understanding the socially constructed nature of oppression and inequality (Davis, 2003).

Central to social workers' knowledge base is a move away from medicalized, individual-ized, purely functional models of human development to *social* models, grounded in an understanding of social, cultural and historical forces. We can only really understand the sit-uations of people in such categories as 'mentally ill' or 'disabled' or 'old' when we understand that these categories are not just medical or biological classifications but socially constructed labels that can result in their being stigmatized and discriminated against and excluded from the full range of life choices. The insights provided by the social model of disability (Oliver, 1990; Barnes and Mercer, 2003) in distinguishing between individuals' functional impair-ment and the social restrictions imposed upon them socially provide us with a powerful means of understanding a range of social processes whereby disability and exclusion are understood not as the personal attributes of individuals but the consequences of discrimina-tory attitudes and institutions in our society. It is important to understand that this social model does not come from social work practitioners or academics but from activists in service user movements who have developed powerful critiques of the way professionals like doctors, nurses and social workers have treated them, problematizing the meaning and nature of 'care' and the 'caring' work at the heart of the social work profession (Beresford, 2008).

A brief history

Social work's origins in the UK are often traced back to the Charity Organisation Society (COS), which was formed in 1869 to regulate the philanthropic contributions made by many middle-class people and voluntary societies in response to the poverty and destitu-tion seen on the streets of Britain's new industrial cities. The COS was concerned that such charity might undermine people's willingness to improve themselves and thereby demoralize them (Stedman-Jones, 1971) and employed visitors to assess potential cases – distinguish-ing between the deserving and undeserving (the latter being thrown onto the mercies of the hated Poor Law). Just how influential the COS really was is open to debate (Cree and Myers, 2008) but its 'casework' method of assessing individuals and households became an impor-tant element of the new profession and its values. Fabian socialists disagreed with the COS's emphasis on individual charity, arguing the need for more state provision (Payne, 2006), and those in the Settlement movement were concerned that communities develop their own responses to hardship (Horner, 2009). Many of these disagreements can still be seen in current political debates.

The reforms introduced by the Liberal Government that came to power in 1906, including the 1908 Children Act, introduced the beginnings of a welfare state and marked an important shift in thinking about the state's role in alleviating social problems. Local authorities began to administer services, although the Poor Laws were still in force. Those laws were finally abolished in 1948 when as part of the Children Act of that year local authority Children's Departments were created and began employing social workers. Social work thus became a state-sponsored profession, part of the new welfare state and its bureaucratic agencies: both reaching their high point in the early 1970s with the creation of large social services departments.

Since then state support for welfare has declined. The economic boom that followed World War II in Western countries came to an end in the 1970s. The subsequent rise in neo-liberalism (the 'New Right') saw welfare services reduced or privatized while those services remaining were much more tightly managed to make workers more efficient and ensure they kept to tight budgets in an ultra-competitive, globalized free-market economy (McDonald, 2006). If social work in the UK was a child of the welfare state, where does it stand in a society where welfarism has been much reduced?

As there has been a loss of confidence, both economically and politically, in the welfare state, so social work has also suffered a crisis of confidence. Harris (1998) argues that in the past the state has accorded social work considerable discretion and autonomy in carrying out its professional role, but it is widely argued that this autonomy is threatened by increasing bureaucratic managerial control and the plethora of performance targets set by central government and local employers. Social workers often talk today about a 'tick box mentality': they are required to use rigid assessment schedules and computer systems which seem to leave little room for professional judgement. Some have argued that social work has been reduced to a series of basic tasks and responses in the name of efficiency, a process noted in wider society as 'McDonaldisation' (Ritzer, 1996) while others argue that social work can never be fully controlled in this way because social work is about relationships with service users or clients and these need to be managed with considerable discretion and flexibility (Harris and White, 2009). This balance between bureaucratic and managerial control on the one hand and the flexible and creative use of interpersonal skills in actual face-to-face encounters is at the heart of social work practice. The social worker in our case study might be given instructions on *what* to do but retains considerable discretion in *how* she does it – how she engages with family members and works with them to resolve the problem

However, it cannot be denied that recent years have seen a steady encroachment on social workers' professional autonomy. The perceived need for bureaucratic efficiency in the use of increasingly scarce resources is an important element in this but another has been the way governments and the profession have responded to a series of high-profile cases where social workers seem to have made disastrous errors and failed to protect children from death or serious injury.

The impact of child abuse inquiries and reviews

One of the key moments in the history of social work was the public inquiry into the death of Maria Colwell in 1973. Maria was 8 years old when she died at the hands of her stepfather. She had spent several years in care, being fostered by an aunt, but was returned to the care of her mother and stepfather despite protests from her wider family. Social workers from the local authority and the NSPCC visited regularly. Neighbours and school teachers had concerns about Maria's safety but the social workers left her in the household with dreadful consequences. For the first time in the modern era social work's practices were exposed to public scrutiny and the inquiry panel expressed shock and bewilderment that apparently clear causes for concern were ignored or misunderstood. As a result of this case the modern system of child-protection procedures was set up to try to ensure that agencies cooperated and shared information (Parton, 2006). Yet there would be other deaths and other inquiries. Procedures were tightened, new guidelines written – such as the *Working Together* guidelines for interagency cooperation which first appeared in 1988 and have been rewritten several times, most recently in 2010 following the Baby Peter case (DCSF, 2010) – yet tragedies continue to occur and the reasons identified have become all too familiar: a lack of interagency communication; poorly supervised staff, operating in stressful conditions; and poor assessments that do not identify needs and risks (Reder and Duncan, 2004).

Hill (1990), writing at a time when there was a series of such inquiries, identified some major improvements arising from these inquiries but he also noted their limitations. He asked if it was possible to learn general lessons from individual cases that were examples of bad practice that might be untypical and that provided no good practice to follow. He was also concerned that a focus on risk factors and procedures created a defensive, authoritarian kind of social work that did not engage families and work with them constructively. A few years later, in 1995, the Department of Health published a series of research studies which suggested that too many families were being drawn into the child protection system and the vast majority were eventually filtered out without being offered any services to address their needs. This prompted a 'refocusing' debate although research suggests this had little effect in changing social workers' practice, which remained heavily focused on child protection at the expense of more preventive work (see, for example, Spratt, 2001).

The death of Victoria Climbié in 2000 prompted widespread changes in legislation and policy, although it was argued that the Labour Government's Every Child Matters reforms, with their focus on more universal early intervention, actually put children at risk by diverting attention from those in need of protection:

What seems clear is that thresholds for intervention change over time as a result of a mix of political and public pressure and clinical judgement and social work as a profession gets blown this way and that according to the prevailing political wind. (Munroe and Calder, 2005)

Deciding if the risks to a child require protective intervention is not an easy or straightforward process. Definitions of child abuse are to a degree socially constructed – that is, defined by social values and expectations (Department of Health, 1995) and involve moral judgements – and while we might agree on certain central features of abuse, its *boundaries*, where those difficult decisions about thresholds for intervention must be made, are highly contested and ambiguous (Munro, 2008). The 1989 Children Act, the key legislation in protecting and safeguarding children, states that legal orders to protect children can only be made if children are suffering, or are likely to suffer in the future, 'significant' harm; but what does 'significant' mean? The government says that 'there are no absolute criteria on which to rely when judging what constitutes significant harm' (DCSF, 2010, p. 36) and the researchers who have analysed Serious Case Reviews (SCRs) for the government point out that 'child protection (does) not come labelled as such' (Brandon et al., 2008a, p. 319). Of the 161 cases they studied in their analysis of SCRs between 2003 and 2005, almost half were seen as below the threshold for intervention; that is, the children were seen as 'in need' rather than 'at risk' (Brandon et al., 2008b):

> Serious Case Reviews are carried out under the *Working Together* guidelines (DCSF, 2010) when a child dies or is injured and abuse is suspected. The guidelines emphasize that these are carried out so that lessons can be learned and the Government has commissioned biennial analyses of such reviews which have become a vital source of research evidence. (Brandon et al., 2008b)

The case study at the beginning of this chapter shows the difficulty of making judgements and decisions about levels of risk and harm. Are these children suffering harm? Is that harm *significant*? Are they likely to suffer such harm in the future? It is unlikely that any group of readers would all agree on the answers to these questions or on what would be the best form of intervention for the children.

Crucial decisions that may be literally life or death decisions in some circumstances have another dimension of difficulty: the circumstances within which they are made. Social workers must form judgements and make decisions in situations in which people are experiencing high levels of distress, fear, anger and uncertainty. Our case study shows all of these factors at work. It has often been noted that child-abuse inquiries and reviews tend to focus on changes in procedures but pay much less attention to the human factors that lie behind failures to protect children. Lord Laming's report on the death of Victoria Climbié (Laming, 2003) was very much like this. Brandon et al. (2008b) found in their analysis that families with longstanding and complex problems had such high levels of need that workers were simply reduced to frozen helplessness. Cooper (2005) argues that Laming ignores the emotional pain of working with abusive adults and abused children, which can traumatize workers and make their judgements unreliable. Ruch (2006) suggests that workers may shut down psychologically and fail to reflect on their practice, a particularly dangerous issue because child protection work is so complex that errors are bound to occur and must always be revisited through supervision and reflection (Munro, 2008). Reder and Duncan (2003) argue that tightening procedures will not overcome the psychological barriers to good interprofessional communication.

Working with other professionals

When we looked at the case study at the beginning of the chapter, we saw that there would be a lot of different professionals involved.

> If you brought together some of the key professionals in this case—the GP, the social worker, the alcohol abuse worker, the domestic abuse worker, the police, the psychiatrist—would they all think the same? Or would they have very different ways of defining what the problem is and how it could best be addressed?
>
> How easy is it for such a varied range of professionals to work together harmoniously? Is there one professional who everyone can agree should be the lead? What kind of conflicts and disagreements might arise? And what – if any – are the benefits of such services for those who need them?
>
> Think about your possible involvement in the case. Given all the different professionals you might have to work with, do you think there might be disagreements over how the family's needs might be assessed and what interventions might be best? How would you feel about working with professionals who are of a higher status than yourself and who perhaps assume that theirs will be the dominant voice? What if you disagreed with them?

A recent review of the literature on interprofessional working (Atkinson et al., 2007) concluded the following:

- There is a lack of evidence of outcomes for professionals, agencies and service users.
- Empirical evidence of improved outcomes for service users is particularly lacking.
- Multi-agency working is so varied in nature, and the research is also so varied that across-the-board comparisons are difficult to make.
- There are both positive and negative impacts on professionals.
- The literature is useful in identifying a range of factors that can hinder or help multi-agency working.
- Some key factors leading to effective practice are identified, such as good resourcing, sustained funding, agreed joint aims and joint training.

This review suggests that the evidence is mixed and sometimes lacking. Yet successive governments have encouraged or even ordered multi-agency working and have seemed convinced of its many benefits.

Many people requiring social services have complex needs and are very likely to require the services of more than one agency. As we have seen, since the 1970s procedural systems have existed to ensure that services involved in the care of children work together and these systems have been progressively tightened and made more comprehensive, often as a result of highly publicized tragic cases. Major changes took place following the inquiry into the death of Victoria Climbié, published in 2003. The report by Lord Laming (2003) emphasized that there had been 'a gross failure of the system (and) widespread organisational malaise' resulting in various professionals failing to work together to protect Victoria. The 2004 Children Act focused on improving those systems that had failed to work safely and effectively with an emphasis on integrating services more tightly and ensuring agencies cooperated fully with each other. The government document *What To Do If You're Worried a Child Is Being Abused* (DCSF, 2006) provides a clear guide as to how cases referred to social work agencies are dealt with. The *Working Together* guidelines (DCSF, 2010) provide a more detailed guide for professionals.

The catalogue of failings in the Victoria Climbié case were very similar to failings in previous child abuse tragedies (Parton, 2006) and events since then, notably the tragic case of Baby Peter, suggest that professionals can still find it hard to work together.

One of the key criticisms of child abuse inquiries, including the Victoria Climbié report, is that they focus on tightening up bureaucratic systems and procedures but pay little or no attention to the complex of psychological issues involved in interprofessional communication or to the high levels of stress and anxiety associated with working with children at risk. Some of the criticisms of the Laming report into Victoria's death have been discussed. Bringing together professionals with different working cultures, levels of pay, working conditions, training and status is bound to cause some problems. Historically, professions have developed separately, each jealously guarding its particular area of expertise, and taking professionals out of their 'silos' and putting them into integrated services is not straightforward. Hudson (2002), for example, highlights the potential for conflict around professional identity, status, discretion and accountability. All professions have their own 'cultures', their own ways of seeing things, their own deeply held values.

Some recent research (Horwath and Morrison, 2007; Frost and Robinson, 2007) argues that integration of services is often rushed, poorly planned and imposed from the top down, leaving professionals feeling deskilled and unmotivated – hardly the ideal position from which to cooperate with other professionals who are suddenly working alongside them. Professionals could find themselves excluded and isolated by, for example, poor information sharing. Setting aside time for proper joint training and team building was important but didn't always happen.

What seems to work best are situations where professional hierarchies have been broken down and replaced by networks or 'communities of practice' (Wenger, 1998), where there is genuine sharing and practical cooperation – people don't just sit at adjacent desks; they actively work together. A commitment to 'knotworking' (Anning et al., 2006) means accepting the inevitability of professional conflicts and ensuring they are not swept under the carpet but openly explored by the team. Such practices are not easy and they require a good deal of commitment from professionals, managers and budget holders. In a later piece of research Hudson (2007) was encouraged by evidence that workers in integrated teams could learn from each other and recognize the commonalities in their professions as well as the differences.

Conclusion

Social workers do complex, demanding and, at times, emotionally exhausting work. As we have seen, social work services are not universal and social workers spend the majority of their time working with some of the most disadvantaged, excluded and vulnerable people in our society. Underpinning their work are values and knowledge which may not be specific to social work but which lie at the heart of their practice in a way that they do not in other professions that operate more universal services. While social workers must work closely with other professionals and agencies, they perform a unique role in protecting and safeguarding children.

> ## Questions for reflective practice
>
> What do you think are the key skills and areas of knowledge you would need to be a social worker with children and families?
>
> Think about your own experiences and deeply held values. How do you think these would help you (or perhaps hinder you) in working with people who may have very different values and experiences from yours?
>
> Why do you think social work gets a bad press? Have a search on the internet for items about social work in the media. Do different newspapers put different slants on stories about social work? Why do you think this is? What do these stories tell you about the public perception of social work? What would your friends and family say if you said you were thinking of training and working as a social worker?

Further reading, resources and/or websites

If you are interested in finding out more about social work as a profession or as a possible career, visit the website of the General Social Care Council, the government body responsible for regulating social workers, at www.gscc.org.uk.

For regular news and articles about social work, the website of *Community Care* magazine is worth looking at: www.communitycare.co.uk.

If you are interested in reading in more detail about some of the issues raised in this chapter, the following texts provide good introductions to understanding social work:

Frost, N., and Parton, N. (2009), *Understanding Children's Social Care: Politics, Policy and Practice*. London: Sage. A detailed but accessible overview of the key issues in social work with children written by two of the UK's foremost social work academics.

Horner, N. (2009), *What Is Social Work? Context and Perspectives*, 3rd edition. Exeter: Learning Matters. An excellent introductory book which looks at social work with many different client groups and which contains a very good historical analysis.

References

Anning, A., Cottrell, D., Frost, N., Green, J., and Robinson, M. (2006), *Developing Multiprofessional Teamwork for Integrated Children's Services*. Maidenhead: Open University Press.

Atkinson, M., Jones, M., and Lamont, E. (2007), *Multi Agency Working and Its Implications for Practice: A Review of the Literature*. Slough: NFER. www.nfer.ac.uk/nfer/publications/MAD01/MAD01_home.cfm?publicationID=68andtitle=Multi-agency%20working%20and%20its%20implications%20for%20practice:%20a%20review%20of%20the%20literature.

Barnes, C., and Mercer, G. (2003), *Disability*. Cambridge: Polity Press.

Beresford, P. (2008), *What Future for Care?* York: Joseph Rowntree. www.jrf.org.uk/publications/what-future-care.

Brandon, M., Belderson, P., Warren, C., Gardner, R., Howe, D., Dodsworth, J., and Black, J. (2008a), The preoccupation with thresholds in cases of child death or serious injury through abuse and neglect, *Child Abuse Review*, 17, (5), 313–330.

— (2008b), *Analysing Child Deaths and Serious Injury Through Abuse and Neglect: What Can We Learn? A Biennial Analysis of Serious Case Reviews 2003–2005*. Nottingham: DCSF.

Cooper, A. (2005), Surface and depth in the Victoria Climbié inquiry report. *Child and Family Social Work*, 10, (1), 1–9.

Cree, V., and Myers, S. (2008), *Social Work: Making a Difference*. Bristol: Policy Press.

Davis, J. (2003), Shared values in interprofessional collaboration. In J. Weinstein, C. Whittington and T. Leiba (eds), *Collaboration in Social Work Practice*. London: Jessica Kingsley.

DCSF (Department for Children, Schools and Families) (2006), *What to Do If You're Worried a Child Is Being Abused*. www.dcsf.gov.uk/everychildmatters/resources-and-practice/IG00182/.

— (2010), *Working Together to Safeguard Children: A Guide to Inter Agency Working to Safeguard and Promote the Welfare of Children*. www.publications.dcsf.gov.uk/default.aspx?PageFunction=productdetailsandPageMode=publicationsandProductId=DCSF-00305-2010.

Department of Health (1995), *Child Protection: Messages from Research*. London: HMSO.

— (2002), *Requirements for social work training*. www.dh.gov.uk/en/Publicationsandstatistics/Publications/PublicationsPolicyAndGuidance/DH_4007803.

Frost, N., and Robinson, M. (2007), Joining up children's services: Safeguarding children in multi disciplinary teams. *Child Abuse Review*, 16, (3), 184–199.

Harris, J. (1998), Scientific management, bureau-professionalism, new managerialism: The labour process in state social work. *British Journal of Social Work*, 28, (6), 839–862.

Harris, J., and White, V. (eds), (2009), *Modernising Social Work: Critical Considerations*. Bristol: Policy Press.

Hill, M. (1990), The manifest and latent lessons of child abuse inquiries. *British Journal of Social Work*, 20, 197–213.

Horner, N. (2009), *What Is Social Work? Context and Perspectives*, 3rd edition. Exeter: Learning Matters.

Horwath, J., and Morrison, T. (2007), Collaboration, integration and change in children's services. *Child Abuse and Neglect*, 31, 55–69.

Hudson, B. (2002), Interprofessionality in health and social care: The Achilles heel of partnership? *Journal of Interprofessional Care*, 16, (1), 7–17.

— (2007), Pessimism and optimism in inter-professional working: The Sedgefield integrated team. *Journal of Interprofessional Care*, 21, (1), 3–15.

Laming, Lord (2003), *The Victoria Climbié Inquiry*. www.nationalarchives.gov.uk/ero/browse.aspx?id=3121andlevel=5.

McDonald, C. (2006), *Challenging Social Work*. Basingstoke: Palgrave.

Morris, K. (2008), *Social Work and Multi Agency Working: Making a Difference*. Bristol: Policy Press.

Morrison, T. (2007), Emotional intelligence, emotion and social work. *British Journal of Social Work*, 37, (2), 245–263.

Munro, E. (2008), *Effective Child Protection*, 2nd edition. London: Sage.

Munro, E., and Calder, M. (2005), Where has child protection gone? *Political Quarterly*, 76, (3), 439–445.

Oliver, M. (1990), *The Politics of Disablement*. Basingstoke: Macmillan.

Parton, N. (2006), *Safeguarding Childhood*. Basingstoke: Palgrave.

Payne, M. (2005), *Modern Social Work Theory*, 3rd edition. Basingstoke: Palgrave.

— (2006), *What Is Professional Social Work?* 2nd edition. Bristol: Policy Press.

Reder, P., and Duncan, S. (2003), Understanding communication in child protection networks. *Child Abuse Review*, 12, (2), 82–100.

— (2004), Making the most of the Victoria ClimbiéInquiry Report. *Child Abuse Review*, 13, (2), 95–114.

Ritzer, G. (1996), *The McDonaldisation of Society*, 3rd edition. London: Pine Forge.

Ruch, G. (2006), Thoughtful practice: Child care social work and the role of case discussion. *Child and Family Social Work*, 12, (4), 370–379.

Scottish Executive (2006), *Changing Lives: Report of the 21st Century Social Work Review*. www.scotland.gov.uk/Publications/2006/02/02094408/0.

Spratt, T. (2001), The influence of child protection orientation on child welfare practice. *British Journal of Social Work*, 31, (6), 933–954.

Stedman-Jones, G. (1971), *Outcast London: A Study in the Relationship Between Classes in Victorian Society*. Harmondsworth: Peregrine.

Thompson, N. (2000), *Understanding Social Work*. Basingstoke: Palgrave.

— (2006), *Anti Discriminatory Practice*, 4th edition. Basingstoke: Palgrave.

Wenger, E. (1998), *Communities of Practice*. Cambridge: Cambridge University Press.

8

The Speech and Language Therapist: Laying the Foundations of Communication

Tracey Marsh

Chapter Outline

Introduction

Communication, language and literacy permeate all aspects of daily living. Consequently these skills are essential for life. If children are not proficient communicators, they are vulnerable to many, varied and significant disruptions to their learning and development in all areas.

Speech and language therapists (SLTs) have become a recognized asset in the interdisciplinary, integrated services provided to young children and their families, as communication and literacy development have become prominent areas of interest. Low language attainment in children nationwide has highlighted concerns that have implications for the entire children's workforce. This has served to elevate the profile of SLTs further, to the benefit of professionals across the sector, children and their families.

This chapter will explore the role of the SLT within contemporary early years service provision and will highlight the changes in policy, theory and practice that have culminated in the current professional context. Brock's (2009) seven dimensions of professionalism will be used as a conceptual framework to examine facets of professionalism within the discipline of speech and language therapy (SLT). Theoretical content will be supported and exemplified by experience and clinical practice.

Why speech and language therapy?

Language surrounds us in all aspects of everyday life and the ability to communicate is an essential life skill. Language is the predominant medium of education, social interaction, emotional development and understanding the world in which we live. Rarely do we stop to consider the complexity of communication or reflect upon our good fortune to have achieved competence in this skill. Quite simply, we routinely take our ability to communicate for granted, we underestimate its intricacy and we do not acknowledge its ubiquitous nature.

There is a legacy of insufficient understanding of the fundamental nature of speech, language and communication among policymakers and commissioners (DCSF, 2008a). It therefore follows that historically, insufficient priority has been attached to addressing speech, language and communication needs (SLCN).

Never before has there been such recognition of the extent of the plight of children with SLCN, their long-term consequences and the cost to the nation of secondary impacts (I Can, 2006a, 2006b, 2007, 2009a). Communication difficulties are life limiting (I Can, 2009b) and a child who struggles to speak will find it hard to read, write, access the curriculum, socialize and make friends (DCSF, 2008a; Tallal and Benasich, 2002). Literacy, behaviour, emotional development and mental health will be at significant risk (National Literacy Trust, 2009; Clegg et al., 2007) and ultimately, employment outcomes may be compromised (Law and Plunkett, 2009).

It is heartening therefore that strengthening children's early language development is now a national, high-profile priority (DCSF, 2008a, 2008b, 2008c) and speech, language and communication are embedded at the heart of children's policy (I Can, 2010). The Bercow Review (DCSF, 2008a) and consequential Better Communication Action Plan (DCSF, 2008b) have been highly influential in England and have generated a great deal of excitement, optimism and energy across the early years SLT division. While SLTs are identified as the key professionals in supporting children with SLCN, both of these documents clearly assert that SLCN are significant and have far reaching implications which necessitate partnerships and working across organizational boundaries. These approaches to practice are given further distinction in the NHS Operating Framework (DoH, 2009) and are clearly supported by the professional body (RCSLT, 2009) and strategic, national commissioning bodies (Commissioning Support Programme, 2010).

What is a speech and language therapist?

SLTs are the lead experts in communication and swallowing disorders across the human lifespan (RCSLT, 2006). This chapter focuses on communication; while dysphagia (a swallowing disorder) is a growing discipline within SLT services, it is not a prominent component of mainstream early years provision.

SLT is a progressive profession whose workforce must integrate in-depth theoretical knowledge, a diverse repertoire of skills and a range of personal attributes. Clinicians rely upon their aptitude for synthesizing theoretical, technical and practical information and utilizing pertinent skills. They have the capacity to apply this knowledge and skill flexibly to plan and deliver high-quality care for people with SLCN and swallowing disorders to make timely and evidence-based decisions. One of the most substantial challenges in this undertaking is ensuring that we do this effectively within a continually changing economic, social and political context, embracing the service-level changes inherent in a dynamic, evolving professional culture.

Typically employed by the NHS, SLTs provide services across the health sector, but do not work exclusively within health contexts and clinical environments. SLT practice is chiefly shaped by Department of Health (DoH) policy and priority, but the responsible SLT must also be diligent in the application of other legislative influences and practice-based policies and frameworks pertinent to their particular clinical field. For SLTs supporting children with SLCN, the stipulations of the DoH need to be in balance with their allegiance to educational obligations.

What does a speech and language therapist do?

Primary clinical responsibilities for the SLT are assessment, diagnosis, intervention and discharge. At each stage, a wealth of options is available to the clinician whose professional skill lies in selecting the most appropriate option for the unique circumstances of each individual. The domains of assessment, diagnosis and discharge remain solely within the remit of the clinician, and while the responsibility for intervention remains with the SLT, the therapist may collaborate with appropriate others at this stage. This may range from the SLT setting a highly prescriptive series of tasks for parents to carry out with their children in between clinical sessions to the SLT handing over an entire programme of individually tailored intervention to a classroom assistant to integrate into the curriculum and implement with the child.

The SLT also has roles working with universal service partners (e.g., education, health and social care) to enhance relevant skills across the children's workforce, supporting the active participation of clients in service planning and improving awareness of ways to overcome communication difficulties – roles which are as important as those of identification, diagnosis and intervention.

Regulatory and professional bodies

In the UK the independent, statutory regulatory body for the SLT profession is the Health Professions Council (HPC). The HPC's primary function is to protect the public and they achieve this through the approval of pre-registration education and subsequent professional registration. An SLT must meet and maintain standards of proficiency (HPC, 2007) in order to register with the HPC, and registration is mandatory in order to practise. There are currently 12,298 registered SLTs in the UK (HPC, 2010a).

In addition to the regulatory HPC, the SLT profession is also fortunate to have an active professional body: the Royal College of Speech and Language Therapists (RCSLT). RCSLT is a member-led, charitable organization, responsible for promoting, maintaining and enhancing the professional practice of SLTs. It provides professional leadership and strategic direction and engages with political campaigning. RCSLT is committed to the definition and development of best practice. By supporting, facilitating and promoting research and evidence-based practice, RCSLT expresses a commitment to safeguarding optimum levels of care for individuals with SLCN and swallowing disorders.

Speech and language therapy services

SLT services are defined by and operate within current policy frameworks. Thus, there is a history of evolving SLT service delivery, responsive to current policy drivers. There have been momentous shifts in culture, models and contexts of service delivery. Thus SLTs have been required to embrace change in order to consistently deliver clinical care of the highest quality (DoH, 2008, 2010a, 2010b). SLTs with specialization in paediatrics, especially the early years, have encountered the significant development and transformation of children's services in parallel with health reforms. Since the advent of Every Child Matters (DfES, 2004) and consequently the National Service Framework for Children, Young People and Maternity Services (DoH, 2004a), change has culminated in SLTs operating within the integrated children's services agenda.

Education and training, knowledge and skill for speech and language therapy

SLT is a graduate profession. In order to practise and use the legally protected title of Speech and Language Therapist, a student must complete an HPC-approved degree programme, which may be accessed at an undergraduate or postgraduate level. It is an intense and rigorous course and, in addition to academic demands, significant personal and professional development is required for successful completion. HPC accreditation is awarded to degree programmes that adequately demonstrate their adherence to the Standards of Education and Training (HPC, 2009a) and can evidence their ability to produce graduates who meet minimum standards of proficiency (HPC, 2007). Course design and delivery is also supported by the guidelines presented by the Royal College of Speech and Language Therapists (RCSLT, 2010a), and the Quality Assurance Agency for Higher Education (QAA, 2001, 2008).

The knowledge base for SLT comprises the following theoretical disciplines:

- Speech and language pathology
- Anatomy, physiology, neurology, medical disciplines
- Linguistics, phonetics, phonology, psycholinguistics
- Psychology
- Sociology
- Research and evidence-based practice skills

Other essential knowledge for effective SLT service delivery revolves around the professional context at a strategic level. In addition, an understanding of the way in which the national context is being interpreted and implemented at the local level is needed, because demographic changes and local variation can be significant and services must consider local impacting factors (e.g. employment, cost of living, housing, transport, levels of deprivation). For example, a family for whom economic survival is challenging may not be able to prioritize SLT appointments when they are uncertain of where their next meal may come from, when they may be able to secure employment, or how their housing situation may improve.

Successful SLT practice is not a matter of theoretical knowledge alone. Theory must be selected appropriately, assimilated and applied sensitively and flexibly to each individual case. Effective SLT practice is therefore reflective and relies upon an array of skills. Table 8.1, which is intended to be illustrative, not comprehensive, provides a list of key skill areas.

SLT is still a profession in its infancy, with the first qualifications emerging in the 1940s at diploma level, followed by the inaugural degree programmes in the 1960s. All areas of SLT practice have undergone and continue to experience transformation as conceptual, theoretical, medical and technological advances continue apace, alongside strategic, political and legislative reform. Such are these changes that SLTs of yesteryear would now struggle to identify their own limited scope of practice, embedded within what has become an entirely different professional landscape.

There is an ongoing requirement to ensure that curriculum changes in pre-registration education and experience continue to reflect the contemporary clinical environment (McAllister and Lincoln, 2004). Newly qualified therapists not only need their core clinical skills and knowledge, but must also be equipped with an aptitude for progressive strategic thinking and openness to workforce redesign. Consideration of commissioning, measuring

Table 8.1 Examples of key skill areas

Technical	Therapeutic/Personal/Interpersonal
Information management	Communication (oral and written)
Data analysis and interpretation	Listening
Critical/analytical thinking	Congruence
Problem solving	Empathy and understanding
Clinical reasoning and decision making	Negotiation
Change facilitation	Reflection, reflective practice
Prioritization	Self-awareness
Time management	Flexibility/adaptability
Creativity	Personal and professional integrity
Research	Teamwork
Observation	Training

outcomes and providing proof of efficacy in a climate that is economically driven are further high-profile priorities (DoH, 2010b).

Early years clinicians need a determination to put the needs of the children and families with whom they work at the forefront of their care. In order to achieve this, graduates must be prepared for partnership, interagency working, the embracement of a universal provision and the increasing adoption of a consultative model of practice in order to ensure the appropriate enskilling of the children's workforce. Promotion of a leadership culture across the allied health professions also dominates current policy (DoH, 2008, 2010b).

The following case example illustrates how an SLT may draw upon and apply knowledge and skill in the management of a child. The referral is not atypical, and while there may be some variation in the management of such a case, it lies within the range of standard practice.

Case Study

Millie was referred to an SLT by her nursery teacher when she was 3 years, 4 months old, owing to concerns about restricted vocabulary and the clarity of her speech. Millie saw the SLT at the local clinic, and attended with her mother.

Since the referral contains little information, the SLT (Clair) needed to plan an assessment session in order to elicit a comprehensive profile of Millie's communicative strengths and difficulties. In order to do this efficiently, Clair had to draw upon her knowledge of developmental milestones, speech and language pathology and likely aetiologies. Clair needed to be systematic and adopt a scientific approach, generating and testing hypotheses.

When welcoming Millie and her mother, Clair needed to present a facilitative and empowering environment, suitable for both mother and child. Clair's interpersonal and communication skills were critical to achieve this. Clair made a detailed assessment by working with Millie herself, and by interviewing Millie's mother. Clinical reasoning, synthesis and interpretation of data all guided Clair through the information-gathering process. In order to engage Millie's mother in the assessment, Clair needed to build and establish rapport and be sensitive in her questioning. With Millie, Clair needed to motivate, support and reward. Clair's appraisal of Millie's receptive and expressive language required Clair to refer to her knowledge of linguistics and language development and, in order to record Millie's speech accurately, conduct a detailed phonetic transcription. Millie's speech did indeed lack clarity, and so in order to rule out any possible physiological cause, Clair performed an oral examination, applying her anatomical and physiological knowledge. Millie became unsettled during the session, resulting in a reluctance to participate in assessment tasks. Clair's observation skills allowed her to recognize this at an early stage and she was therefore flexible in her approach, adapting activities to mirror Millie's interest and earn her continued cooperation.

Clair analysed and interpreted the detailed and comprehensive data gathered so that she could hypothesize on the cause of Millie's difficulties and reach a diagnosis. In order to share this, Clair needed to provide feedback to Millie's mother on the assessment findings in a succinct and meaningful way, drawing on examples to illustrate the difficulties Millie was experiencing. Millie's mother had been reluctant to attend the appointment as she didn't share the teacher's concerns about Millie, and so when Clair confirmed an expressive language delay and disordered patterns of speech, she was resistant and became distressed. Clair was required to listen to and counsel Millie's mother in order to maintain trust and respect. Clair had a thorough understanding of the options for intervention and the local service delivery models, and was thus able to talk knowledgeably about these. By the conclusion of the hour-long session, Clair had established a respectful rapport with Millie's mother and a productive relationship with Millie, made a comprehensive assessment, reached a preliminary diagnosis and put in place a package of clinical care.

Continuing professional development (CPD)

Educational provision is designed not only to address learning needs during the qualifying course, but also to equip students with the ethos of lifelong learning, which in turn will support them to meet the demands and challenges of professional life. CPD is the primary means by which standards of clinical practice are enhanced and clinicians retain their capacity to practise safely, effectively and legally within their evolving scope of practice (HPC, 2010b; RCSLT, 2010b). CPD is essential to safeguard the development and renewal of the profession and is a mandatory requirement for all practising SLTs who must continue to augment subject expertise and technical skill throughout their career.

Crucial to the development of the profession is also the expansion of a robust evidence base to underpin clinical practice, and so research and scholarly activity are both promoted and encouraged within the profession. Generating, discovering and evaluating new theoretical and empirical evidence and applying this to the management of individuals with SLCN and swallowing disorders are highly regarded professional activities.

Autonomy in the speech and language therapy profession

The role and identity of the SLT is predominantly autonomous, irrespective of clinical context. For the majority of time, the SLT works independently and is self-governing in caseload management. SLTs must comply with all standards prescribed by the HPC (HPC, 2006, 2007, 2008, 2009a) and are mandated to operate within a framework of clinical governance, dictated by employing bodies. Within these parameters, however, the SLT has scope and flexibility to operate with a great deal of independence and choice. This high level of autonomy does not equate with a lack of support or isolation. Clinical support, mentoring and supervision are typically well-established components of service management.

Traditional SLT services fell within the medical model, while contemporary practice is more aligned with the vision and values of a social model of care. This clearly places the child and family at the centre of any intervention, embraces holistic management of the child and family in their broad context and is underpinned by partnership and empowerment. As a result of this, SLTs were well prepared to operate effectively within current integrated children's services. Table 8.2 illustrates the transition from the medical to the social model of care.

As Table 8.2 illustrates, the social model of service provision necessitates that the SLT has the skills necessary for integrated working and collaborative practice and empowers clinicians to work within a collegiate, team-based ethos, embracing the team around the child. This model of practice is given distinction in the latest Department of Health white paper, 'Equity and excellence: Liberating the NHS' (DoH, 2010b).

Threats to autonomy pervade SLT practice and require sensitive management in order to avoid an erosion of professional value. Inherent in the philosophies and policy underpinning current early years service provision is the consultative model of practice, which obligates the SLT to share expert knowledge in order to equip and empower other professionals to create developmentally appropriate, supportive and stimulating environments in which children can enjoy experimenting with and learning language (DCSF, 2007, 2008c, 2008d). This must not be confused with either a devaluing or deskilling of the expert nature of SLT input, nor with a dilution of services to children, neither of which is a valid assertion.

A further potential hazard in relation to autonomy is the increased access to communication technologies and the internet. This has resulted in the SLT no longer being the exclusive holder of expert knowledge. The role of the SLT must now incorporate the management of this material, ensuring that only reliable and reputable sources are given attention.

Though the SLT profession is exhorted to be autonomous, the increasing levels of surveillance present something of a paradox and further challenge a clinician's autonomy. Current

Table 8.2 An illustration of the transition from the medical to the social model of care

Traditional/Medical Model of SLT provision	Contemporary/Social Model of SLT provision
Work in isolation with child, in a didactic relationship.	Work in partnership with child and significant others; for example, parents, teacher.
Child removed from natural environment (e.g. clinic room, or removal from classroom to medical room).	Work within the natural environment and context and use this environment to support intervention.
Work disconnected from natural communicative circumstances.	Intervention uses natural communicative circumstances to ensure meaningful and contextual outcomes that can be immediately generalized into the child's communicative repertoire and meet situational needs.
Child is the passive recipient of services.	Child and significant others become empowered, active partners in the therapeutic process, with shared goal setting and intervention options discussed, negotiated and jointly agreed.
Little or no collaboration, consultation, or negotiation about 'treatment' given.	
Professional considered expert in all matters, resulting in unequal relationship.	Value and embrace the expert status that the child and family hold regarding their own unique circumstances, needs and perceptions. Foster an equitable, reciprocal and mutually supportive therapeutic relationship.
Deficit based, impairment focused therapy.	Functional, contextual and integrated intervention that builds on strengths and takes into account communicative environments.

emphasis is upon quality and productivity (DoH, 2010a), which are arguably imperative obligations for the profession, yet can present, in themselves, a conflict.

Values in speech and language therapy

Value in SLT is notoriously difficult to demonstrate, owing to its complexity and incongruence with objective, tangible measurement tools. Many people involved in the strategic planning, commissioning or reviewing of services are not familiar with SLT, its objectives, the needs of clients, the principles driving the profession or the evidence base (RCSLT, 2009). This can lead to a failure to appreciate the value of the profession at a strategic level, which impacts upon service contracts and commissioning. Reassuringly though, when removed from the context of objective measurement instruments and evaluative analytical tools, the value placed upon us by our clients is indisputable. The qualitative, yet irreplaceable difference that SLT can make to an individual's quality of life is immense.

There is an entirely misguided perception among the general public that SLT equates with elocution; that we are 'the nice ladies to help with talking'. Also, the 'twin set and pearls' perception of SLTs, however erroneous, is still live, which does not help in the promotion of the profession or in establishing its true identity and worth. However, perhaps these inaccurate perceptions are preferable to an unfortunate mistake made by a child who, on seeing me visiting his school, announced 'yippee, it's the speech terrorist!!!'

The misperception surrounding the role and remit of the SLT may contribute to the homogeneity within the profession. There is a well-established pattern of white, middle-class females forming a significant majority, despite a long-standing effort to attract greater diversity, especially the engagement of men. It may be that with the evolving scope of practice in dysphagia, acute medical care, and the proliferation of technological advancements in assessment, diagnostics and intervention, the profession may benefit from the ability to attract a more diverse pool of applicants. This may be further supported by the increased role and profile of scientific, evidence-based approaches, research and scholarly activity. We must remain optimistic that these trends will further enhance diversity within the profession.

The SLT working in the early years sector could be forgiven for having something of a professional identity crisis as a consequence of their successful integration into the team around the child. I was often conscious of a 'no man's land' between the health and education sectors. I remember working in Sure Start Local Programmes in the early 2000s, when the primary guiding principles were almost exclusively the Every Child Matters five outcomes. At that time, I recall having to fight my corner to be included in work pertaining to 'Enjoy and Achieve', because in those early days it was inaccurately assumed that as a health professional, my contributions would be exclusively restricted to 'Be Healthy'. Today, ten years later, the SLTs who have established themselves effectively in early years teams may have to work hard to retain their identity as health professionals, such is now their influential role across health, educational and social aspects of care.

The shift away from traditional models of practice that focused entirely and exclusively on the clinical population and care pathways also denote an altered identity for the early years SLT. Conventionally, the role, remit and practice of the SLT was exclusively applied to children with identified difficulties, where the customary assessment, diagnosis, intervention and discharge protocol of care was adopted. Contemporary practice is much more inclusive. In addition to the targeted intervention for children with identified needs, the SLT has an imperative role in prevention and enrichment. Working universally, raising the profile of the critical nature of speech, language and communication and working consultatively to improve communicative environments and the skills of early years staff, the SLT now contributes to enhance what is already good and prevent the establishment of long-term difficulties in those children vulnerable to SLCN. For example, the establishment of narrative groups, rhyme time, listening and sound discrimination groups, for all nursery children, alongside staff training and environmental modification (DCSF, 2008c, 2008d, DfES, 2006).

Ethics in speech and language therapy

'All healthcare practice takes place in the ethical realm' (Seedhouse, 2002, p. 253). Modern healthcare continues to be built upon a solid ethical foundation (DoH, 2009), requiring all

NHS staff to model exemplary ethical practice (DoH, 2010a). By its very nature, the SLT profession is routinely engaged with individuals for whom language presents a specific difficulty. Thus, ethics presents a particularly interesting challenge, as many of the practical and clinical manifestations of ethical practice are conveyed via the medium of language, for example, client consent.

It is beyond the scope of this chapter to make a detailed examination of theoretical, conceptual and principled accounts of bioethics; the intention here is to offer an insight into a selection of the most prevalent ethical issues in paediatric practice. Ultimately, SLT practice must adhere to the HPC's Standards of Conduct, Performance and Ethics (HPC, 2008, 2009b) and any SLT in breach of these standards will place his or her registration in jeopardy. Ethics are so closely related to morality, values and conscience that even the public declaration of broad ethical codes doesn't define practice within a framework that is black and white, or right and wrong. Conflicting and differing reactions to ethical dilemmas are therefore frequent, and it is for this reason that clinicians may lack confidence or moral and professional courage in their approaches (Body and McAllister, 2009). Yet, it is often only through the rich debate stimulated by these differences that the best outcomes emerge.

While many of the ethical themes prevalent in paediatric clinical practice are not the high-profile, high-impact ones deserving of media attention, they are no less important. However mundane, the ethical tensions in mainstream paediatric practice must not and cannot be ignored. Chief among the everyday ethical encounters are the issues of consent and confidentiality. Both of these subjects have libraries' worth of literature written on them, but the thorny practical issues of establishing consent for SLT practice and for appropriate information sharing is a continual challenge, which often remains inadequately addressed.

Many staff-room discussions have centred upon the debate around the applications and implications of consent, particularly when SLTs are routinely working in the educational context. Schools are not governed in the same ways when it comes to consent and this can give rise to tension between the school and the SLT. It is a common experience for an SLT to visit a school to see a particular child already on the SLT caseload with parental consent in place, but on discovering that this child is not in school, the SLT is asked to see a different child – 'you are here now anyway, can we have the appointment time for another child we have concerns about?' When the SLT is unable to comply with this request (which appears logical from a practical standpoint) tension can result. Without parental consent, an SLT cannot have any direct involvement with a child. Hopefully relations between the school and the SLT are robust enough to withstand this temporary frustration, but I have known it to cause quite some consternation.

Confidentiality is probably the most commonly cited of ethical considerations, even by student therapists, yet when it comes to the complexities of information sharing and the interface with the Data Protection Act (1998) and the Freedom of Information Act (2000), experience suggests that many of us become less clear and less confident in our boundaries.

At a more strategic level, the ethics surrounding resource allocation are complex and sensitive. Being required more than ever before to improve care within an increasingly tight fiscal climate (DoH, 2010c) challenges the provision and prioritization of services even further. Financial responsibility is a key personal, professional and moral responsibility, and so securing and allocating resources must be as effective as possible (DoH, 2010a, 2010b). At the coalface, the distribution of services affects all SLTs who, within the strategic boundaries imposed, are responsible for equity and parity within their own caseload. 'Rationing of healthcare resources and prioritization of client groups and individual clients seem inevitable consequences of contemporary healthcare' (Body and McAllister, 2009, p. 169). In my own clinical practice, I have been continually aware of an inner conflict arising as a result of quality versus quantity and the 'more for less' doctrine permeating from 'on high'. There seems to be increasing emphasis upon and monitoring of throughput (numbers seen), with an apparent lack of credence given to quality (outcomes). I am concerned that the imposed service priorities undermine the values of my profession and therefore test my professional integrity. Compromise is often essential, and whether it is parity of provision or an individual's needs that are implicated offers little solace to the therapist who must reach the agonizing decision.

Integrated services, joint working, multi-, inter- and transdisciplinary approaches within contemporary children's services emphasize the ethical issues surrounding protection of professional interests, role boundaries, delegation and supervision. Sensitive and subtle in nature, these debates are only just emerging but will need continued attention in order to safeguard all concerned.

Reward for speech and language therapists

SLT is a profession typified by change, and the financial reward is no exception. Prior to a successful equal pay claim in the 1990s, SLT salaries were low. However, pay for SLTs now falls within the NHS pay structure – Agenda for Change – and reward is commensurate with the levels of responsibility, autonomy, accountability and clinical expertise. Newly qualified practitioners will typically be employed on Band 5 of the structure and the career progression is structured, with a maximum clinical salary, usually including managerial responsibility, taking an SLT to Band 8 (NHS, 2010). The NHS Knowledge and Skills Framework (DoH, 2004b) arises directly from the Agenda for Change pay structure and lies at the heart of the career and pay progression of NHS staff. It provides a single, consistent, comprehensive and explicit framework on which to base review and development.

While the financial reward is fair, anecdotal evidence suggests that SLTs are not typically exclusively motivated by remuneration. Typical conversations on the matter will include phrases such as 'it's a good job we're not in it for the money' and 'you just cannot put a price on the difference we make to some lives. That's what gets me out of bed in a morning'.

For many SLTs, alternative rewards and additional benefits are of great value. Foremost among these is the satisfaction associated with facilitating change, supporting improvement

Figure 8.1 A speech and language therapist at work

and guiding children and their families to achieve better outcomes. Within the Every Child Matters framework (DfES, 2004), the SLT is fortunate to be able to vicariously appreciate holistic gains across all five outcomes. The central role of communication is such that an improvement permeates all areas of development and thus impacts positively across all outcomes. The satisfaction associated with this never appears to be underestimated, yet is not feasible without engaging in a meaningful, trustful and empowering relationship with a child and family. This alone is valued as a privileged position for any professional to be in.

The collaborative, integrated and team-based working practices characteristic of the early years sector undeniably offers the SLT great reward, specifically from the perspective of support, joint planning, problem solving and sharing of good practice. An SLT working exclusively within integrated children's services may be vulnerable to professional isolation, but there is compensatory value in the interdisciplinary team support providing richness of experience, diversity of skill and variety of priority, perspective and professional direction.

There are two further non-fiscal incentives commonly cited by clinicians. The first of these pertains to the ever-present opportunities and encouragement of professional development, both in the sense of the advancement of the profession and individual development as a professional. The second is rated highly among SLTs and relates to the highly varied vocation, which is created by the dynamic working environment and the complexity of caseloads, made only more fascinating by the concession of working with people, embracing their diversity.

Conclusion

The pace of policy development and reform across the early years sector is a testament to the modernization agenda in public services. The professionals working within this culture of change can be justifiably proud of their ability to drive up the quality of care against such a backdrop of transformation.

SLTs have been fortunate and privileged to witness and influence such developmental, progressive and fundamental change in early years culture and practice. Change can be exhausting, but the evident improvements continually made to services and outcomes for children have positively contributed to morale, motivation and commitment to excel. This relies upon the key tenets of professionalism and illustrates the SLT's loyalty and dedication to uphold the reputation, integrity and rigour of the profession.

Questions for reflective practice

How can you disseminate the critical importance of language and communication skills for young children's holistic development?

What do you perceive to be the benefits to the child when a speech and language therapist adopts a social model of care?

Further reading, resources and/or websites

Brock, A., and Rankin, C. (2008), *Communication, Language and Literacy from Birth to Five*. London: Sage.

Kersner, M., and Wright, J. A. (2001), *Speech and Language Therapy. The Decision Making Process When Working with Children*. London: David Fulton Publishers.

—. (2002), *How to Manage Communication Problems in Young Children*, 3rd edition. London: David Fulton Publishers.

www.afasicengland.org.uk.

www.ican.org.uk.

References

Body, R., and McAllister, L. (2009), *Ethics in Speech and Language Therapy*. Chichester: Wiley-Blackwell.

Brock, A. (2009) Eliciting early years educators' thinking: How do they define and sustain their professionalism? Unpublished thesis. Leeds: University of Leeds.

Clegg, J., Brumfitt, S., Parks, R., and Woodruff, P. (2007), Speech and language intervention in schizophrenia: A case study. *International Journal of Language and Communication Disorders*, 42, (1), 81–101.

Commissioning Support Programme (2010), *Commissioning Community Health Services – Commissioning Better Health for Children and Young People*. London: Commissioning Support Programme.

DCSF (2007), *The Early Years Foundation Stage. Setting the Standards for Learning, Development and Care for Children from Birth to Five*. Nottingham: DCSF Publications.

— (2008a), *The Bercow Review. A Review of Services for Children and Young People (0–19) with Speech, Language and Communication Needs*. Nottingham: DCSF Publications.

— (2008b), *Better Communication. An Action Plan to Improve Services for Children and Young People with Speech, Language and Communication Needs*. Nottingham: DCSF Publications.

— (2008c), *Every Child a Talker: Guidance for Early Language Lead Practitioners*. Nottingham: DCSF Publications.

— (2008d), *Inclusion Development Programme. Supporting Children with Speech, Language and Communication Needs: Guidance for Practitioners in the Early Years Foundation Stage*. Nottingham: DCSF Publications.

DfES (2004), *Every Child Matters*. Nottingham: DfES Publications.

— (2006), *Communicating Matters Trainer's Pack*. Nottingham: DfES Publications.

DoH (2004a), *National Service Framework for Children, Young People and Maternity Services*. London: Department of Health Publications.

— (2004b), *The NHS Knowledge and Skills Framework (NHS KSF) and the Development Review Process*. London: Department of Health Publications.

— (2008), *High Quality Care for All. NHS Next Stage Review Final Report*. London: Department of Health Publications.

— (2009), *The Operating Framework for the NHS in England 2010/11*. London: Department of Health Publications.

— (2010a), *NHS 2010–2015: From Good to Great. Preventative, People Centred, Productive*. Norwich: The Stationery Office.

— (2010b), *Equity and Excellence: Liberating the NHS*. Norwich: The Stationery Office.

— (2010c), *The NHS Quality, Innovation, Productivity and Prevention Challenge: An Introduction for Clinicians*. London: Department of Health Publications.

HPC (2006), *Your Guide to Our Standards for Continuing Professional Development*. London: Health Professions Council.

— (2007), *Standards of Proficiency – Speech and Language Therapists*. London: Health Professions Council.

— (2008), *Standards of Conduct, Performance and Ethics*. London: Health Professions Council.

— (2009a), *Standards of Education and Training*. London: Health Professions Council.

— (2009b), *Guidance on Conduct and Ethics for Students*. London: Health Professions Council.

— (2010a), *Registration Statistics*. www.hpc-uk.org/aboutregistration/theregister/stats/. Accessed 3 April 2010.

— (2010b), *Continuing Professional Development and Your Registration*. London: Health Professions Council.

I Can (2006a), *Communication Disability and Literacy Difficulties*. I Can Talk Series – Issue 1. www.ican.org.uk/upload2/i%20can%20talk%20-%20communication%20disability%20and%20%20literacy%20difficulties.pdf. Accessed 3 February 2010.

— (2006b), *The Cost to the Nation of Children's Poor Communication*. I Can Talk Series – Issue 2. www.ican.org.uk/upload2/chatter%20matter%20update/mcm%20report%20final.pdf. Accessed 3 February 2010.

— (2007), *Language and Social Exclusion*. I Can Talk Series – Issue 4. www.ican.org.uk/upload2/publications/language%20and%20social%20exclusion%20report.pdf. Accessed 3 February 2010.

— (2009a), *Speech, Language and Communication and the Early Years*. I Can Talk Series – Issue 7. www.ican.org.uk/Resources/~/media/ICAN%20website/7%20Info%20Resources%20%20%20Publ/Publications/7%20Speech%20Language%20and%20Communication%20Needs%20and%20the%20Early%20Years.ashx. Accessed 3 February 2010.

— (2009b), *Impact Report 2008–2009*. London: I Can Publications.

— (2010), *Speech, Language and Communication Needs (SLCN)*. www.ican.org.uk/about%20us/speech%20language%20and%20communication%20needs.aspx. Accessed 5 April 2010.

Law, J. and Plunkett, C. (2009), *The Interaction Between Behaviour and Speech and Language Difficulties: Does Intervention for One Affect Outcomes in the Other?* Technical Report. Nuffield Speech and Language Review Group.

McAllister, L. and Lincoln, M. (2004), *Clinical Education in Speech-Language Pathology*. London: Whurr Publishers.

National Literacy Trust (2009), *Guidance for Developing a Strategic Approach to Speech, Language and Communication in the Early Years*. www.literacytrust.org.uk/talk_to_your_baby/resources/439_strategy_guidance_paper. Accessed 3 March 2010.

NHS (2010), *NHS Terms and Conditions of Service Handbook. Pay Circular (AforC) 2/2010*. Amendment number 17. London: The NHS Staff Council.

QAA (2001), *Benchmark Statement : Healthcare Programmes, Speech and Language Therapy*. Gloucester: The Quality Assurance Agency for Higher Education.

— (2008), *The Framework for Higher Education Qualifications in England, Wales and Northern Ireland*. Mansfield: The Quality Assurance Agency for Higher Education.

RCSLT (2006), *Communicating Quality 3. RCSLT's Guidance on Best Practice in Service Organisation and Provision*. London: Royal College of Speech and Language Therapists.

— (2009), *Resource Manual for Commissioning and Planning Services for SLCN*. London: RCSLT.

— (2010a), *Guidelines for Pre-Registration Speech and Language Therapy Courses in the UK, Incorporating Curriculum Guidelines*. London: Royal College of Speech and Language Therapists.

— (2010b), *CPD Toolkit*. www.rcslt.org/members/cpd/toolkit_download. Accessed 5 April 2010.

Seedhouse, D. (2002), Commitment to health: A shared ethical bond between professions. *Journal of Interprofessional Care*, 16, 249–260.

Tallal, P. and Benasich, A. A. (2002), Developmental language learning environments. *Development and Psychopathology*. 14, 559–579.

9

The Librarian: A Key Partner in Promoting Early Language and Literacy

Carolynn Rankin

Introduction

This chapter discusses the work of librarians who specialize in providing services and resources to support the needs of babies, young children and their families. These practitioners will usually be employed in the public library service or in Children's Centres. They may have a variety of different job titles, for example, children's librarian, early years librarian, community librarian and outreach librarian. In this chapter the term 'librarian' is used for convenience to include all practitioners who are the active intermediaries in providing library services and resources to newborns and young children up to 8 years old. Brock's seven dimensions of professionalism will be used as a conceptual framework to discuss the professionalism of library and information professionals.

What librarians do – take them to the library

Library practitioners are at the forefront of promoting children's rights and play a key role in disseminating information about the importance of early literacy to parents, child care providers, early childhood educators, children's advocates and political decision makers. Libraries and librarians are a vital aid to literacy development and the generic message is that reading with young children is important irrespective of first language, heritage or cultural background (Rankin and Brock, 2009).

Since the late nineteenth century, public libraries in the UK have been at the centre of their local communities, providing services for children and young people, reflecting the diversity of the population they serve (Brophy, 2007). Communities give purpose to libraries and it is important that libraries seek to reach out to the local community beyond the library walls. There is much interest now in the social impact of what libraries are doing and how they can contribute to the social cohesion and development of their communities. Good library services will put the community at the heart of developing and delivering services, engaging with people and responding to their needs. In reflecting the needs of the population they serve, libraries impact greatly upon people's lives as learning centres, cultural centres and information centres (IFLA, 2009).

> Public libraries make a measurable and substantial contribution to local economies, and help to bridge social divides. They support well-being, encourage reading, spread knowledge, contribute to learning and skills and help to foster identity, community and a sense of place for people of all ages, backgrounds and cultures. (MLA, 2008, p. 2)

A library service should provide a positive experience for local people. Public library provision is a statutory duty for local councils. The Public Libraries and Museums Act 1964 came into force in April 1965 making it a statutory obligation for a local authority to provide 'a comprehensive and efficient' public library service for its community. This act remains the statutory framework for the delivery of library services in England and Wales (McMenemy, 2009, p. 33). In order to meet key legal requirements, a local library service must serve both adults and children and provide value for money working in partnership with other authorities and agencies. Libraries give identity to a community and should provide opportunities for everyone within it. A good library service will deliver against key policy objectives by providing a positive future for children and young people; strong safe and sustainable communities; equality, community cohesion and social justice; health improvements and well-being (CILIP, 2009c). The physical location is also important as libraries are seen as trusted institutions;

both users and non-users identify public libraries as inclusive, non-threatening, non-judge-mental spaces which can engage 'hard-to-reach groups' with their own services, and provide access to these groups for other public services (Burns Owens Partnership, 2009).

The election of the New Labour Government in 1997 was generally seen as an opportunity for public libraries to be placed back on the political agenda as combating social exclusion was at the heart of the political mission. The role of the public library was identified in aiding this mission (DCMS, 1999; McMenemy, 2009, p. 6).The publication of the first-ever national public library strategy, Framework for the Future, provided a long-term strategic vision that public libraries in England could aspire to by 2013; this included the core role of the service in the promotion of reading and informal learning (DCMS, 2003). The public library is also seen as a trusted community resource providing a universal entitlement to the skills and joy of reading, essential information, learning and knowledge at all stages of life and involve-ment in the social, learning and creative life of the community (Dolan, 2007). The Start with the Child report (CILIP, 2002) recognised the contribution libraries can make in delivering government policies on lifelong learning and combating social exclusion and improving the quality of life of children and young people in the UK. In responding to the needs of their communities, public libraries have introduced new services and outreach programmes built up over established core services such as book lending, referral points and providing access to information and communication technology (ICT) facilities. In terms of cognitive skills development, librarians have a contribution to make to the early years by providing activities that support the development of literacy and speech, language and communication skills. These services are focused on helping to deliver the Every Child Matters (ECM) agenda. The support for developing family literacy extends into later life, across all age ranges, alongside activities that contribute to the development of other adult basic skills, such as numeracy, ICT skills and health literacy (Burns Owens Partnership, 2009). The *Modernisation Review of Public Libraries* (DCMS, 2010), published under the New Labour Government, recom-mended that all libraries provide a universal core offer, with local authorities shaping their offer around local need. A number of proposals related to making connections to other local services and policy priorities; this included local authority leaders actively considering how their library service could contribute effectively to other local services for children, schools and families, and championing the partnership agenda for libraries to help deliver improved services. However, the prevailing financial climate under the Coalition Government presents very difficult challenges for public library funding.

The role of the librarian is gathering greater agency, born out of policy directives and a cultural climate which questions the role of the public library offering in relation to the fam-ily. Developments under the previous Labour Government (in power from 1997 to 2010) saw a significant increase in the activity around early years provision. Multi-agency working and integrated service delivery have been key aspects of the government strategy to improve standards in the early years. Agency partnerships are helping parents to support their chil-dren's early language and literacy, as well as communicating important messages about emo-tional and social development and health issues. The public library is the prime community access point designed to respond to a multitude of ever-changing information needs (Koontz and Gubbin, 2010), and the challenge is for librarians to implement policies in libraries and work with partner organizations to achieve the effective delivery of services. As discussed in Chapter 2, partnership working takes time to develop and space needs to be devoted to planning (Frost, 2005).

> Everybody assumes that a social worker is really important and children's speech and language therapists are important but librarians have a role too and I am working hard on finding and building these partnership contacts. (Development librarian)

Recent UK Government policy has required a focus on working across professional and organizational boundaries as there is the potential to address complex societal problems such as social inclusion and the lifelong-learning agenda. Partnership working and increased interagency working has been promoted with legislation aimed at increasing this type of cooperation at strategic and operational levels. Library and information practitioners have a tradition of networking with other professional groups and developing communities of practice. A key message here is that librarians can play an important role as connectors, working in intra-organizational teams in their local communities (Rankin et al., 2007).

Challenging assumptions and the sex stereotype

A strand of discussion in Chapter 2 considered how interdisciplinary teamwork requires professionals to be open and flexible to different ways of working. A lack of knowledge concerning each other's roles can lead to misunderstanding and negative stereotypes, but an understanding of each other's roles, philosophies and ideologies can lead to trust and respect between professionals (Frost, 2005). On the basis that preconceived ideas and assumptions influence attitudes and practices, it is likely that stereotypes and preconceptions exist for librarians working with babies and young children. Here is an issue of professional identity. Librarianship is seen as a primarily female profession and practitioners are often conventionally associated with just 'providing books'. However, they are now recognized as playing a key role in outreach work in the community. Qualified librarians take on specialist roles, rather than managing the day-to-day running of the library branches.

> There is no typical day as an early years librarian – my job is full of variety, and there are several different areas of responsibility. Probably about 40 per cent of my time is spent on outreach work in the community – I visit parent and toddler groups, Children's Centres, nurseries, young mums' groups and so on. It's all about trying to get over to parents the importance of reading and helping young children to develop a love of books and reading. (Early years librarian)

Katrina is an experienced community librarian working in a city library service. She is outgoing and proactive, yet, to her frustration, regularly encounters a lack of knowledge in partner organizations:

> A lot of time it is quite shocking that you are at a Children's Centre talking about library services and you tell them it is free to join and you can borrow twenty books, and the early years people there say, 'Oh you can have babies joining? I didn't know that' and I think that's a worry that they didn't already know about this. (Community librarian)

> Chris was appointed last year as a children's librarian and he is the first male children's librarian that we have had. This is great as he usually takes the 'Saturdads' sessions where dads can spend more time with their kids away from home, just like mums at mothers and toddlers groups, So I think it really helps when you are dealing with groups like that to have a good role modelling. (Early years librarian)

> There are still very few male children's librarians so we share them out across the branches! When I went to the Children's Centre I brought Chris and he was telling the stories to the children; it was mainly families from ethnic minorities that were there last time, and it was really nice because they didn't see men as natural storytellers. So at first they were saying 'man?' but he was really well received. (Community Librarian)

Figure 9.1 A children's librarian taking a storytelling session

Libraries are key partners alongside Children's Centres in encouraging family reading, and children's librarians provide collaborative activities such as storytelling events, toy libraries, family literacy activities, craft activities and puppet shows. Popular additions are interactive library sessions using rhyme, rhythm, songs and music. This is an important element of early language development; 'rhyme time' interactive sessions also encourage interaction between parent and baby. Most cultures have their own long-established rhymes and songs, and singing in different home languages can promote bilingualism and also provide a link to the children's heritage. Many public libraries have strong links with writers, illustrators and storytellers and library practitioners get involved in holding events which draw in the local community. Providing a welcoming community facility is an important aspect of the job as the library is competing with other local 'attractions' for family time. A key message is that libraries are engaging, informative, creative and memorably enjoyable places for people to visit and use (MLA, 2008).

> I love to see how the kids interact at my library now the children's section has been refurbished. From my office there is a little porthole and you can see kids literally running to grab books and then dive on the furniture to sit there and enjoy the books. There's a big beanbag that they can throw themselves on, and they will keep doing that. They will sit and read. You will see parents in there. I will sometimes go in to choose a book on something I am doing and then I will go back an hour or two later and they are still there because it is such a comfy environment and the parents can sit there and watch the children play. (Development librarian)

Knowledge base – what makes librarians unique

Every professional organization needs a knowledge base describing what members of the profession must know in order to practise. CILIP has established the unique knowledge base which distinguishes library and information professionals from other professionals (CILIP, 2004). The librarian practises within a specific environment in which ethical, legal, policy and organizational issues need to be understood at an appropriate level. Children's services are receiving a high profile today as policymakers are concerned about the level of reading skills and effective education for the information age. Early childhood is now high on the political agenda in many countries of the world. This has happened because of the growing awareness of the importance of the first years of life for intellectual, social and emotional development. Many different disciplines are interested including health, psychology, education, social policy, social care and neuropsychology (Rankin and Brock, 2009). Librarians have always been interested in a 'reading child', but now due to new understandings about child development and emergent literacy they also need to be aware of the needs of babies and toddlers and provide opportunities to support their learning.

I'm the first point of contact for our library branch staff for any queries about early years' services. For example, staff may need advice on the sessions they run for babies and toddlers in their library and I can suggest suitable resources to use. I'm very happy to go along and help run activities and explain our evaluation processes. (Early years librarian)

Librarians know that reading to babies and young children is one of the most effective ways of enhancing language development in a child (Brock and Rankin, 2008; Walter, 2009). Librarians have a number of great 'selling points' when encouraging parents and carers to bring their babies and toddlers to the library as they provide free access to books and other resources! It is never too early to start encouraging the development of early language skills in children, but this also means providing support and guidance for parents and carers.

There can be a huge impact when you work with groups that do not access books or access libraries. For example, chatting to a parent who has just put their child in front of the TV for four hours on a morning while they are doing the housework and who has never shared a story in a book. Giving them the ideas about sharing a book and seeing their reaction, and their child's reaction and hearing them say 'I never thought about doing things like that before'. (Early Literacy coordinator)

The librarian can help parents and carers to understand they are the best teachers to help their children to enjoy books and prepare to learn to read. Parents are in the best position to introduce their children to the world of words. Reading together and sharing books encourages talking which helps develop speaking and listening skills. We know that fluent readers are more likely to do well in school, and reading and literacy skills will stand them in good stead for life in the twenty-first century. The benefits of sharing books last longer than a lifetime, since children who are brought up to value reading are likely to pass their love of reading (and their good literacy skills) on to the next generation.

I get rewards from the job when I've helped someone – I feel I have affected their lives. I really enjoy working with children, getting them to repeat things after me and joining in the stories. (Children's librarian)

Partnerships – making the most of networking

Librarians who specialize in providing services to children are actively involved in taking their provision and resources out to the local community. Much of their time is spent on outreach work as they leave the library premises to visit parent and toddler groups, Children's Centres, nurseries and young mums' groups.

> I have two 'office' desks based in different library branches across the city, but my daily work environment can range from a nursery to, for example, the local community centre where I'm going later today to act out a reading of *We're Going on a Bear Hunt* with a parent and toddler group. Some weeks I'm rarely actually in a library! (Community librarian)

The idea of professionals working in partnership sounds very positive and provides networking and outreach opportunities for many librarians. However, we need to be aware that this way of working can present difficult challenges and ethical dilemmas for professionals, particularly in cross-sector partnerships where participants from different organizations may have different strategic priorities and political drivers and levels of knowledge.

> It is worrying how little people know about libraries and what we can offer. Sometimes they just want us to go in and do lots of things. I have a Children's Centre who have just sent me an email asking if we could have a meeting so that I could set up their library service, provide books for them, do the story times and set up a toy library. I had to have a diplomatic discussion about how we have agendas and they have agendas, and are there any that we can join up together? Because to me that is what partnerships are about. There has got to be something in it for us and something in it for them – you have got to try and work out what agendas you are sharing. That's the whole point of partnerships. We deal with a lot of people with whom we have shared agendas and limited resources so if we can team up then it is a win-win. (Community librarian)

There are issues though about breaking down barriers to professionals' partnerships:

> There are lots of preconceptions about librarians when you go into early years settings – sometimes I have found going into Children's Centres – when you walk in, you can feel the hostility if they have had literacy problems or had a bad experience with a library, straight away they think you are going to come in and preach at them – how they are not reading enough and they are not clever enough. There are these preconceptions. And if you go in a very formal way, 'Yes, I am from the library, you must come and join' attitude, then the barriers will be reinforced, so you have to be a bit daft, relaxed with it and get them to relax. (Community librarian)

The needs of parents and carers are also provided through special collections of information about childhood services and resources about parenting. A recent partnership initiative is the provision of the Baby Café in some public libraries. The Baby Café is a network of breastfeeding support, drop-in centres where mums can access high-quality health advice from health visitors and peer support from trained volunteers. In a public library setting, local mums can come to see the health visitor, seek advice, borrow books, have a coffee or use the many other facilities the library has to offer.

Many early years librarians in the UK will be involved with Bookstart, run by the national charity Booktrust. Bookstart is the national early intervention and cultural access programme for every child. This is the first national baby book-gifting programme in the world and encourages all parents and carers to enjoy books with their children from as early an age as possible. Bookstart for babies 0–12 months aims to provide a canvas bag to every new baby born in the UK containing baby books, a booklet for parents setting out information and advice on sharing stories with young children, a Children's Centres leaflet and a booklist and invitation to join the local library. These packs are distributed through health visitors, libraries and early years settings. Usually a health visitor will give babies their first book pack at 6 to 12 months and another book pack to toddlers at 2 to 2½ years. Preschoolers aged 3–4 years usually receive their My Bookstart Treasure Chest through an early years setting. The Bookstart packs are also available from the local library. The contents of the packs and Treasure Chests have been carefully chosen to include everything parents and carers need to get started sharing stories, rhymes and songs.

> Things like being aware of all the government initiatives such as Every Child a Talker. We naturally do a lot of work with speech and language therapists because they do a lot with Bookstart as well. I have regular meetings with them and with early years because they partly fund the Bookstart programme. So lots of government initiatives, like when we did Book Head last year we did boys into books, so giving out free book packs for nurseries and Children's Centres as well. And also financial illiteracy is a big thing at the moment and how that affects health, that's where we are using the 'count me in' bags. (Early years librarian)

> Sometimes because I do Bookstart, I am seen as the free book lady or that lady who does silly voices ... (Early years librarian)

As an extension to the book gifting, *Booktouch* packs are available for blind and partially sighted babies and *Bookshine* packs are available to help parents of deaf babies and children discover books together. Librarians welcome the very youngest members of their communities by inviting them to take part in the Bookstart Book Crawl. This encourages children under 5 to join the library and to borrow books by rewarding them with stickers and certificates. As a pioneering initiative in children's book gifting, the programme has been of interest to researchers investigating its impact on language and literacy development in babies and toddlers, and the Bookstart idea has been copied internationally.

Resources – books and more

Librarians need to have knowledge about children and their families' culture, heritage, language and interests to ensure that a breadth of valuable resources are provided; this is known as collection development. Picture books are the core of an early years library collection and are important as they enable us to explore the world around us. These books provide opportunities for multicultural content and can help to reflect the cultural heritage of families in the local area as well as a view of the wider world. The well-planned early years library will provide a range of books, toys, story sacks, treasure baskets and other creative resources for young users and their families. Librarians know that the constructive use of toys can help a child's development. Toy libraries can engage parents who otherwise might not use early years play services, but they also provide a chance to see and try out different toys and can help parents in selecting toys for their child's stage of development. Parents can be supported by knowing that playing with toys can stimulate language skills and helps to develop hand/eye coordination.

The IFLA's *Guidelines for Children's Library Services* recommend that librarians should choose materials which are of high quality and are age appropriate. 'Children's libraries should include a variety of developmentally appropriate materials in all formats, including printed materials (books, periodicals, comics, brochures), media, (CDs, DVDs, cassettes), toys, learning games, computers, software and connectivity' (IFLA, 2003, p. 9). However, there is also the ethically challenging issue of choosing materials that reflect a variety of values and opinions and the local community culture. Some public library authorities leave book selection up to commercial suppliers, while others still rely on the decisions of professional librarians. In collection development many of the choices that selectors make have strong ethical implications (Hauptman, 2002). Ethical selection policies require that librarians choose appropriate materials while attempting to ignore social and personal prejudices that may cause the censoring of 'unacceptable' materials.

Qualifications and rewards

So far this chapter has outlined the work undertaken by librarians who specialize in providing services and resources to support the needs of babies, young children and their families. Successful practitioners may come from a variety of professional backgrounds as there is no requirement for particular qualifications. Librarians wishing to gain professional qualifications can undertake postgraduate or undergraduate courses accredited by the Chartered Institute of Library and Information Professionals (CILIP). These courses are recognized internationally. Those seeking further recognition can work towards chartered status by undertaking a further period of continuing professional development and presenting the evidence base for scrutiny by a Chartership Board.

> We do shadowing. I wouldn't just go into an early years setting completely on my own at the start. Like the first time I went to a post-natal group, I went with a development librarian who had been doing it for a long time. I do lot of reading as well, and do various training courses. We do a lot of buddying up when we do things for the first time to try and get everyone involved in training. (Development librarian)

Achieving professional qualifications in librarianship does not necessarily lead to higher prestige or increased remuneration but, for many, seems to indicate a strong sense of vocation. Anecdotal evidence would suggest that although many librarians working in the early years sector have teaching qualifications, they may not be members of CILIP or undertake the route to chartership. This has implications in relation to professional status and results in inconsistencies in the local authority employment market.

Skills – children's librarians as multitaskers

The skills of the children's librarian go far beyond storytelling. The decisions a professional makes affects large numbers of people, our patrons, our stakeholders, our societies, and this clearly differentiates professionals from lay persons (Buchanan and Henderson, 2009, p. 95). In order to apply specialist and domain-specific knowledge and skills CILIP says the information professional may need a range of generic and transferable skills. These include computer and information literacy; interpersonal skills; management skills, especially relating to human and financial resources; marketing ability; training and mentoring skills; and familiarity with research methods (CILIP, 2004). The International Federation of Library Associations (IFLA) has a very proactive children and young adults' group which emphasizes that effective and professionally run children's libraries require trained, flexible and committed staff. As we have already noted, library and information practitioners have a tradition of networking with other professional groups and developing communities of practice.

Librarians need good managerial and technical skills. It is important to have an understanding of the parent organization's strategy and business plan and be able to implement decisions. The effective library practitioner needs to develop good political and advocacy skills but this is an area where the profession may still be lacking:

> I think traditionally librarians aren't that good at advocacy because we are too nice and too self-depreciating. We don't like to brag and the more we do that and get better at that the more strategic people will be aware and the more it will get passed around, but we are not traditionally very good at shouting about our work. We are aware now that it is not our forte, so we should put a lot more work into advocacy and more professional advocacy. (Development librarian)

Good management and leadership skills are also important as librarians need not only to work in a team with the other librarians but also to promote ongoing discussion and negotiation with members of staff in other services. As already discussed in this chapter librarians will liaise with people who work in 'partner' organizations, such as health visitors, nursery teachers and staff from various children's projects, and many are actively involved in delivering the Bookstart scheme. The development of the Children's Centre network has presented the opportunity to become an integral part of the multi-agency services helping parents to support their children's early language and literacy, as well as communicating important messages about emotional and social development and health issues.

> Obviously working really closely with Children's Centres and family outreach workers there are a lot of vulnerable families and you become aware of issues that may be arising. We do story time sessions over a period of twelve weeks and you have the same people coming – you build up relationships with them and you do find out what is going on in their lives. They are also building relationships with other people they might not know in the group. They are making their own support systems as well, so that is good. (Development librarian)

Ethical issues and values

A professional's ethical practice is dependent on professional knowledge acquired through education, qualification and experience, which will have generated specific skills, values and beliefs (Brock et al., 2011). Gorman (2000) proposes eight values that that offer foundational support to librarianship: stewardship, service, intellectual freedom, rationalism, literacy and learning, equity of access, privacy and democracy. One of the hallmarks of a profession is the framework of values that underpin the work of practitioners; the International Federation of Library Associations has compiled a collection of professional guidelines for librarians and other library employees adopted by national library or librarians associations or implemented by government agencies. CILIP has developed a set of twelve Ethical Principles and a Code of Professional Practice for Library and Information Professionals in the UK. The introduction to the CILIP code states that library and information professionals are frequently the essential link between information users and the information or piece of literature which they require and therefore occupy a privileged position which carries corresponding responsibilities. The purpose of the Principles and Code is to provide a framework to help library and information professionals who are members of CILIP, to manage the responsibilities and sensitivities which figure prominently in their work. A consideration of ethical issues is an essential quality of the 'reflective' practitioner. McMenemy et al. (2007) point out that ethical codes are useful documents for two specific reasons. First, they offer members of the professional association a model of behaviour that is expected of them, establishing the parameters of acceptable behaviour. Second, they communicate a set of values to the wider world, including employers and other stakeholders. However, although ethical codes are in place for librarians in the UK, it is not known how useful and relevant they are in terms of supporting and guiding the everyday work of practitioners when facing ethical dilemmas. Hauptman states:

> Codes, rules, regulations and even laws do not create or foster an ethical environment; a true commitment on the part of the organization and its individual members is mandatory if we are to operate fairly, and offer all patrons and clients the service that they deserve while avoiding social harm. (Hauptman, 2002, p. 135)

The notion of using a personal moral compass as an ethical guide is addressed in professions such as health and social care, yet there is little evidence of research and theory within librarianship although the profession is well served by codes of practice.

As discussed earlier in this chapter, the library profession does suffer from stereotyping but many proactive and innovative early years library professionals have a vocation for an occupation that brings satisfaction, enjoyment and a commitment to others. Professional practice fundamentally involves practitioners in making judgements, but they also need to be effective advocates for the value and impact of their services and programmes. This advocacy is particularly powerful when promoting the value and impact of library services to senior managers, politicians and other financial decision makers.

> I think libraries are always the poor relations in terms of funding resources and staff when you look at how other people seem to be doing. You probably don't come into the public library service for financial rewards; you probably come into it for the warm happy glow, the feeling of satisfaction. (Community librarian)

The economic climate and funding cuts imposed by the Coalition Government have required local authorities to look ever more critically at the services they provide and what can be offered within the budgets available. Although there is evidence to show the value a public library service and its staff can offer to their local community, other services will be making equally persuasive claims for their provision and there are difficult times ahead.

Conclusion

Evidence has shown that library practitioners have a key role to play in supporting the development of language and literacy in young children. Professional practice fundamentally involves practitioners in making judgements and they are good at reaching 'hard-to-reach' groups, successfully building partnerships based on reading and family learning. Children's librarians present themselves as well-rounded professionals who have a good knowledge of their client group, understand theories of children's learning and development and recognize and support the needs of their diverse communities. However, there are critical challenges ahead in finding the resources to continue delivering publicly funded library services in times of economic strictures. Librarians may be effective and reliable partners in providing services that the public appreciate, but they are rarely recognized as the lead agency and as such do not yet have the same political voice in promoting their professional worth. There is much interest now in the social impact of what libraries are doing and how they can contribute to the social cohesion and development of their communities. Library practitioners are at the forefront of promoting children's rights and as such are a vital aid to literacy development.

Questions for reflective practice

How can you support the development of language and literacy of young children who visit the library?
What are the challenges in reaching families and how can you promote effective partnerships?
How can librarians work in partnership with other professional colleagues?
What challenges may impact a librarian's capacity to undertake continuing professional development?

Further reading, resources and/or websites

Rankin, C., and Brock, A. (2009), *Delivering the Best Start: A Guide to Early Years Libraries*. London: Facet.

— (eds) (2011, in press), *Library Services for Children and Young Adults: Challenges and Opportunities in the Digital Age*. London: Facet.

Bookstart www.bookstart.org.uk/Home.

Chartered Institute of Library and Information Professionals. www.cilip.org.uk.

Every Child a Talker (ECaT). http://nationalstrategies.standards.dcsf.gov.uk/search/earlyyears/results/nav%3A46542.

National Literacy Trust. www.literacytrust.org.uk.

Talk to Your Baby Campaign. www.literacytrust.org.uk/talk_to_your_baby.

References

Brock, A., and Rankin, C. (2008), *Communication, Language and Literacy from Birth to Five*. London: Sage.

Brock, A., Rankin, C., and Swiniarski, L., (2011), Are we doing it by the book? Professional ethics for teachers and librarians in the early years. In Chapter 2 pf A. Campbell and P. Broadhead (eds), *Working with Children and Young People: Ethical Debates and Practices Across Disciplines and Continents*. New International Studies in Applied Ethics. Oxford: Peter Lang, 15–36.

Brophy, P. (2007), *The Library in the Twenty-first Century*, 2nd edition. London: Facet Publishing.

Buchanan, E., and Henderson, K. (2009), *Case Studies in Library and Information Science Ethics*. Jefferson, NC: McFarland.

Burns Owens Partnership (2009), *Capturing the Impact of Libraries*. Final report prepared for DCSM by BOP. http://www.culture.gov.uk/images/publications/Capt uring_the_impact_of_libraries.pdf.

CILIP (2002), *Start with the Child*. http://www.cilip.org.uk/filedownloadslibrary/groups/ylg/startwiththechild.pdf.

— (2004), *Body of Professional Knowledge: Setting Out an Adaptable and Flexible Framework for Your Changing Needs*. London: CILIP. www.cilip.org.uk/sitecollectiondocuments/PDFs/qualificationschartership/BPK.pdf.

— (2009a), *Code of Practice*. www.cilip.org.uk/get-involved/policy/ethics/pages/code.aspx.

— (2009b), *Ethical Principles for Library and Information Professionals*. London: CILIP. www.cilip.org.uk/get-involved/policy/ethics/pages/principles.aspx.

— (2009c), *What Makes a Good Library Service? Guidelines on Public Library Service Provision in England for Portfolio Holders in Local Councils*. London: CILIP. www.cilip.org.uk/get-involved/advocacy/public-libraries/Documents/What_makes_a_good_library_service_CILIP_guidelines.pdf. Accessed 3 September 2010.

DCMS (1999), *Libraries for All: Social Inclusion in Public Libraries: Policy Guidance for Local Authorities in England*. Department for Culture, Media and Sport. http://webarchive.nationalarchives.gov.uk/+/http://www.culture.gov.uk/images/publications/Social_Inclusion_PLibraries.pdf.

— (2003), *Framework for the Future: Libraries, Learning and Information in the Next Decade*. London: Department of Culture, Media and Sport.

— (2010), *The Modernisation Review of Public Libraries: A Policy Statement*. London: The Stationery Office.

Dolan, J. (2007), *A Blueprint for Excellence: Public Libraries 2008–2011: Connecting People to Knowledge and Inspiration*. London: MLA.

Frost, N. (2005), *Professionalism, Partnership and Joined-up Thinking: A Research Review of Front-line Working with Children and Families*. Totnes, Research in Practice. http://leedsmet.ac.uk/health/socialwork/people/images/frostreview8.pdf.

Gorman, M. (2000), *Our Enduring Values: Librarianship in the 21st Century*. Chicago : ALA Editions.

Hauptman, R. (2002), *Ethics and Librarianship*. Jefferson, NC: McFarland and Co.

IFLA (2003) *Guidelines for Children's Library Services*. International Federation of Library Associations. http://archive.ifla.org/VII/s10/pubs/ChildrensGuidelines.pdf.

— (2009), *Multicultural Communities: Guidelines for Library Services*, 3rd edition. International Federation of Library Associations. http://www.ifla.org/files/library-services-to-multicultural-populations/publications/multicultural-communities-en.pdf.

Koontz, C., and Gubbin, B. (eds) (2010), *IFLA Public Library Service Guidelines*.Berlin: IFLA Publications 147 Saur.

McMenemy, D. (2009) *Public Library*. London: Facet Publishing.

McMenemy, D., Poulter, A., and Burton, P. (2007). *A Handbook of Ethical Practice*. Oxford: Chandos.

MLA (2008), *Framework for the Future MLA Action Plan for Public Libraries – "towards 2013"*. London: MLA. www.mla.gov.uk/what/strategies/~/media/Files/pdf/2008/library_action_plan.

Rankin, C., and Brock, A. (2009), *Delivering the Best Start: A Guide to Early Years Libraries*. London, Facet.

Rankin, C., Brock, A., Wootton, C. and Halpin, E. (2007), *The Role of the Early Years Librarian in Developing an Information Community: A Case Study of Effective Partnerships and Early Years Literacy Within a Sure Start Project in Wakefield*. Published in 2007 conference proceedings of the Canadian Association for Information Science. www.caisacsi.ca/proceedings/2007/rankin_2007.pdf.

Walter, V. (2009), *Twenty-first-Century Kids, Twenty-first-Century Librarians*. Chicago: ALA.

Part III
Conclusion

10

A Future for Interdisciplinary Professional Work: Mainstream to Oppositional?

Nick Frost

Introduction

The period of the British New Labour Government (1997–2010) witnessed an unprecedented growth in, and reform of, children's services (Frost and Parton, 2009). This growth was informed by a number of themes, including a belief in 'early intervention', a faith in the role of the state as a positive force for change and an attempt to address chronic problems such as 'anti-social behaviour' and 'social exclusion'. Underpinning all these developments, and arguably the central technique in delivering change, was that addressed by the contributors to this book – multi-professional working with children and families. The New Labour project in relation to this can be summarized as follows:

> Positive calls for interconnectedness and negative critiques of old-style public service monoliths generated a new mantra for policymakers: 'joined-up working'. The idea was that 'joined-up working' or 'thinking' acknowledged the interrelatedness of children and family needs in the fields of health, education, social services, law enforcement, housing, employment and family support. The aim was to reshape services. The belief was that joined-up working would make services more

flexible, more responsive to local demographics and priorities, more efficient by reducing overlap of treatments, diagnoses and records, and ultimately more effective. (Anning et al., 2006, p. 4)

The challenges of interprofessional working have generated a large volume of literature over the past decade. The literature tends to reflect the evolution of interprofessional working in the field – with the early literature being exploratory, mid-period literature being developmental and reflective and the later literature attempting to theorize the work and assess outcomes (see Atkinson et al., 2007, and Robinson et al., 2008).

This book was brought together at a pivotal moment in the history of British interprofessional working: the period of transition from the New Labour Government (1997–2010) to the Coalition Government elected in May 2010. As such it provides a key space for reflecting on the future of interprofessional working. As we live through a period of fundamental political, social and economic change, what does the landscape of interdisciplinary working look like?

From mainstream to oppositional?

It will be argued here that during this period of transition interdisciplinary working has been travelling a continuum from mainstream to oppositional. What do we mean by this?

Interprofessional working was certainly mainstream during the New Labour period. All the key initiatives under the Every Child Matters banner were interdisciplinary: Sure Start, Children's Centres, Connexions, Youth Offending Teams, Family Intervention Projects and many of the initiatives explored in this book. This approach to professional working reflected a number of wider social trends and changes.

First, there was a fundamental attempt by the state to tackle seemingly long-standing and intractable social problems. These problems – including youth crime, social exclusion and poor educational outcomes – were seen as being multifaceted, having social, individual and economic and community aspects. If the problems were multifaceted, then it followed that they required a multi-factoral response. This way of thinking had a global aspect with similar initiatives being taken worldwide (e.g., in the Republic of Ireland, see Rafferty and Colgan, 2009).

Second, it became clear that the traditional approach to professionalism was become increasing implausible. Traditional claims to professionalism rested on uniqueness: that each profession had unique claims to knowledge, skills and expertise that signify their difference from other professionals (see Brock, Chapters 1 and 3 in this volume). Traditional claims to professionalism rest on difference and on unique forms of expertise. This 'silo' mentality became increasingly implausible as we entered the late twentieth century. The growth of information technology, the complexity and connectedness of social problems, the imperviousness of profound social problems to traditional interventions and the decline of deference to professionals all combined to make interprofessional working increasing imperative.

Third, wherever society faced 'scandals' involving professionals it became increasingly clear that many of them were underpinned by the perceived failings of 'silo' professional working. In the field of child and family work this was particularly high-profile in the child-abuse deaths discussed in this volume by Saltiel (see Chapter 7). Professions – in social work, health, education and the police – were repeatedly found to have failed to communicate effectively. While these failures were perceived as being individually based, they reflected wider structural issues – based in organizations with different approaches, different values and different forms of working. Thus 'silo' working was perceived as failing children and young people; a shift towards interprofessional, or integrated, working became increasingly imperative and was given a strong development direction following the Laming Inquiry into the death of Victoria Climbié (Laming, 2003).

Here we see some powerful – and perhaps irresistible – forces working towards inter-disciplinary working. Thus interdisciplinary, or more strongly integrated, working became mainstream – a dominant method of addressing intractable social problems.

The New Labour approach to interdisciplinary work remains effectively summarized in the 'onion' diagram – an official method of representing the policy, as we see in Figure 10.1 below.

Figure 10.1 The 'onion' diagram: children's services under New Labour (1997–2010)

This diagram can be described as follows. The inter-agency circle relates to leadership of services which took organizational form in the shape of Children's Trusts. These trusts bring together the wide range of organizations working in each local authority area with children and young people. The Children's Trusts were introduced in 2006 and became mandatory in the Apprenticeship, Skills, Children and Learning Act 2009, but the Coalition Government announced its intention to rescind this legislation during the life of the first parliament and for Children's Trusts to be elective rather than mandatory. This approach to deregulation and 'localism', characteristic of the Coalition Government, was also reflected in its policy of 'integrated' strategy. Labour had introduced the Children and Young Person's Plan, mandated by a regulation, which the Coalition Government was able to withraw in 2010. The 'integrated processes' circle represents actual methods of working together, two of which have been referred to by the contributors to this book: the Common Assessment Framework (CAF) and Contact Point. The latter programme was ended by the Coalition Government on 6 August 2010. Contact Point was an electronic database containing data on all 11 million children in England. The abolition of Contact Point perhaps perfectly reflected the values of the Coalition Government. The abolition reflected the ambition of the Conservatives to roll back the state and also to reduce public expenditure. On the Liberal Democrat side, the abolition of Contact Point was seen as reducing state surveillance of citizens and therefore promoting civil liberties. The circle closest to the outcomes for children and young people represents the actual concrete settings that professionals work in: Children's Centres, Youth Offending Teams and so on. At the centre of the circle are the five outcomes for children: being healthy, staying safe, enjoying and achieving, making a positive contribution and achieving economic well-being.

Having described this model, which underpins the contributions to this book, let us move on to provide a critical commentary, which will examine the strengths of the 'onion' approach and explore potential critiques.

This diagram represents a powerful model of state intervention in childhood. It reflects an optimistic belief that the state can improve the life of every child in the country under the mantra 'Every Child Matters'. The breadth of ambition expressed by the 'onion' model and in the Children's Plan (2007) is remarkable (see Table 1.5: Milestones of policy initiatives that have impacted on early childhood in the UK, 1999–2010). Significantly for this book the main vehicle for delivering the five outcomes and for restructuring childhood are professions – or to be more precise, interdisciplinary professional working. New Labour expressed this remarkable faith in interdisciplinary professional work not only in rhetoric but also in reality in many of the initiatives explored in the previous chapters. The investment in professional development was indeed highly significant, for example, through

- the National Professional Qualification in Integrated Centre Leadership, for Children's Centre leaders;
- the formation of the Children's Workforce Development Council;

- the formation and development of the National College for School and Children's Services Leadership;
- the Early Years Professional scheme.

This investment in human resources took place alongside significant financial investment in Children's Centres, the Building Schools for the Future programme and the Child Trust Fund, among many others initiatives.

We can perhaps summarize New Labour childhood policy as a fundamental belief that

> Childhood can be successfully reconstructed by the state, through investment in enhanced, integrated professional intervention, backed by financial investment in infrastructure and direct benefits. (see Frost, 2011, for an expansion of this argument)

Having explored the New Labour programme and pointed out some of its ambitions and strengths, let us move on to provide a more critical perspective.

First, while the programme is ambitious, one could also argue that it is naive in many ways. It can be argued that the state cannot successfully penetrate the deepest reaches of people's private lives, including sexuality (in the case of teenage pregnancy) or diet ('be healthy'). This belief in the state perhaps underplays the role of the market, which has a profound impact on children's life chances and lifestyle choices.

Second, the 'onion' diagram can be read in a different way: as a system of surveillance and normalization. Drawing on the incredibly prescient work of Foucault and Donzelot, it can be argued that the five outcomes are a system of normalization that is creating societal norms which parents aspire too. Foucault and his followers see normalization as creating forms of governing and regulating populations. Such norms can be policed through systems of surveillance of which Contact Point represents an example – possibly unprecedented in the Western world and more reminiscent of a gigantic East German system of gathering data on entire populations. The 'onion' can then be re-imagined as a system of surveillance and regulation with the child trapped in the middle of the 'onion', or perhaps more pointedly, what looks like a 'dartboard'. While the case is no doubt overstated here, the Foucauldian analysis provides a necessary corrective to a naive welfarist analysis of New Labour policy towards children.

Third, in terms of critique, of course the 'onion' remains an ideal type – an aspiration model which was never effectively delivered in any concrete setting. The reality was uneven with some Children's Trusts almost reaching the aspirations and others falling far short. In reality, if one were to devise an 'onion' for each authority, it would produce a range of different onions: different sizes and shapes, some lacking shape and some failing to form a coherent whole.

Fourth, and perhaps most powerfully, we can now look back on the Every Child Matters agenda as being seriously derailed by the misguided New Labour response to the sad death of Baby Peter. Baby Peter died when living with his mother and her resident partner. The details of this case can be read in the published Serious Case Reviews and the state response can be seen in the Laming Report and the resultant government policy statements. The Secretary of State Ed Balls played a high-profile role in leading the government response to the death of Baby Peter. He took a number of steps, including the following:

1) ordering a Joint Area Review (JAR) of children's services in Haringey, the London borough where Baby Peter died;
2) asking Lord Laming to produce a report on the state of children's services in the wake of Baby Peter's death;
3) accepting each of Laming's recommendations and producing a plan for implementing them;
4) intervening personally to dismiss the Director of Children's Services Sharon Shoesmith.

During the election campaign of 2010, Ed Balls was to refer to these events as the most challenging of his political career. In retrospect this period was a turning point in the Every Child Matters policy. In summary, the result of Balls's high-profile intervention was to:

1) increase the number of care proceedings and children coming into care;
2) create a harsher and more rigorous Ofsted inspection regime;
3) create a period of defensive practice in which children's services reacted to critical Ofsted inspections by increasing regulation and managerialism;
4) return to an emphasis on 'child protection' in the narrowest sense at the expense of the wider 'safeguarding' regime;
5) produce an environment of sustained media attack on the role of social workers and their managers.

Having argued that multi-professional work was 'mainstream' – that is, consistent with the dominant themes of government policy under New Labour – it may well now be argued that it has become 'oppositional' – that is, outside mainstream government thinking. What evidence is there for this assertion?

First, one of the first acts of the Coalition Government was to change the name of the Department for Children, Schools and Families to the Department for Education. This act was both symbolic and deeply materially significant. It was symbolic in the sense that it represented a shift from a 'joined-up' approach to children's services to a specific and privileged emphasis on education.

Second, the decision to withdraw regulations making Children and Young Person's Plans mandatory, and the planned intention to amend primary legislation making Children's Trusts mandatory, flag a withdrawal from the mainstream emphasis on integrated professional working.

Third, and perhaps most significantly, changes to the organization of health services (with a stronger emphasis on general practitioner commissioning) and education (creating 'free' schools) will make multi-professional delivery of services increasingly challenging.

Fourth, the decision has also been made to withdraw state funding from the Children's Workforce Development Council (CWDC), which has been one of the main drivers of interdisciplinary professional working with children and their families.

These policy shifts have profound implications for each profession mentioned in this book, as demonstrated by Jarvis and Holland in Chapter 4, for example. The policy is informed by a shift towards less bureaucracy, more professional autonomy and localism, and has many positive aspects but will undoubtedly undermine interdisciplinary working.

Taken together, these policy decisions seem to represent a major retreat from the 'strong' integration model pursued by the previous Labour Government and represented diagrammatically by the 'onion'. This is why it is argued here that interdisciplinary work has moved, in a very short period during the spring and summer of 2010, from being 'mainstream' to being 'oppositional'.

The Brock framework

The emphasis on interdisciplinary work has profound implications for how we think about professionals and professionalism. This book and the debates within it about interdisciplinary working has been informed by the Brock framework, which will now be examined in terms of how our view of the professional has been changed by the shift towards interdisciplinary working. The Brock framework consists of seven key themes: knowledge, education and training, skills, autonomy, values, ethics and reward (see Chapter 3 in this volume).

Knowledge

Knowledge is at the core of professionalism: the traditional profession makes certain knowledge claims without which professionalism would lack a core purpose. Interdisciplinary working has a major impact on knowledge: how it is formed, how it is shared and how it is structured. We have seen in the preceding chapters how knowledge is shared across professions: professionals can learn and develop from working alongside each other. This knowledge transfer and transformation is arguably enhanced where there is integration and co-location (Anning et al., 2010), such as in schools, Youth Offending Teams or Children's Centres. Thus integrated working changes and transforms the nature of professional knowledge.

Education and training

Traditionally education and training for professions has taken place in 'silos', with profession-specific training taking place in universities or colleges. While many universities and colleges now provide differing forms of interprofessional education, it remains the case that the emphasis remains on single-profession education. The growth and development of interdisciplinary and/or integrated working presents a challenge to traditional forms of initial professional education. Continuing professional development has perhaps been more successful in delivering multi-professional forums, particularly in relation to child protection.

Skills

As with sharing knowledge, skill sharing and development is also enhanced where integration and co-location exists, although it is also potentially present whenever professionals work together. Professionals based in integrated settings report being able to share skills and being able to develop and diversify their skill base and their experience. Professionals working together are able to be coached and mentored to develop new skills appropriate to the setting in which they are working. The sharing of skills and knowledge will be enhanced by effective teamwork, and reflective practice provides a useful framework for exploring these issues (see Chapter 2, Rankin and Butler, and Chapter 6, Smith and Karban, in this volume).

Autonomy

Whereas interprofessional working can be seen as enhancing knowledge and skill development, it can arguably also be seen as reducing professional autonomy. Ground-breaking research by Glisson and Hemmelgarn (1998) argued that some interprofessional settings can reduce professional autonomy, largely through an increased emphasis on the procedures and policies required for joint working. The Glisson and Hemmelgarn evidence suggests that procedural approaches to reduce autonomy can have an adverse impact on actual outcomes for children and young people.

Values

A key element of the professional 'silo' identity rests in the values of each profession; while these sometimes overlap and are consistent, there can be important incidences of differences, clashes and inconsistencies. Where there is conflict and difference between professionals, these are often based in value issues. It is important to note that while values seem to be abstract, they have a real, concrete impact on modes of practice and therefore their significance is more than abstract. The core theme of the United Nations Convention on the Rights of the Child and the Children Act 1989, 'the best interests of the child', has a connecting and unifying theme for those working with children. The child should be at the centre of effective interdisciplinary practice, which should ensure that British childhood is experienced more positively (see Brock, Chapter 1, in this volume).

Ethics

Professional ethics and ethical practices are also core to 'silo' approaches to professionalism. Ethical positions are often challenged in interprofessional settings, particularly when it comes to issues around confidentiality and information sharing. Medical and health-based professions often hold a strict position on confidentiality which can bring them into conflict with other professions.

Reward

The issue of reward is a challenging one for interprofessional working. Where professionals are increasingly working together, being members of the same team and even undertaking the same tasks, such as the Common Assessment Framework (see Chapter 2, Rankin and Butler, in this volume), they can be expected to demand more equality of reward and status. The legacy of differential pay and conditions will be carried over into newly integrated team settings, thus creating possible tensions and conflicts. However, Brock is clear that reward also has a non-financial element: the reward that comes from working effectively and creatively with children and their families. There is evidence that professionals identify greater rewards from working in multi-professional settings: the rewards arising from feeling more effective, learning from each other and being able to mobilize resources more effectively (Brock et al, 2009).

Conclusion

This book makes an original contribution to our knowledge of professionals working together by examining in detail a whole range of professionals practicing with young children and their families. Underpinning the chapters is the framework devised by Brock, which we have explored above, to help us understand professionalism and the future of interdisciplinary practice. It has been argued above that the shift from the New Labour Government (1997–2010) to the Coalition Government formed in May 2010 represents a major shift in policy and practice around interdisciplinary working. The direct outcomes of these shifts remain to be seen.

References

Anning, A., Cottrell, D., Green, J., Frost, N., and Robinson, M. (2006, first edition; 2010, second edition), *Developing Multi-professional Working for Integrated Children's Services*. London: Open University Press.

Atkinson, M., Jones, M., and Lamont, E. (2007), *Multi-agency Working and Its Implications for Practice: A Review of the Literature*. Reading: Centre for British Teachers.

Brock, A., Frost, N., Karban, K., and Smith, S. (2009), (TIPS)*Towards Interprofessional Partnerships: A Resource Pack*. Leeds: Leeds Metropolitan University.

DCSF (2007), *The Children's Plan*. London: Department for Children, Schools and Families.

DfES (2004), *The Children Act, 2004*. London: Department for Education and Skills.

Frost, N. (2011), *Rethinking Children and Families*. London: Continuum.

180 Professionalism in the Interdisciplinary Early Years Team

Frost, N., and Parton, N. (2009), *Understanding Children's Social Care*. London: Sage.

Glisson, C., and Hemmelgarn, A. (1998) The effects of organizational climate and interorganisational coordination on the quality and outcomes of children's service system, *Child Abuse and Neglect*, 22(5), 401–421.

Laming, H. (2003), *The Victoria Climbié Inquiry*. London: HMSO.

— (2009), *The Protection of Children in England: A Progress Report*. London: TSO.

Ofsted (2008), *Joint Area Review of Haringey*. London: Department for Children, Schools and Families.

— (2009a), *Comprehensive Area Assessment: Annual Rating of Council Children's Services for 2009*. London: Ofsted.

— (2009b), *Inspections of Safeguarding and Looked After Children Services*. London: Ofsted.

— (2009c), *Unannounced Inspections of Contact, Referral and Assessment*. London: Ofsted.

Rafferty, M., and Colgan, A. (2009), *Organisational Case Studies of Inter-Agency Co-operation in the Delivery of Children's Services*. Dublin: CAAB.

Robinson, M., Atkinson, M., and Downing, D. (2008), *Supporting Theory Building in Integrated Services Research*. NFER.

Index